THE
ORIGINS
OF
HAPPINESS

THE
ORIGINS
OF
HAPPINESS

The Science of Well-Being
over the Life Course

Andrew E. Clark, Sarah Flèche,
Richard Layard, Nattavudh Powdthavee,
and George Ward

Princeton University Press   *Princeton & Oxford*

9838250446

Copyright © 2018 by Princeton University Press

Published by Princeton University Press,
41 William Street, Princeton, New Jersey 08540

In the United Kingdom: Princeton University Press,
6 Oxford Street, Woodstock, Oxfordshire OX20 1TR

press.princeton.edu

Jacket image courtesy LZT / Alamy Stock Vector

All Rights Reserved

ISBN 978-0-691-17789-2

British Library Cataloging-in-Publication Data is available

This book has been composed in Sabon and Scala Sans

Printed on acid-free paper. ∞

Printed in the United States of America

1 3 5 7 9 10 8 6 4 2

TO GUS O'DONNELL
CHAMPION OF WELL-BEING

CONTENTS

PART III. SO WHAT?

THE
ORIGINS
OF
HAPPINESS

"*I can't wait to grow up and be happy.*"

Introduction: The New Paradigm

All great truths begin as blasphemies.

—*George Bernard Shaw*

In April 2016, the German chancellor, Angela Merkel, launched a big national consultation. It was called "What Matters to Us?" Was she mad, or are we actually quite confused about what matters most to us and what real human progress would look like?

Money is a very visible indicator, and until recently many people would have given it pride of place. But now, worldwide, people are demanding a better concept of progress. They are rejecting wealth and income as the overriding goals for policy development—and for personal lifestyles. And they are turning instead to the much broader idea from the eighteenth-century Anglo-Saxon Enlightenment: that we judge our progress by how much people are enjoying their lives.

This noble and humane ideal has been a central strand in modern Western civilization for over two hundred years. And it has profound implications for how we should live our own lives, and for how our policy makers should make their choices. For individuals it provides the ethical principle that we should create as much happiness in the world as we can, and as little misery.[1] And for policy makers it becomes the principle that they should create the conditions for happy and fulfilling lives. In fact, as Thomas Jefferson once said, "The care of human life and happiness . . . is the only legitimate object of good government."[2]

We agree with him. But how to implement this objective? Until recently it was not easy. There was no agreed way of measuring whether people were enjoying their lives, and there was even less knowledge about what conditions would help them to do so. But now all that is changing. The last forty years have seen a burgeoning new science of "subjective well-being." On the one hand, this has shown that in many countries, including the United States and West Germany, people get no more enjoyment from life than forty years ago or more.[3] On the other hand, the science tells us a great deal about what can actually be done to increase well-being.

The main purpose of this book is to set out that knowledge as clearly as possible and to lay out in quantitative terms what is known about the causes of well-being. This is crucial for us as individuals—and also for policy makers.

Imagine a policy maker trying to allocate extra resources between youth training or mental health. Or the chief executive of an NGO choosing the balance between care of the elderly or support for young mothers. How can such choices be made in a rational way? Clearly there has to be some way of comparing the benefits of each alternative, using some common measure of benefit. Only if this is done can the policy maker attempt to generate the maximum total benefit from the available resources.

Until recently the recommended measure of benefit was the amount of money people would be willing to pay for the outcome. This may make some sense for some types of expenditure, but it could never make sense for much of public expenditure—on health care, elderly care, child protection, law and order, parks and the environment, and welfare payments. Indeed one major reason why these activities are undertaken by the state is that individual choice would not always produce the most efficient or equitable outcomes.[4] For health care many countries have for some years used nonmonetary measures of benefit, like Britain's Quality-Adjusted Life Years (QALYs).[5] But everywhere the key issue is: What is the best measure of the quality of life?

Measuring Happiness

In our view we should evaluate people's happiness as they themselves evaluate it. People are often asked, "Overall, how satisfied are you with your life these days?" They answer on a scale of 0–10, where 0 means "not at all satisfied" and 10 means "extremely satisfied." Or they are asked to make a mark on a line running from 0 to 10—which gives very similar results.[6] In many countries the question has been asked in unofficial surveys for up to fifty years. But now it is asked of large samples in regular official statistics in most advanced countries.[7]

When people answer this question, they are evaluating their own overall well-being. That is why we like this question. But well-being is often measured in other ways. One approach is to try to catch people's mood—their current hedonic feelings of enjoyment or discomfort. This approach is necessarily limited to a specific, and usually short, period of time.[8] But it is extremely useful in illuminating the quality of life as it is experienced moment by moment.[9] A third approach is to ask people how worthwhile they consider the things they do in their life—the measure of so-called eudaimonia. These measures are interesting, but we prefer life-satisfaction as our measure of well-being for a number of reasons.

First, it is comprehensive—it refers to the whole of a person's life these days. Second, it is clear to the reader—it involves no process of aggregation by researchers. Third, and most important, it is democratic—it allows individuals to assess their lives on the basis of whatever *they* consider important to themselves. It does not impose anybody else's views on what emotions or experiences are valuable. This is particularly important if we want policy makers to use these results. In a democracy politicians should not make judgments about what is good for people—they should create the conditions where people are satisfied with their lives.

Increasingly, policy makers feel comfortable about this approach to their role. After all, enlightened policy makers have for years been asking citizens how satisfied they are with their public services. From there it is a smallish step to ask how satisfied they are with their lives as a whole. In fact, policy makers would be well advised to do this, since our analysis of European elections over the last forty years shows that the life-satisfaction of the population is the best explanation of whether the government gets reelected. In fact, as Table 0.1 shows, life-satisfaction predicts better than any economic variable.[10]

But how reliable is the measure? Do different people use the scale in the same way when they answer the question? To some extent they must do so because, as the book will show, we can predict a person's measured life-satisfaction with some accuracy using a whole range of relevant factors.[11] Equally, life-satisfaction is itself a good predictor of many outcomes—not only voting for the existing government, but also, for example, longevity.[12]

Table 0.1. Factors explaining the existing government's vote share (partial correlation coefficients)

Life-satisfaction	**0.64**
Economic growth	**0.36**
Unemployment	**−0.06**
Inflation	**0.15**

Can we also use life-satisfaction when we measure the well-being of children? Clearly the quality of life they experience is intrinsically as important as that experienced by adults (and it is even more important if we also include its effect on the resulting adult). But children are less able than adults to make judgments about their experience. That is why younger children are not asked questions about life-satisfaction. They are however asked batteries of questions about their mood and feelings.[13] Similar questions about the child's mood and feelings are asked of their parents and teachers. So we aggregate these answers as our measure of child well-being.

Thus, to summarize so far, we are interested, for all individuals, in their well-being over their lifespan. In adulthood that is measured by life-satisfaction, and in childhood by mood and feelings.

Causes of Happiness over the Life Course

Having measured happiness, the next key step is to explain it—to understand why some people flourish, while others languish. The main purpose of this book is to set out a comprehensive map of the causes of well-being—in a novel way.

Putting it bluntly, most existing well-being research focuses on only one cause at a time (often with some controls) and shows that it influences well-being in a statistically significant way. Not only that, but well-being is generally measured in different ways in different studies.

Our approach is different. First, we use only one measure of well-being, so that we can unambiguously compare the effects of different factors. And, second, we estimate the effect of all these factors simultaneously, so that we can really isolate the effect of changing each one of them on its own. This is really crucial because most policies are targeted at specific variables, like income or health. To know the effects of changing any one of these, we will often want to assume that the others remain constant.

So our analysis will show the relative importance of the different factors within one single framework. This is important for us as individuals—and for policy makers. Once policy makers have identified key areas of concern, they should of course undertake controlled experiments of new policies, and such experiments are discussed in Part III of the book. But, before that, we need a model of how our well-being is determined over the course of our lives. We need to answer questions like:

- Which dimensions of childhood are the more important—intellectual, behavioral, or emotional?
- Which aspects of life should be targeted, at what ages?

Our model of life (excluding old age) is described somewhat crudely by Figure 0.1. An individual is born to parents who have given characteristics—like income, parenting

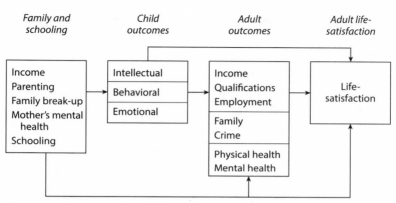

Figure 0.1. Determinants of adult life-satisfaction

skills, a harmonious home, and good mental health. And the child is then educated in schools that do or do not promote well-being. These influences (plus the genes) then determine the way the child develops over three main dimensions—intellectual, behavioral, and emotional. (The emotional dimension is also the way we measure child well-being.) We call these dimensions of development "child outcomes." Emotional development and behavior we measure at age 16, but we measure intellectual development by the highest qualification ever obtained. The child then develops into an adult, with many new dimensions of success—income, employment, family formation, noncriminal behavior, and health (both physical and mental). And these "adult outcomes" then determine the person's life-satisfaction.

This description of life corresponds to the central horizontal arrows in the graph. However, all earlier stages of life also continue to exert direct influences on later life, as shown by the other arrows in the graph. Each stage of life is determined by everything that preceded it.

If we are interested in affecting life-satisfaction, we want to know how we could affect it by intervening at different stages of life.

- We could intervene in *adulthood*, in which case we want to know how altering adult outcomes affects life-satisfaction, holding constant everything that went before;
- we could intervene on *child outcomes*, in which case we want to know how altering them affects life-satisfaction, holding constant family and schooling;
- we could intervene on *family or schooling*.

To answer these three questions we need to estimate the three corresponding relationships:

(1) how life-satisfaction *is affected by* adult outcomes, given the child outcomes and family/schooling;
(2) how life-satisfaction *is affected by* child outcomes, given the family/schooling;
(3) how life-satisfaction *is affected by* family/schooling.

The other interesting relationships are those that explain adult outcomes and child outcomes (including child well-being):

(4) how adult outcomes *are affected by* child outcomes and family and schooling;
(5) how child outcomes *are affected by* family and schooling.

Evidence on all these relationships is invaluable in suggesting which areas we should consider for new policy development aimed at improving adult or child well-being.

But to evaluate a specific new policy we need to conduct a proper controlled experiment. This experiment will normally tell us only the short-run effect, so the model is also useful in enabling us to simulate the longer-term effects that would be likely to follow any short-run effect.

This Book

So in this book our prime aim is to provide quantitative evidence about relationships (1) to (5)—and much else besides. The evidence we use is international and comes from many countries, including especially Britain, the United States, Germany, and Australia. Britain is especially rich in data about how people develop over their lifetimes and provides us with "birth cohort surveys" that have followed children born in Britain in 1970 and 1991–92.[14] In addition many countries have for decades conducted "household panel" surveys, which follow people from around the age of 15, on a year-by-year basis (Britain, Germany, and Australia).[15] We use all these surveys and other international data.[16] There is online material that includes details of all the surveys and questionnaires used and also provides the complete tables corresponding to every single table and figure in the book.[17]

In terms of structure, the first chapter sets the scene with an overview of the whole life course, showing what matters more and what matters less. The rest of the book is in three distinct parts.

- Part I is about *adulthood*. We ask how much each separate adult outcome matters for happiness. We also ask "Do people adapt to it?" and we ask "Do people mainly compare this outcome with that of other people?"—both crucial questions if we wish to increase the amount of happiness in the world. We also ask "How much do social norms matter, and other people's behavior?" And we ask "What outcomes of childhood most influence the resulting adult?"

- Part II is about *childhood* itself. How do parents affect their children's happiness, behavior, and academic performance? And what is the impact of schools and teachers, compared with parents?

- Part III shows how all this information can be fed into *policy making*, and why we need a totally new way of making policy. The last chapter summarizes our conclusions.

Cautions

Our aim is ambitious—it is to revolutionize how we think about human priorities. Inevitably the findings at this stage are approximate. But it is better to be roughly right about what really matters than to be exactly right about what matters less. Our findings should therefore be judged not by comparison with a state of perfect knowledge but with the prevailing ignorance.

This said, the whole book is subject to certain cautions. First, the aim is of course to show how much something affects happiness—to measure a causal relationship. And causal relationships are most easily established by controlled experiments where the "something" is varied and the result observed. But we have few such experiments in all social science and even fewer on happiness. So in this book we rely on naturalistic evidence, subjected to multiple regression analysis. But we still use the language of causality. We say that something "affects" happiness by some specific amount. This makes for easier reading, but the reported result is neither more nor less valid than the equation from which it comes.

Second, all the "effects" are averaged across people, even though they are certainly different for different people (for some people larger and for others smaller). Moreover most of the equations are broad-brush linear equations without interactions—they are early overall maps of a new and largely unmapped territory. In particular, we say little about male-female differences, partly because most of the equations are remarkably similar for men and women. But, for those who wish to explore this issue, we provide in the Online Materials the full tables for Chapter 1 separately for men and women.

Third, there are many important issues for which life-course surveys are not very helpful. These include the environment and housing, and also differences across ethnic groups where the sample sizes are generally too small. We do not address any of these issues. And fourth, this book is about developed countries only.

Where we use the word *happiness*, we always mean life-satisfaction (for adults) or emotional health (for children). Most of the effects we show are quite small, but this does not mean they are unimportant. If we could raise the life-satisfaction of humanity by 1 point (out of 10) in the next twenty-five years that would be a massive rate of progress.

Conclusion

Is any of this remotely useful? Can we really persuade policy makers to focus on the life-satisfaction of the people?

The answer is surely Yes. Already the OECD urges governments to have as their goal the well-being of their people, and some governments use well-being as a criterion for policy making.[18] But most policy making worldwide still proceeds by a series of ad hoc arguments, with no attempt made to make one argument commensurate with another. At one time Margaret Thatcher attempted to establish wealth creation as an overreaching criterion in Britain. But this did not work because no one believed that the main objective of health care, or child protection, or elderly care, or law and order, or parks was to increase wealth. People had some wider, fluffier concept of what things mattered, but no way to compare them.

Today well-being research offers real evidence to fill that vacuum. It is early days yet, and the numbers in this book are offered to stimulate further refinement rather than as final answers. But no one can doubt that they offer a significantly different perspective from traditional beliefs.

Can they actually be used to evaluate policies? Again the answer is Yes. When existing methods of cost-benefit analysis were first proposed sixty years ago, they seemed impossibly ambitious. But, within the limits to which they apply, they have been constantly refined. As a general approach they are now unquestioned. The same will happen to policy appraisal based on well-being. It will eventually become totally accepted as the standard way to evaluate social policies, and much else besides. And hopefully experimentation will become the standard prelude to policy change. The consequences will be massive.

As Angela Merkel said "What matters to people must be the guideline for our policies."[19] That requires evidence from well-being research, and policy makers brave enough to apply it. If that happens, we can surely build much happier societies.

" Money was down again in relation to love and happiness. "

1 Happiness over the Life Course: What Matters Most?

All human life is here.

—News of the World

The central aim of this book is to supply a perspective on what makes people happy—to make it possible to compare the importance of any one factor with any other. So, before we look at each factor in detail, let us try to see the wood for the trees—to discover what matters more and what matters less.

In this chapter we shall estimate the five sets of relationships discussed in the Introduction, using only two of our surveys. We shall first estimate relationships (1) to (4), using the British Cohort Study data (BCS) on children born in 1970. Then we shall estimate relationship (5), using data on the British cohort born mainly in the county of Avon in 1991–92.[1] These are of course results for Britain, but, as we shall see in later chapters, they are typical of what is found across the advanced world.

The analysis in this chapter is purely cross-sectional, but we discuss panel estimation at length later on. (In panel estimation all effects are smaller, but the ranking of factors is generally similar.) Further explanation and discussion appears in later chapters. At this point the key lesson is the power of these studies to shed a completely new perspective on human life.

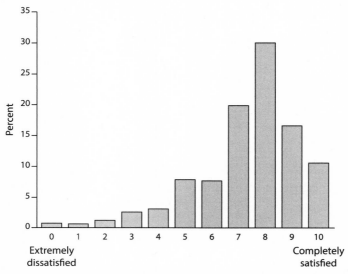

Distribution of life-satisfaction (0–10) at ages 34 and 42 (British Cohort Study)

Interpreting the Results

Throughout the analysis we start from the huge variation in well-being in the population. This is large even within one country, and wider still across the whole human race.[2] The graph above is based on the British Cohort Study and, like the figures that follow, uses observations on the sample at both ages 34 and 42.[3] The standard deviation of life-satisfaction in the sample is 1.9 (on the scale of 0–10).

So what explains this variation? The method of explanation is called multiple regression. This provides estimates of an equation such as

$$\text{Life-satisfaction} = (\propto_1 \times \text{Income}) + (\propto_2 \times \text{Education}) + \text{etc.} \quad (1)$$

where income is measured in dollars and education in years. From this type of equation we can predict that one extra dollar of income will increase life-satisfaction by α_1 points (measured as usual on the scale of 0–10). And likewise one extra year of education will produce an extra α_2 points of life-satisfaction. And so on.

This is essential knowledge if we are to compare the effects of alternative policies to raise well-being—by, for example, raising earnings, expanding education, reducing unemployment, improving health, and so on. In each case we need to know how many points of additional life-satisfaction result from each type of improvement.

A quite different issue is how far do inequalities in income, education, employment, health, and so on explain the huge variation in happiness shown in the diagram. In this case we have to take into account not only the effect of having extra income, which is measured by α_1, but also the extent to which income varies in the population. The most natural measure of such variation is the standard deviation (SD).[4] So one natural measure of the variation in life-satisfaction produced by income inequality (other things equal) is α_1SD (Income). And that amount of variation relative to the overall variation of life-satisfaction is what we shall call β_1 where

$$\beta_1 = \frac{\alpha_1 SD \ (Income)}{SD \ (Life\text{--}satisfaction)}$$

And so on for each other factor.

These β-coefficients are partial correlation coefficients. They show the correlation of, for example, income and life-satisfaction, holding all else constant. They are also the coefficients in an alternative version of equation (1) in which all the variables are "standardized"—that is they are divided by their standard deviations.[5] The standardized regression equation is now

$$\text{Life-satisfaction} = (\beta_1 \times \textit{Income}) + (\beta_2 \times \textit{Education}) + \text{etc.,} \quad (2)$$

where all the variables are italicized to show that they are standardized.

As we have said, these β-coefficients are useful because they tell us how important the different factors are in explaining the overall variation in life-satisfaction. In fact, if the variation in life-satisfaction is measured by its "variance," we can split up the explained variance exactly into the sum of the squared β-coefficients plus some other terms.[6]

In some parts of the book we shall show α-coefficients and in others β-coefficients, as appropriate.[7] When we show β-coefficients, we shall always indicate this in the table heading. If we have not shown it, this means that the regression is based on natural units (i.e., it shows α-coefficients). All of this is explained more fully in online Annex 1.

Every coefficient estimate is only approximate, but the true value is 95% likely to lie within two standard errors (s.e.'s) of the coefficient estimate. So the standard errors are shown in brackets after most of the coefficients. When any coefficient estimate has over 90% probability of being different from zero, the coefficient is printed in bold.[8] Whenever we report an estimated equation, the results of the equation appear as a single vertical column of numbers.

Improving Adult Happiness

So what can we say about what determines the life-satisfaction of an adult? We begin with relationship (1), which includes the "proximate" determinants, as well as the more "distant" ones. In Figure 1.1 we focus only on the co-efficients on the "adult outcomes," in order to see what can be done to improve life-satisfaction once someone is already an adult. (We turn later to what can be done when people are children.)

The dependent variable is life-satisfaction. We begin with economic influences. As Figure 1.1 shows, the logarithm of equivalized household income has some effect on life-satisfaction—similar in Britain to that found in most other countries. But it explains under 1% of the overall variance of life-satisfaction in the population, while all the factors we can identify together explain around 15% of the variance. The direct influence of educational qualifications is smaller still, though they do of course have further indirect influence, for example, through their effect on income. As important as income or education is whether or not you are unemployed.

We turn next to behavior. Being partnered makes a big difference. Equally, criminal behavior (measured by criminal arrests since 16) clearly leads to social exclusion and lower life-satisfaction.

Finally comes health, which involves mental as well as physical health. Mental illness is a specific diagnosable condition. It is one of many factors that can produce low life-satisfaction. They are not the same thing. For example women have on average more well-being than men but more mental illness. The most convincing measure of

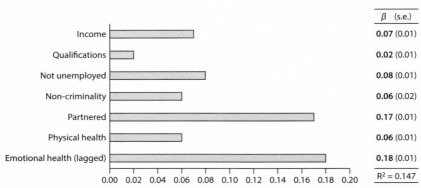

	β (s.e.)
Income	**0.07** (0.01)
Qualifications	**0.02** (0.01)
Not unemployed	**0.08** (0.01)
Non-criminality	**0.06** (0.02)
Partnered	**0.17** (0.01)
Physical health	**0.06** (0.01)
Emotional health (lagged)	**0.18** (0.01)
	R² = 0.147

Figure 1.1. How adult life-satisfaction at 34 and 42 is affected by adult outcomes at these ages (British Cohort Study)

mental illness is one based on an actual diagnosis (and this is the measure that we mainly use in Chapter 6). However in the British Cohort Study we have to rely on 24 self-reported answers to questions. This is a weakness, and we therefore lag this measure (using the answers the individual gave to these 24 questions at ages 34 and 26) to remove the simultaneous effect of temporary mood on reports of mental health and life-satisfaction. Even so, the estimated effects of mental health are large and similar to the estimates in Chapter 6.[9] Moreover they are, both here and later, larger than the explanatory power of physical health, as measured by the number of health conditions the person is experiencing.

So how can policy makers influence these proximate determinants of well-being? Clearly policies directed at adults are important—policies on poverty, adult education, employment, crime, family support, and health. But another vital, and complementary, approach is to intervene earlier, in childhood, in order to improve the later outcomes. This

brings us to the more "distant" causes of human happiness
—in childhood.

Which aspects of childhood should receive the most
attention? There are broadly three main aspects of child
development—intellectual (or cognitive), behavioral, and
emotional. Intellectual development is about knowledge
and task-oriented skills. Behavioral development is primar-
ily about behavior to others. And emotional development
is about how the child feels. Which of these is the most important as a predictor of subsequent life-satisfaction?

In Figure 1.2, we estimate relationship (2) showing how
adult life-satisfaction is explained by life up to age 16, or
in the case of intellectual performance the highest qualification obtained (including where relevant a university degree).[10] Behavioral development is measured by 17 questions
answered by the mother, and emotional development by 22
questions answered by the child and 8 by the mother.[11] In
the table we show the coefficients on the three dimensions
of child development. As can be seen, the strongest childhood predictor of a satisfying adult life is emotional health
in childhood. Less powerful predictors are intellectual development and behavior. These findings have obvious relevance to educational policy.[12]

Finally, we can look further back using relationship (3)—
to the effect of a person's family working its way through everything that followed (see Figure 1.3). For parents we look at
economic status, labor-market activity, parenting style, family stability, and the mother's mental health. Parents' education is measured by their terminal age of full-time education, and equivalized family income is averaged throughout
childhood. Father's unemployment is averaged throughout childhood, and so is mother's work. Parenting style is

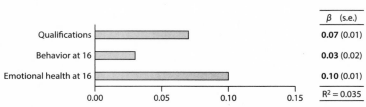

Figure 1.2. How adult life-satisfaction is affected by child outcomes (British Cohort Study)

measured by parents' involvement with the child, and family stability by whether the parents were still together when the child was 16. Mother's mental health is based on 24 questions and is averaged throughout childhood.

As Figure 1.3 shows, most of these factors have similar predictive power, but two findings stand out. Whether the mother works or not has no significant effect one way or other on whether the child becomes a happy adult. This important finding is discussed at length in a later chapter. On the other hand the mental health of the mother turns out to be crucial.

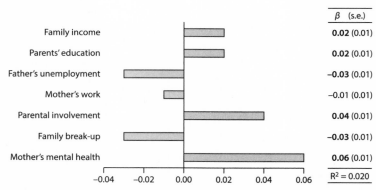

Figure 1.3. How adult life-satisfaction is affected by family background (British Cohort Study)

The Causes of Adult Outcomes

Equations (1) to (3) give us a good idea of the effect of intervening at different stages in a person's life. But it is also important to understand what is going on inside the black box. How, for example, are all the different adult outcomes determined? Even if you do not think happiness is a valuable outcome, you may want to know how to affect adult income, education, employment, crime, family life, and health. Figure 1.4 shows how these adult outcomes are affected by the outcomes of childhood: it represents equation (4).

There is a very clear pattern. Intellectual development is the most powerful predictor of income, qualifications, and employment. Behavioral development is the best predictor of prosocial living and attachment to a partner. And emotional development is much the best predictor of mental and physical health. This is important because mental health is the strongest proximate influence on life-satisfaction, and therefore the aspect of childhood that best predicts adult mental health (i.e., childhood emotional health) is also a good predictor of adult life-satisfaction.

The Causes of Child Outcomes

Finally we can examine what determines the child outcomes themselves (equation 5). This is crucial. Childhood is not a dress rehearsal. It is life itself—to be lived to the full. So what produces a happy, emotionally healthy child?

In Figures 1.5 (a) and (b) we look at how each of the child outcomes at 16 depends on the experience of family

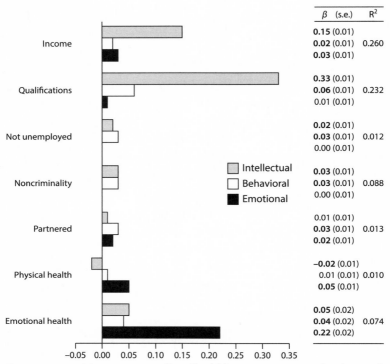

	β	(s.e.)	R²
Income	**0.15**	(0.01)	
	0.02	(0.01)	0.260
	0.03	(0.01)	
Qualifications	**0.33**	(0.01)	
	0.06	(0.01)	0.232
	0.01	(0.01)	
Not unemployed	**0.02**	(0.01)	
	0.03	(0.01)	0.012
	0.00	(0.01)	
Noncriminality	**0.03**	(0.01)	
	0.03	(0.01)	0.088
	0.00	(0.01)	
Partnered	0.01	(0.01)	
	0.03	(0.01)	0.013
	0.02	(0.01)	
Physical health	**–0.02**	(0.01)	
	0.01	(0.01)	0.010
	0.05	(0.01)	
Emotional health	**0.05**	(0.02)	
	0.04	(0.02)	0.074
	0.22	(0.02)	

Intellectual
Behavioral
Emotional

Figure 1.4. How adult outcomes are affected by child outcomes at 16 (British Cohort Study)

and school. The analysis is based on the more detailed information provided by the Avon Study, which includes more data on family finances, parenting behavior, family conflict, and, crucially, schooling. All these variables are included in three separate multiple regressions for intellectual performance at 16, behavior at 16, and emotional health at 16. Intellectual performance relates to the point score at GCSE, behavior comes from the relevant parts of the Strengths and Difficulties Questionnaire (SDQ), and emotional health from the Short Mood and Feelings Questionnaire (SMFQ).

All the determining variables are averaged over the child's life up to 16. The results of each regression are presented in Figures 1.5 (a) and (b).

In Figure 1.5 (a) we report the impact of the family variables on each of the three child outcomes. Strikingly, the determinants of intellectual performance are very different from the determinants of behavior and emotional health (which are much more similar).

We can begin with economic variables like family income and the family's financial problems. These are very important for intellectual performance, and much less so for behavior or emotional health. The same is true of the effects of parents' education.[13]

We then come to the vexed question of how children are affected if their mothers work. Our results confirm the findings of other studies that, if their mothers work (except in their first year after the child is born), children on average do better in school, but their behavior suffers somewhat. There appears to be no significant effect on their emotional well-being.[14]

Another key issue is how the parents relate to the child. Standard propositions are that parents should be (i) "involved" in the child's cognitive development and (ii) "authoritative," that is, warm but reasonably strict. In the Avon study we have good data on involvement (reading to the child, teaching the child, going on outings, singing to the child). This is good for all three outcomes. Unfortunately we do not have good data on authoritative parenting, but we can identify overauthoritarian and aggressive parenting (shouting and hitting). This is correlated with bad behavior and poor emotional health (though there may also be elements of reverse causation at work here).

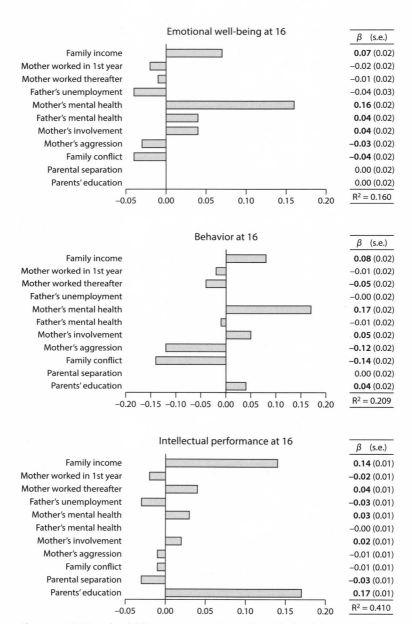

Figure 1.5 (a). How the child's outcomes at 16 are affected by family background (Britain, ALSPAC)

The next issue is how the parents relate to each other. There is clear evidence that parental conflict produces badly behaved and unhappy children. So what about family break-up, which the British Cohort Study identified as important? The answer is that the measured effect of family break-up is largely a proxy for family conflict, which is highly correlated with it. But, where there is already conflict, does family break-up make things even worse for the children? As we show in Chapter 13, it depends how bad the conflict is. If the conflict is terrible, break-up helps; if the conflict is mild, break-up adds to the damage.

Finally how are children affected by the psychological make-up of the parents, and especially their mother? The mother's mental health matters relatively little for children's academic performance, but it matters greatly for their behavior and their emotional health. Their father's mental health generally matters less.

So parents matter. But what about schools? Many people think schools only affect academic performance and behavior, but probably not the emotional health of the child, since this depends so heavily on the family. This view is totally wrong. In the Avon study we know which primary school and which secondary school each child went to. So we can see in Figure 1.5 (b) what difference these schools made.[15] The effect of schools is huge, holding constant the child's family background. Even at the age of 16 the primary school still had an enduring influence—and for behavior and emotional health it had as great an influence as the secondary school.

It might be interesting to compare the importance of schools with that of parents. But we cannot do this because, while each school has many children in the sample, making

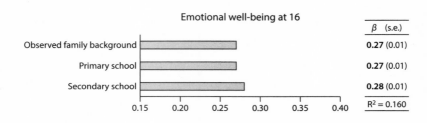

Emotional well-being at 16

	β (s.e.)
Observed family background	**0.27** (0.01)
Primary school	**0.27** (0.01)
Secondary school	**0.28** (0.01)
	$R^2 = 0.160$

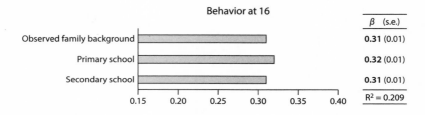

Behavior at 16

	β (s.e.)
Observed family background	**0.31** (0.01)
Primary school	**0.32** (0.01)
Secondary school	**0.31** (0.01)
	$R^2 = 0.209$

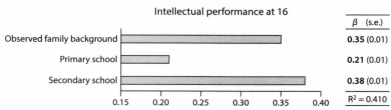

Intellectual performance at 16

	β (s.e.)
Observed family background	**0.35** (0.01)
Primary school	**0.21** (0.01)
Secondary school	**0.38** (0.01)
	$R^2 = 0.410$

Figure 1.5 (b). How child outcomes at 16 are affected by family and schooling (Britain, ALSPAC)

it possible to identify its average effect on all those children, each parent had only one child in the sample. However we can summarize the overall effect of those family characteristics that we can identify. As the graphs show, the size of this effect is similar to that of the secondary school—meaning that the true effect of parents must be larger. One should add of course that this includes the effect of the genes they share with their children.

So much for the determinants of outcomes at age 16. But childhood is an ongoing experience. It is therefore interesting to look also at the determinants of outcomes earlier in childhood—at 5 and at 11. These are shown in the online Full Tables 10.1–10.3. The determinants are very similar to those we have seen at age 16.

In fact we can, remarkably, trace the long-term influence of the primary school teacher each pupil had both when they were aged 8 and 11. First, we can measure for each teacher the value-added that their pupils derived from the teacher—in that year of teaching—by looking at the teacher's average impact on their emotional health, behavior, and math scores at the time. Interestingly the teacher had more effect on their emotional health than on their mathematical knowledge (in terms of explained variance). And then we can show that the teacher's value-added at ages 8 and 11 was still influencing the pupils at age 20—both in terms of their entry to higher education and their employment record. But more on this in Chapter 14.

Conclusions

From the present whistle-stop tour, some key conclusions are already clear.

- Income explains only a relatively small part of the variation in the happiness of the population.
- Human relationships are much more important, especially close personal partnering.
- Mental health is the most important single factor explaining the variation in the happiness of the population.

- If we go back to childhood and ask what is the best predictor of an enjoyable adult life, the best predictor is the child's emotional health, which, with the child's behavior, is significantly more important than all the qualifications the person ever obtains.
- And finally children are of course affected by their parents (especially their mother's mental health). But schools and individual teachers also have an enduring impact.

PART ONE

What Makes a Happy Adult?

"Thanks, but I still want a dollar."

2 Income

Wealth is like seawater. The more we drink, the thirstier
we become.

—*Schopenhauer*

Does more money buy more happiness? It does, but less than
many people might think. There are two extreme views,
both equally fallacious. On the one hand there are careless
studies claiming that money makes no difference. This is
certainly wrong, if we are talking about life-satisfaction as
the outcome. On the other hand, there are millions of individuals who think that more money would totally change
their well-being. For most people, this too is a delusion.

The effect of income on happiness is in fact one of the
best-measured effects in all happiness research. In this chapter we present the evidence. This is the first of five chapters,
all of which follow a fairly standard format. Each chapter
takes the effects of one factor (here income) and begins
with evidence from the British Cohort Study, mostly cross-
sectional. It then goes on to time-series data on individuals
drawn from three panel studies for Britain, Germany, and
Australia, as well as cross-section data on the United States.
For every factor we also examine the key role of social comparisons and adaptation, before tracing how the factor itself
is determined by earlier childhood experiences.

There is one other important general point. From now
on we measure life-satisfaction not in terms of its standard
deviation (as in Chapter 1) but in its natural units, running

from 0 to 10. This reflects a major purpose of this book—to encourage people to think of well-being as a concrete entity, with units that every policy maker can recognize and can therefore try to maximize. We are confident that, with sufficient exposure, this will become standard practice in policy making. In the seventeenth century there was no clear concept of temperature, but today we all know what 75°F is like and how it differs from 32°F. Indeed most car owners know the difference between temperature levels that are quite close to each other. The same will become true of life-satisfaction.

So what causes it? We begin with income, not because it is the most important determinant of well-being, but because so many people have for so long thought it was. Indeed some economists have taken "full income" as equivalent to well-being.[1]

Of course it would be so if everyone were the same and everything that mattered to their well-being could be bought with money. Neither is true. We are born different. And, as we shall see, many key things that matter for us just happen to us—we do not choose them. They are, in the language of economists, "external effects." These include how other people behave, how they influence our tastes, and the myriad of nonchoice factors affecting our mental and physical health. And, even in many areas where choice operates, there are problems of "asymmetric information" and imperfect foresight, where the happiness resulting from a choice is different from what the person expected. In all these areas we can learn what causes happiness only by studying it directly.[2]

So happiness is not the same as income. But income does affect happiness. By how much?

Life-Satisfaction

Our first empirical analysis uses data from the British Cohort Study (BCS), which covers people born in one particular week of April 1970.[3] Adult well-being in the BCS is
measured by the following *life-satisfaction* question:

> Here is a scale from 0–10. On it "0" means that you
> are completely dissatisfied and "10" means that you are
> completely satisfied. Please tick the box with the num-
> ber above it which shows how dissatisfied or satisfied
> you are about the way your life has turned out so far.[4]

Information on life-satisfaction is currently available for
the BCS sweeps that were carried out when the respondents were aged 26, 30, 34, and 42. For the reasons that
were explained in Chapter 1,[5] we concentrate our analysis
here on the data for when the respondents were 34 and 42.
The standard deviation of life-satisfaction in this group is
1.9. So anything that alters life-satisfaction by 1 point is having a large effect (shifting someone up 21 percentile points,
starting from the mean). Even an increase of 0.1 point in
life-satisfaction from the mean raises someone by 2 percentile points.

Income and Life-Satisfaction

So how much extra life-satisfaction can extra *income* bring?
The closest relationship is between life-satisfaction (measured in natural units) and the logarithm of income.[6] This
means that the gain in happiness from an extra dollar of

income varies greatly with income. In fact the gain in happiness is inversely proportional to income. So when a poor person gets a dollar from someone who is ten times richer than him or her, the poor person gains ten times more happiness than the rich person loses. This so-called Diminishing Marginal Utility of Income was an article of faith in nineteenth-century economics and was a central argument for the redistribution of income. It is now substantiated by hard evidence, both across individuals (see below) and across countries (see Chapter 8).

But how big is the effect? How much of the variation in happiness is due to income inequality? For this purpose income is measured in the BCS as household disposable income per adult-equivalent[7] in the household.[8] The distribution of this income in the BCS is the familiar bell shape—not perfectly "normal" but fairly symmetrical, as Figure 2.1 shows. The standard deviation of log income is 0.74.[9] (We use the word log somewhat loosely throughout, to mean natural logarithm, i.e., log to the base e.)

There is a clear relationship between income and happiness. This can be seen in Figure 2.2, which distributes the whole adult population according to income and life-satisfaction. As it shows, of the richest third of the population, only 16% have life-satisfaction of 6 or less, while for the poorest third this figure is 29%. However, the overall correlation between log income and life-satisfaction is only 0.05—the variance of log income "explains" only 0.25% of the variance of life-satisfaction.

To evaluate the effect of a policy change it is clearest if we measure how extra income affects life-satisfaction when this is measured in absolute units (0–10). If we regress life-

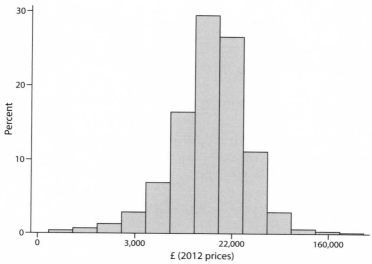

Figure 2.1. The distribution of individuals aged 34 and 42 by annual equivalized income (British Cohort Study)

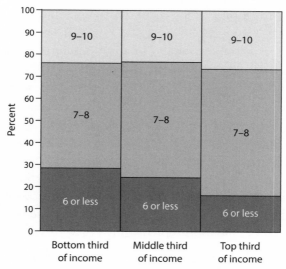

Figure 2.2. Distribution of life-satisfaction among adults in each third of incomes (British Cohort Study)

satisfaction (thus measured) on log income and nothing else beyond age and gender, we are estimating the relationship

$$\text{Life-satisfaction} = \alpha_1 \log \text{Income} + \text{constant}$$

holding constant only gender and age. The coefficient α_1 estimated this way is 0.30—a similar figure, as we shall see, to figures found around the world.[10] If this were the whole story, it would mean that a doubling of income would increase life-satisfaction by 0.21 points (since when income doubles log income rises by 0.7).

But this is a maximum estimate, since other things were not held equal in the equation. To do this, we need to estimate the multivariate relationship.

$$\text{Life-satisfaction} = \alpha_1 \log \text{Income} + \alpha_2 \text{Qualifications} + \text{etc.}$$

including the whole battery of adult outcomes, child outcomes, and family variables. The results are shown in the first column of Table 2.1, which reproduces Figure 1.1 from the last chapter—but with all the variables appearing where possible in their natural units as labeled in the table. The coefficient on log income now falls from 0.30 to 0.20, reflecting the correlation between income and other determinants of life-satisfaction like mental health or family background. Clearly some of these other variables (like parental education) are simply correlated with income and they should be included in the equation: they are "confounders." But some other variables (like mental health) may be affected by income and therefore can "mediate" the effect of income on life-satisfaction. To the extent this is true their effect should not be removed, and those mediating variables should not be included in the equation. It would be nice if we could say how far the other factors are "mediating" an effect of income or are simply correlated with it (i.e., confounders). If we assume they are all confounders we can infer that if we double someone's income (cet. par.) we could raise their life-satisfaction by about 0.14 points.[11] Equally if we raised their income by 10% we would raise their life-satisfaction by 0.02 points— not a huge amount for a substantial cost.[12]

These are fairly standard results of cross-sectional analysis. But cross-sectional analysis is always at the mercy of omitted personal variables. Those omitted variables that do not change over time can be controlled for by including a personal fixed effect, provided we can obtain two or more observations on the same individual. The BCS provides such observations at ages 34 and 42, and Table 2.1 reports in the next column the results of a fixed effects analysis using these data. As expected, the estimated effects are reduced, and the impact of log income falls from 0.20 to 0.13.

However, much better panel data can be found in the *household surveys* carried out repeatedly on the same households in Britain, Germany, and Australia—the British Household Panel Survey (BHPS),[13] the German Socio-Economic Panel (SOEP), and the Household, Income and Labour Dynamics in Australia (HILDA) survey.[14] These are not birth cohorts, so we cannot include childhood characteristics as we can in the BCS. Nor do these panels include data on criminality. But the other variables are defined to be as close as possible to those in the BCS. In addition we include US data from the Behavioral Risk Factor Surveillance System (BRFSS). This is not a panel survey but a large annual survey of different samples of people each year. In this

Table 2.1. How life-satisfaction (0–10) is affected by adult outcomes
(British Cohort Study)

	Units	*Cross-section*	*Panel*
Income	ln	**0.20** (.03)	**0.13** (.04)
Qualifications	SD (index)	**0.04** (.02)	
Not unemployed	1, 0	**0.89** (.13)	**0.35** (.15)
Noncriminality	Minus no. of arrests	**0.05** (.01)	
Partnered	1, 0	**0.69** (.03)	**0.40** (.05)
Physical health	No. of conditions	**0.12** (.01)	0.03 (.02)
Emotional health (lagged)	SD (index)	**0.35** (.01)	
Emotional health	SD (index)		**0.11** (.02)
Observations		17,812	17,812
Individual fixed effects		No	Yes
R^2		0.147	
Within R^2			0.018

and the next two chapters we confine the analysis to people of working age (aged under 65 but above 25).

The results are in Table 2.2. The first column shows the results of pooled cross-sectional analyses including every observation on every sample member, with time and regional dummies added in to the equation. As can be seen, these cross-sectional results are similar to those we have already seen in the British Cohort Study. But the fixed-effects estimates for both Britain and Australia are really small.[15]

Table 2.2. How life-satisfaction (0–10) is affected by log income (household panel data)

	Cross-section	*Panel*
Britain	**0.16** (.01)	**0.04** (.01)
Germany	**0.26** (.01)	**0.08** (.01)
Australia	**0.16** (.01)	**0.06** (.01)
USA	**0.31** (.01)	**NA**

There are always problems of measurement error and timing here, and the truth probably lies somewhere between the cross-sectional and the fixed-effects results.

The cross-sectional results in the table are fairly typical of those found in other countries. Such analyses have by now been carried out in most countries in the world and are tabulated in online Annex 2. They always show a positive impact of log income on life-satisfaction (0–10), and the simple coefficient (with no cet. par.) is generally around 0.3. Holding other things constant, the coefficient is nearer 0.2.

The Easterlin Paradox

It would seem to follow that, if average real income in a country rises substantially, as it has in most countries since the second World War, life-satisfaction would also rise substantially. Yet in many countries, including the United States, this has not happened. Figure 2.3 gives the evidence for the United States and the three countries whose panel data we have been looking at. In all of them income per head has risen substantially, while average life-satisfaction has not.[16]

This is the paradox first identified by Richard Easterlin as long ago as the 1970s.[17] The paradox contrasts two stylized facts:

- Within a country at a point in time, richer people are on average happier.
- Within a country over time, as everyone has become richer, people have not become happier.

The first of these stylized facts is certainly true, as we have seen. The second is true of some countries, but not all. On average world happiness has indeed risen, and at the same time the world has become richer. But has happiness increased more in those countries where economic growth has been higher? The answer here is a matter of dispute.[18] If we look only at countries with long series of data on happiness, there is no relationship between economic growth and increases in happiness, whether the countries are all rich or all poor, or mixed. Indeed in China, which has experienced the fastest growth of any major country, happiness is the same now as in 1990.[19] However the analysis is different if we include countries with shorter time-series—but in shorter time series it becomes difficult to disentangle the cyclical effects of boom and bust on happiness (which certainly exist) from the effects of the long-term rate of economic growth.

In any case none of us lives in an average country; and in the many countries to which the Easterlin paradox applies it is important to understand why this has been the case. There could of course be many adverse factors that have offset the undoubted benefits an individual obtains from increased income.[20] But there are two general factors intrinsic

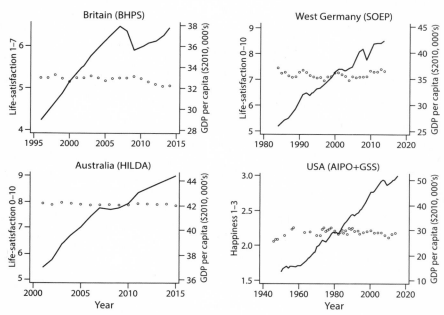

Figure 2.3. Average income (——) and well-being (∘∘∘∘∘) over time

to income that may be at work, and both of these were mentioned in Easterlin's original article. He hypothesized that there were two possible adverse factors at work.

- *Social comparisons.* If others become richer, this reduces the enjoyment I get from a given income. And if in the extreme case people care only about their relative income, then economic growth can bring no overall increase in happiness.
- *Adaptation.* The enjoyment I get from a given income is lower the higher my previous income—owing to habituation. If there is "full adaptation,"

a person's happiness is the same whatever their income, once they have experienced it long enough. However there cannot be full adaptation to income because, if there were, richer people would not be happier than poorer people, nor richer countries happier than poorer countries (cet. par.).

Both social comparisons and adaptation are major potential factors limiting the benefits from higher income. The same may be true of the benefits of education, employment, partnering, or health if they too are subject to social comparisons or adaptation. So in each of this sequence of chapters we investigate the scale of social comparisons and of adaptation.[21] This is important because, if we want to improve human happiness, we should focus especially on those areas where there is less social comparison and less adaptation.

Social Comparisons and Adaptation

In Russia there is a story of a peasant whose neighbor has a fine cow. God asks the peasant how he can help him, and the peasant replies, "Kill the cow." In academia, in 2008 a website was established through which it was possible for all University of California employees to discover their colleagues' salaries. Hardly anyone knew about it until, as an experiment, the prize-winning economist David Card and colleagues informed a random selection of University of California employees that the site existed.[22] Shortly afterward, they surveyed these employees and a control group. Employees with less than the average pay for their occupation and department were substantially less satisfied with their job if they knew the site existed (and thus their colleagues' salaries) than if they did not.

There is now a major literature on social comparisons, and it would require a whole book to do it justice.[23] But as the survey by Clark, Frijters, and Shields (2008) shows, comparisons with other people's incomes play a big role in most people's life-satisfaction. We can do no more than illustrate this from the surveys we are using in this book.

Table 2.3 is a more general version of our standard pooled cross-section equation, where we include comparison effects for income, education, unemployment, and family formation. For log income comparisons we use the average income in the same sex, age group, region, and year in question.[24] The negative effects of comparator income show up clearly (even with regional and year dummies included). The size of the effects is remarkable. In Britain, Germany, and Australia the negative effect of comparator income is roughly as large as (or even larger than) the positive effect of your own income. This means that all you care about is your income relative to that of your comparators. If this is true, economic growth cannot increase average happiness since the average of relative income is by definition constant. In such a case only reduced inequality of income can increase average happiness.[25]

In the United States absolute income also matters, but, if someone's income increases, the total social benefit is substantially less than the private benefit to that individual. For example, taking the US estimates, when one individual raises his or her income 10% he or she gains 0.031 points. But the other N comparators find that their average comparator income has risen by 10%/N. So their total loss of life-satisfaction is N times 0.17 times 10%/N. The net social gain is 0.031–0.017, which is roughly half the private gain.

Table 2.3. How life-satisfaction (0–10) is affected by own income and comparator income (household panel data) (pooled cross-section)

	Britain	*Germany*	*Australia*	*USA*
Log own income	**0.16** (.01)	**0.26** (.01)	**0.16** (.01)	**0.31** (.01)
Log comparator income	**–0.23** (.07)	**–0.25** (.04)	**–0.17** (.06)	**–0.19** (.03)

At this point, one might of course ask: Does everyone care equally strongly about how much other people have? Or do these comparisons become more important when you are well off, while poorer people worry more about their absolute income? There is some evidence of this in Britain, where the estimated coefficient on log comparator income is 0.05 points more negative at the upper quartile of income than at the lower quartile.[26] The same is true in Germany. But the implications are the same as those we have already noted.

Another issue is whether people compare themselves not to the average of a comparator group but for example to some particular part of the income distribution, like for example top incomes. In this case we should have to include some measure of inequality (like top incomes relative to mean incomes) in the happiness equation. However, attempts to disentangle the effects of inequality on individual happiness have not been particularly successful, and a discussion of this issue is left to Chapter 8.[27]

What of adaptation? This can only be studied by exploiting the time-series aspect of the panel data. So we add to a standard individual fixed-effects regression a variable for comparator income plus another equal to the average of own log income over the previous three years (see Table 2.4).

Table 2.4. How life-satisfaction (0–10) is affected by own income, comparator income, and own previous income (household panel data) (fixed effects)

	Britain	*Germany*	*Australia*
Log own income	**0.06** (.01)	**0.19** (.01)	**0.06** (.01)
Log comparator income	–0.09 (.06)	**–0.12** (.04)	0.01 (.04)
Log previous 3 years' income	–0.02 (.02)	**–0.08** (.01)	–0.01 (.01)

As expected, all the coefficient sizes are reduced, but social comparisons dominate adaptation in both Britain and Germany (while in Australia both become very small).

What Determines Someone's Income?

Finally, how are family incomes determined? What aspects of your earlier life predict your standard of living? To investigate this, we return to the BCS and estimate an equation in which the log of equivalized income is regressed on all three child outcomes as well as family background. Bear in mind that this is not an individual earnings equation: equivalized household income also reflects the income of their partner and the size of their family. And it explains the resulting income by everything we know about a person's childhood and background. The main influences are shown in Table 2.5.[28]

As expected, the dominant influence is the child's intellectual performance. This is measured simply by whether the person had or did not have an O-level equivalent (grades

Table 2.5. How log income is affected by childhood outcomes and family background (British Cohort Study)

	Units	*β-coefficients*	*Unstandardized coefficients*
Intellectual performance (16)	1, 0	**0.15** (.01)	**0.30** (.02)
Behavior (16)	SD (index)	0.02 (.01)	0.01 (.01)
Emotional health (16)	SD (index)	**0.03** (.01)	**0.02** (.01)
Family income	Ln	**0.09** (.01)	**0.12** (.02)
Parents' education	Age	**0.11** (.01)	**0.04** (.00)
Father's unemployment	Fraction of waves	–0.02 (.01)	**–0.08** (.04)
Mother's employment	Fraction of waves	0.01 (.01)	0.01 (.02)
Parental involvement	SD (index)	0.01 (.01)	0.01 (.01)
Family break-up	1, 0	–0.00 (.01)	–0.00 (.02)
Mother's mental health	SD (index)	0.01 (.01)	0.01 (.01)
Number of siblings	Number	–0.01 (.01)	–0.01 (.01)
Postmarital conception	1, 0	–0.00 (.01)	–0.00 (.02)
Female	1, 0	**–0.45** (.01)	**–0.62** (.01)
Ethnicity: white	1, 0	**–0.02** (.01)	**–0.12** (.05)
Low birth weight	1, 0	**–0.02** (.01)	**–0.07** (.03)
Observations		12,378	12,378
R^2		0.260	0.260

A*–C) at age 16. Yet this one characteristic predicts that you receive an extra 30% on your income.[29] By contrast behavior and emotional health in childhood are weak predictors of adult income. The next best predictors are parents' income and father's unemployment. If we omit the childhood outcomes, the effects of the family variables increase, but only slightly.

Conclusions

We have covered much ground. But three conclusions stand out. First, life-satisfaction (0–10) depends linearly on the logarithm of income. This means that an extra dollar is 10 times more valuable (in terms of life-satisfaction) to a poor person than to someone who is 10 times richer.[30] Before happiness research, economists merely speculated about the "declining marginal utility of income." Now we can measure it.

Second, income is very salient, and so it becomes a major preoccupation. But most studies suggest that by doubling their income people can gain no more than 0.2 additional points of life-satisfaction.

Moreover, at the level of society, if everyone doubles their income, the effect is very much less because so much of the positive effect of income on happiness is an effect of income relative to others. And for society as a whole the average of relative income cannot change.

This last finding has huge policy relevance. It affects the importance of all policies whose aim is to increase economic growth.[31] One such is educational policy, since education is the most important determinant of an individual's income. But does education also affect happiness directly, as well as via income? Let us see.

"Don't cry, Mom. Lots of parents have children who didn't get into their first-choice college, and they went on to live happy, fulfilled lives."

3 Education

We must educate our masters.

—*Robert Lowe, Chancellor of the Exchequer (1868–73)*

Education is the route to a career, and that is a major reason for its importance. It benefits society, and society pays the educated individual for those benefits. In the 1950s under 10% of Britons went into higher education; now it is nearly a half. A similar educational explosion has happened worldwide (see Figure 3.1). So is education mainly a route to higher productivity and better pay; or is it also a good in itself?[1]

Education certainly raises income, as we saw in the last chapter. And this effect has been remarkably sustained despite the huge increase in the number of highly educated people. Clearly the demand for educated workers has increased at least as much as the supply, at least in the United States and the UK.[2] And it is this wage premium that, in part at least, draws people into higher education.

But education also provides more than just extra income to the person who is educated. It provides an interesting and potentially enjoyable experience for students; it educates people as citizens and voters; it generates higher tax payments; it reduces crime (see Chapter 7). And it provides for the individuals concerned a personal resource, interesting work, and additional capacity for enjoyment throughout their life.[3] In this chapter we investigate only this last set of ("direct") benefits, using our standard framework of

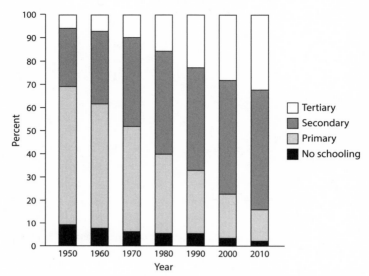

Figure 3.1. Highest educational attainment of the adult population in advanced countries (%)

analysis. So what is the direct impact of extra education per se on how much we enjoy our lives?

The measure of education we use in the BCS is qualifications. The BCS tell us the highest qualifications that a person has achieved. There are altogether five levels of qualifications,[4] but we need to create a single continuous variable. So we weight each qualification by the weight it attracts in a wage equation.[5] This is the index of qualifications that we use for the BCS. We always present it in standardized form. In the household panel studies we measure education more simply by years of full-time education and confine the analyses to people under 65. For purposes of translation one standard deviation of qualifications is approximately equal to 2.5 years of schooling.[6]

Table 3.1. How life-satisfaction (0–10) is affected by qualifications (British Cohort Study)

	Effect of 1 SD of qualifications
Holding nothing else constant	**0.19** (.02)
Holding everything constant	**0.04** (.02)

How Education Affects Life-Satisfaction

In the British Cohort Study, education is well correlated with life-satisfaction, provided no other variables are included. As Table 3.1 shows, one standard deviation more of education is associated with 0.19 extra points of life-satisfaction.

However, this overestimates the direct impact of education per se on life-satisfaction, for two reasons. First, some of those 0.19 points are an indirect effect of education via other things (like income) that education affects and that then affect life-satisfaction. These are "mediating" variables and reflect a genuine effect of education but one that is indirect. Second, there are other variables, like father's unemployment, that are correlated with education and also affect life-satisfaction. These are "confounding" variables.

To obtain the direct effect of education on life-satisfaction we have to hold all these other variables constant. When this is done, the effect of one standard deviation of education falls drastically to 0.04 points of happiness. This may seem small, but one must remember that it lasts over a very long period.

On top of this there is the indirect effect via things like income. How big is this indirect effect of education on happiness? To answer this requires a "decomposition analysis." This is a very useful technique that we also use extensively in Part II of the book. The idea is very simple and explained more fully in online Annex 3b. Suppose that the full estimated equation is

$$\text{Life-satisfaction} = a_1 \text{ Education} + a_2 \text{ Income} + \text{etc.}$$

but we also estimate the simple relationship

$$\text{Life-satisfaction} = b_1 \text{ Education}$$

Then b_1 will be larger than a_1 and the difference will equal a_2 times the "effect" of education on income, plus all the other similar terms for all the other variables. Some of these variables will be "mediating" variables, and some will be "confounders" (where for example the "effect" of education on father's unemployment is clearly not a causal relationship).

The variables that have a good claim to be mediating variables are those listed in Table 3.2. Some of the relationship between education and these variables is not causal, but we cannot separate out the part that is confounding. Treating the whole as a mediating effect we find the total effect of education on happiness as shown in Table 3.2. This total is less than the simple estimate of 0.19, and the residual is due to the role of confounding variables, like father's unemployment.

Thus, to conclude our BCS analysis, education in itself has a small positive direct effect on life-satisfaction, but a bigger overall effect due to its effect via income and other mediating variables.[7]

Like the BCS, the household panel surveys also find that happiness is moderately affected by education per se. The

Table 3.2. How life-satisfaction (0–10) is affected by qualifications (British Cohort Study)

		Effect of 1 SD of qualification
Direct effect		**0.04**
Mediated effect via	income	**0.03**
	not unemployed	**0.00**
	partnered	**0.00**
	noncriminality	**0.01**
	physical health	**0.00**
	mental health	**0.02**
Total		**0.10**

British, German, and US estimates are similar; the Australian estimate is actually negative (see Table 3.3).

Taken together with the mediated effects, a total effect averaging say 0.07 points of life-satisfaction throughout life is a worthwhile contribution for one extra year of education.[8] However, there is one major problem: social comparisons. In Table 3.4 we investigate how people's life-satisfaction is affected by the years of education of others in the same age group, gender, and region.

Looking at the first column for each country, the effect of other peoples' education is consistently negative.[9] In Britain

Table 3.3. How life-satisfaction (0–10) is affected by years of education (household panel data) (pooled cross-section)

	Britain	*Germany*	*Australia*	*USA*
Years of education	**0.03** (.00)	**0.05** (.00)	**–0.01** (.00)	**0.03** (.00)

Table 3.4. How life-satisfaction (0–10) is affected by years of education (household panel data) (pooled cross-section)

Education	Britain		Germany		Australia		USA	
Own	**0.03**	**−0.16**	**0.05**	0.07	**−0.01**	**−0.13**	**0.03**	−0.02
	(.00)	(.07)	(.00)	(.05)	(.00)	(.05)	(.00)	(.01)
Others'	**−0.09**	**−0.27**	**−0.05**	−0.02	**−0.03**	**−0.14**	**−0.01**	**−0.06**
	(.02)	(.07)	(.01)	(.06)	(.01)	(.05)	(.01)	(.02)
Own × others'		**0.01**		−0.00		**0.01**		**0.01**
		(.01)		(.00)		(.00)		(.00)

it is larger than the total of positive effects. In the other countries it is also substantial.

So what is happening here? Are people just going to higher education because their friends go and it would therefore hurt not to go? We investigate this hypothesis in the second column for each country. We do indeed find some evidence that the more other people are going to further education, the more you gain in happiness by going yourself.

To sum up, extra education brings considerable benefits (direct and mediated) to the individual. But these are substantially offset by the negative effect of one person's education on others in the peer group. However that is not the end of the story: there are other external effects.

Most important may be the development of a better informed and more rational set of citizens and voters. Second, there are the tax externalities. More education leads to higher incomes and therefore higher taxes, which can be used to provide better public services or higher disposable income to other families. If the latter, this could add at most

0.01 points to the social return from one year of education for one person.[10] Finally, education reduces crime. We investigate the issue of crime in Chapter 7. From those estimates we can infer that one extra year of education for one person may reduce crime enough to generate 0.14 extra point-years of life-satisfaction for the population.[11] When spread over say sixty years of life, this makes little difference to the overall assessment. As educators we had hoped the case for general educational expansion was stronger than appears to be the case.[12]

Causes of Educational Success

Finally we turn to the causes of educational success. These have been much studied; but it is still useful to fit them into our overall framework, using the British Cohort Study.[13]

Our aim is to explain a person's highest educational qualification (measured as usual in standardized form). The results are in Table 3.5. As explanatory factors, we include all three measures of child development at 16. Here intellectual performance is measured by a simple variable reflecting whether or not the person had any O-level equivalent (grades A*–C). Not surprisingly people with this achievement at 16 reach a final level of educational qualification nearly one standard deviation higher than other people do. Unlike emotional health, behavior is also a significant predictor.

Family background also matters. If your family is three times richer, your qualifications are on average 0.2 standard deviations higher. If your father is continuously unemployed, they are 0.3 standard deviations lower. No other

Table 3.5. How highest qualification (standardized) is affected by childhood outcomes and family background (British Cohort Study)

	Units	*β-coefficients*	*RH variables unstandardized*
Intellectual performance (16)	1, 0	**0.33** (.01)	**0.94** (.03)
Behavior (16)	SD (index)	**0.06** (.01)	**0.06** (.01)
Emotional health (16)	SD (index)	0.01 (.01)	0.01 (.01)
Family income	Ln	**0.10** (.01)	**0.21** (.03)
Parents' education	Age	**0.19** (.02)	**0.10** (.01)
Father's unemployment	Fraction of waves	**−0.05** (.01)	**−0.29** (.06)
Mother's employment	Fraction of waves	**−0.03** (.01)	**−0.08** (.04)
Parental involvement	SD (index)	**0.04** (.01)	**0.04** (.01)
Family break-up	1, 0	−0.02 (.01)	−0.05 (.03)
Mother's mental health	SD (index)	**0.03** (.01)	**0.03** (.01)
Number of siblings	Number	**−0.03** (.01)	**−0.03** (.01)
Postmarital conception	1, 0	**0.02** (.01)	**0.08** (.04)
Female	1, 0	0.02 (.01)	0.04 (.02)
Ethnicity: white	1, 0	**−0.05** (.01)	**−0.33** (.09)
Low birth weight	1, 0	−0.02 (.01)	−0.07 (.05)
Observations		8,943	8,943
R^2		0.232	0.232

variables have a particularly large effect, except for mother's mental health and being white, which in that cohort was an educational disadvantage.[14] If we leave out the effect of childhood outcomes, the effects of the family variables rise on qualifications, but only slightly.[15]

Conclusion

Education raises the income of individuals and of nations.[16] But does it do more than this? Extra education per se raises the happiness of the educated person somewhat, over their whole lifetime. But it lowers the happiness of the rest of the population. There are, however, effects in reducing crime, which we investigate in Chapter 7. And there are hopefully positive effects on our national civic life, which we are unable to investigate with data only on individuals in one country. Moreover, as we show in Chapter 14, the quality of education matters even more than its quantity.

So where are we so far? We have examined two of the most common indicators of progress in most people's minds—higher income and more education. And we have found that they contribute less to life-satisfaction than most people suppose. Can it be that, relative to these rather economic variables, we have underestimated the role of human relationships—at work, in the family, and in the community? This is what we turn to in the following chapters.

"I've stopped carrying a briefcase. I don't like to flaunt my employment."

4 Work and Unemployment

The insupportable Labour of doing nothing.

—*Sir Richard Steele*

Full-time workers spend at least a quarter of their waking life at work.[1] But sad to say, on average, they enjoy that time less than anything else they do. The worst time of all is when they are with their boss.[2]

Even so, people hate it even more if they are unemployed. This is not just because they lose money from being out of work. They lose something even more precious—a sense of contributing, of belonging, and of being wanted.

In this chapter we explore all these issues, focusing again on people under 65. We first look at unemployment—how much it hurts, whether you can adapt to it, what legacy it leaves, the role of local unemployment rates, and what determines who becomes unemployed. Only then do we turn to the quality of work.

Unemployment

The pain caused by the experience of unemployment is one of the best-documented findings in all happiness research.[3] Most unemployed people are struggling and less happy than when they were in work. For the same reason they become happier when they get back to work.[4] We can document this most clearly from the panel studies, but first we can use the British Cohort Study to look at how satisfied

Table 4.1. How life-satisfaction (0–10) is affected by labor-force status (British Cohort Study)

Compared with full-time workers	Cross-section	Cross-section	Panel
Unemployed	**−1.55** (.13)	**−1.06** (.15)	**−0.30** (.15)
Part-time workers	−0.01 (.05)	0.05 (.05)	0.09 (.07)
Self-employed	**0.19** (.05)	**0.25** (.09)	**0.34** (.08)
Out of labor force	−0.08 (.06)	−0.09 (.10)	**0.26** (.09)
Controls	Age, gender	All	All + fixed effect

people are with all the different possible positions in the labor force.

In Table 4.1 we compare the life-satisfaction in each group with that of people with full-time jobs, holding constant only age and gender. The unemployed are less happy by a staggering 1.5 points, see column (1). By contrast self-employed people are happier by nearly 0.2 points.[5] However the effect of unemployment falls to around 1 point when, in column (2), all the other standard factors (including income) are introduced. So unemployment hurts for many reasons beyond the loss of income.

Similar results are obtained in the panel datasets for Britain and Germany (see Table 4.2).[6] When all the data for each country are pooled and subjected to cross-section analysis, unemployment reduces life-satisfaction by 0.7 of a point in Britain, 1 whole point in Germany and rather less in Australia and the United States.

However all cross-section estimates are subject to bias from omitted personal variables. We can remove this bias by introducing a fixed personal effect for each individual. The

Table 4.2. How life-satisfaction (0–10) is affected by labor force status—compared with full-time workers (household panel data)

	Britain	*Germany*	*Australia*	*USA*
Pooled cross-section				
Unemployed	**–0.70** (.04)	**–0.99** (.03)	**–0.31** (.03)	**–0.45** (.02)
Part-time workers	0.03 (.02)	–0.03 (.02)	**0.08** (.02)	NA
Self-employed	**0.06** (.03)	**–0.08** (.03)	0.01 (.03)	**0.08** (.01)
Out of labor force	**–0.29** (.02)	**–0.10** (.02)	–0.04 (0.2)	**–0.23** (.01)
Panel				
Unemployed	**–0.46** (.04)	**–0.71** (.03)	**–0.18** (.02)	
Part-time workers	–0.01 (.02)	**–0.11** (.02)	0.01 (.01)	NA
Self-employed	–0.04 (.03)	–0.04 (.04)	0.03 (.02)	
Out of labor force	**–0.14** (.03)	**–0.14** (.02)	–0.04 (.02)	

estimates now tells us what happens on average every time the individual changes his or her labor-force status. We now estimate that, compared with full-time employment, unemployment in Britain reduces life-satisfaction by 0.3–0.4 points (see Tables 4.1 and 4.2). The German estimate is higher at 0.7, while the Australian one is lower at around 0.2.

Adaptation and Scarring

If unemployment hurts, do you get used to it after a while so that it becomes less painful? The answer is No. That is the finding of previous literature,[7] and here we investigate it for men using the household panel data.[8]

We study those individuals in the sample who had at least one spell of unemployment, and we observe their well-being in the years before their first spell began and the subsequent years (up till their next spell of unemployment).[9] For the whole sample we now estimate a standard regression that measures the level of life-satisfaction in these years, using a fixed effect to remove any selection biases.[10] The equation tells us how happy on average the sample were in the years before unemployment set in, and then how happy those people were who were still unemployed one year later, two years later, three years later, and four or more years later. The results are plotted in Figure 4.1.

As can be seen, in Britain and Germany the onset of unemployment reduces life-satisfaction by nearly 1 point, and life-satisfaction remains at least this low so long as the person remains unemployed. In none of the three countries is there any adaptation to unemployment.

What happens once a person is reemployed? Does the experience of unemployment still linger, reducing the person's life-satisfaction? This is the issue of *scarring*. We investigate this by including in our regressions a variable reflecting the amount of time a person was unemployed previously. For the BCS we have a complete record at age 30 for the proportion of time the individual has been unemployed since joining the labor force. When we introduce this into our standard equation, it attracts a coefficient of −1.47 (s.e. = .18). This means that each previous year of unemployment is reducing current life-satisfaction by about 0.1 points (1.47/14)—one-tenth of the pain it causes at the time.

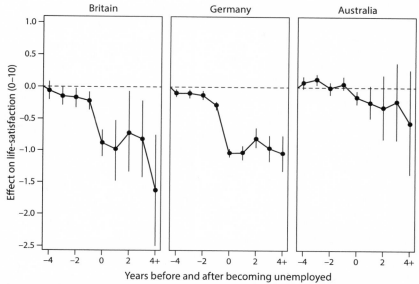

Figure 4.1. Adaptation to unemployment. (household panel data) (men).
Note: The value of 0 corresponds to more than four years before becoming unemployed.

Very similar estimates are found in the household panel data. In Table 4.3 we add to each pooled cross-section equation a variable representing the proportion of the last five years for which the person was unemployed.[11] The estimated coefficients are all about 0.6, meaning again that

Table 4.3. How life-satisfaction (0–10) is affected by current and previous unemployment (household panel data) (pooled cross-section)

	Units	*Britain*	*Germany*	*Australia*
Current unemployment	1, 0	**−0.74** (.07)	**−0.82** (.03)	**−0.37** (.04)
Previous unemployment	0–1	**−0.44** (.13)	**−0.73** (.05)	**−0.53** (.10)

each previous year of unemployment is reducing current life-satisfaction by about 0.1 point. Thus unemployment causes pain not only at the time but also to a lesser extent over the years that follow, even after the person is back in work.[12]

Local Unemployment

When jobs are scarce, this makes some people unemployed; but it also creates fear and uncertainty for many more people, even if they currently have work. In consequence, when unemployment rises in a region, this reduces the life-satisfaction of the employed population in the region. Table 4.4 shows this effect in the first row of the table.[13] It implies that in Britain a 10% local unemployment rate reduces the life-satisfaction of the employed population by 0.14 points—and rather more in Germany and less in Australia.

At the same time, for those who are unemployed, a high unemployment rate reduces their sense of shame at being unemployed, and it also expands the social group with whom they can interact.[14] Does this help? We investigate this issue in the second row of the table, and the answer is Yes, it helps but not by much. For example, in Britain, using the bottom two rows of the table we find the following. If the local unemployment rate is 10%, unemployed people suffer in total a loss of 0.69 points (i.e., 0.73–0.038), while when the unemployment rate is zero they suffer by 0.73 points. This is not much comfort, and even though the estimated interaction effect is bigger in Germany and Australia, we conclude that social comparisons are not a big issue for the effects of unemployment.

Table 4.4. How life-satisfaction (0–10) is affected by your own unemployment and by the regional unemployment rate (household panel data) (pooled cross-section)

	Units	Britain	Germany	Australia	USA
Own unemployment	1, 0	**−0.73** (.09)	**−0.93** (.07)	**−0.48** (.11)	**−0.49** (.06)
Regional unemployment rate	0–1	**−1.38** (.56)	**−1.58** (.36)	−0.37 (.42)	**−1.44** (.47)
Regional unemployment rate × own unemployment	(0–1) × (1, 0)	0.38 (1.36)	−0.67 (.75)	2.85 (1.74)	0.93 (1.18)

Note: Regional unemployment rate is for same age group and gender.

But the spillovers on the rest of the population are severe. So if we look at the total well-being cost when a person becomes unemployed, it is 0.7 points for the unemployed person and another 2.0 points in aggregate among the rest of the population.[15]

From this analysis, unemployment emerges as an unalloyed bad. It reduces well-being and is not mitigated by habituation or by social comparisons.

Causes of Individual Unemployment

But what determines which individuals become unemployed?[16] The main issue is to explain who has a history of unemployment, not who is unemployed at a particular moment. To explain lifetime well-being, we need to explain lifetime unemployment—or at any rate the amount of unemployment over a longish spell of years. As we have seen, the BCS give us data on a person's complete unemployment history up to the age of 30. So in Table 4.5 the dependent variable is the percentage of that time the person spent unemployed—in other words their average unemployment rate. For ease of exposition, we measure it this time as a percentage (rather than a proportion).

In Table 4.5, column (1) we give the β-coefficients. As this shows, the biggest single determinant of your unemployment rate is your father's unemployment rate. (The effect is measured here with childhood outcomes held constant, but this has little effect on the impact of the family variables.) So, turning to column (2), if your father's unemployment rate averaged 10%, your own unemployment rate will average 0.6% points higher than if your father was never unemployed. The rate of intergenerational transmission (measured by the β-coefficient of 0.09) is thus only modest.[17]

Quality of Work

But do people enjoy their work? Only recently has social science shown how little most people do in fact enjoy their work, compared with many other activities. This has been discovered through time-use studies pioneered by, among others, the Nobel Prize–winning psychologist Daniel Kahneman. Table 4.6 shows the results of his team's first time-use study,[18] of around nine hundred women in Texas. They were asked to divide the previous working day into episodes, like a film: typically they identified about fourteen episodes. They then reported what they were doing in each episode and who they were doing it with. They were also

Table 4.5. How an individual's percentage of time unemployed up to age 30 is affected by childhood factors (British Cohort Study)

	Units	β-coefficients	All variables unstandardized
Intellectual performance (16)	1, 0	**−0.04** (.01)	**−1.40** (.41)
Behavior (16)	SD (index)	**−0.06** (.02)	**−0.71** (.20)
Emotional health (16)	SD (index)	**−0.04** (.01)	**−0.47** (.17)
Family income	Ln	**−0.03** (.01)	**−0.81** (.34)
Parents' education	Age	0.02 (.01)	0.15 (.08)
Father's unemployment	Fraction of waves	**0.09** (.02)	**6.39** (1.26)
Mother's employment	Fraction of waves	**−0.05** (.01)	**−1.94** (0.42)
Parental involvement	SD (index)	**−0.04** (.01)	**−0.43** (0.17)
Family break-up	1, 0	0.01 (.01)	0.54 (.45)
Mother's mental health	SD (index)	−0.03 (.01)	−0.31 (.17)
Number of siblings	Number	**0.04** (.01)	**0.39** (.15)
Postmarital conception	1, 0	0.02 (.01)	0.71 (.46)
Female	1, 0	**−0.07** (.01)	**−1.69** (.26)
Ethnicity: white	1, 0	−0.01 (.01)	−0.70 (1.24)
Low birth weight	1, 0	−0.00 (.01)	−0.24 (.60)
Observations		9,811	9,811
R^2		0.046	0.046

Table 4.6. Happiness in different activities (sample of Texan women)

Activity	Average happiness	Average hours a day
Sex	4.7	0.2
Socializing	4.0	2.3
Relaxing	3.9	2.2
Praying/worshipping/ meditating	3.8	0.4
Eating	3.8	2.2
Exercising	3.8	0.2
Watching TV	3.6	2.2
Shopping	3.2	0.4
Preparing food	3.2	1.1
Talking on the phone	3.1	2.5
Taking care of my children	3.0	1.1
Computer/e-mail/ Internet	3.0	1.9
Housework	3.0	1.1
Working	2.7	6.9
Commuting	2.6	1.6

asked how they felt in each episode, along twelve dimensions that can be combined into a single index of good or bad feeling.

The table shows what they liked most (sex), and what they liked much less. Bottom, bar one, comes work. This is of course an average over all the hours of work.

This finding has since been confirmed in many studies of more representative samples including those in the US government's official American Time Use Survey.[19] Work always comes very near to the bottom of the list.

Table 4.7. Happiness while interacting with different people
(sample of Texan women)

Interacting with	Average happiness	Average hours a day
Friends	3.7	2.6
Relatives	3.4	1.0
Spouse/partner	3.3	2.7
My children	3.3	2.3
Clients/customers	2.8	4.5
Coworkers	2.8	5.7
Alone	2.7	3.4
Boss	2.4	2.4

Equally distressing is how people experience their boss. As Table 4.7 shows, the worst time in the day for the Texan women was when they were with their boss. This too has been found elsewhere for more representative samples.[20] Apparently most bosses fail to inspire their subordinates or make them feel appreciated. This raises real questions about modern methods of management.

Not surprisingly people prefer shorter hours to longer hours. Figure 4.2 shows the effect on life-satisfaction of different hours of work in our four household panel countries. It would appear that, in all these countries, shorter is better other things equal. The difference in life-satisfaction between those working over 50 hours a week and those working 11–20 hours averages nearly 0.2 points of life-satisfaction, everything else (including household income) held constant.

So how can work be made more enjoyable? Clearly any business has to make money. Its sole aim cannot be to make

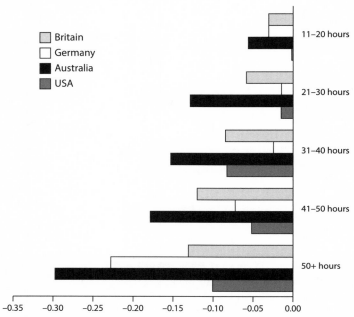

Figure 4.2. How life-satisfaction (0–10) is affected by weekly hours of work—compared with 0–10 hours (household panel data) (pooled cross-section)

its workers happy, or even its customers. But there is increasing evidence that making workers happy and engaged does help a firm to make money. For example, one study focused on the 100 US companies that (based on employee surveys) were judged to be the "100 Best Places to Work" in 1985. The share prices of those companies were followed for the next twenty-five years and compared with the share prices of all other US listed companies. After twenty-five years, money invested in the 100 Best Places to Work was worth 50% more than the same amount of money invested in other companies.[21]

So what does make somewhere a good place to work? This is a whole subject in itself. Roughly speaking, a good workplace needs to offer:

• good work organization, including

  clear goals for the work
  adequate autonomy in doing it
  support and appreciation for doing it
  adequate skill and time to do it
  sufficient variety of work
  safety at work

• good work/life balance, including

  reasonable hours of work
  flexibility for family objectives

• good pay, promotion prospects, and job security

There have been countless studies of job satisfaction that lie behind this.[22] But the acid test is whether the workplace makes people contented with their life as a whole. Here there have been few studies of the effect of the workplace on overall life-satisfaction.

To study this, a good source is the European Social Survey (2004 and 2010), which asked detailed questions about the different dimensions of workplace experience. Table 4.8 studies employed people and shows the regression of life-satisfaction (0–10) on a set of questions that cover most of the standard characteristics of good practice that were listed earlier. Interestingly all the characteristics show up with fairly similar sizes of effect, and the effects are big.[23] Questions relating to work-life balance are particularly strong predictors of life-satisfaction across these European

Table 4.8. How life-satisfaction (0–10) is affected by various dimensions of workplace quality (European Social Survey)

	Life-satisfaction
Wages (log)	**0.19** (0.06)
Work hours per week	−0.14 (0.19)
Supervisor	**0.10** (0.04)
Job is secure	**0.23** (0.03)
Good opportunities for promotion	**0.25** (0.06)
Job has high autonomy	**0.23** (0.02)
High variety in work	**0.25** (0.03)
Coworkers are supportive	**0.27** (0.03)
High time pressure	**−0.11** (0.03)
Job interferes with family life	**−0.49** (0.04)
Worry about work at home	**−0.32** (0.04)
Job is dangerous	**−0.37** (0.06)
Country and wave dummies	Yes
2-digit industry dummies	Yes
2-digit occupation dummies	Yes
Observations	21,590
R^2	0.273

countries. So this table offers plenty of suggestions for employers who wish to improve the atmosphere at the workplace.[24]

Using the coefficients in Table 4.8 we can calculate a quality-of-work index for each member of the sample. We can then compute how one standard deviation in the quality of work alters life-satisfaction. It raises life-satisfaction by 0.4 points—a substantial effect.

Conclusion

If it is important to make work more enjoyable, it is even more important to make sure that those who want it have it. Unemployment is one of the most bruising of all experiences. It cannot be adapted to, and it leaves psychological scars. Public policy should aim not only to stabilize unemployment but to make it permanently lower. That is the most important objective for economic policy. But it is time to move beyond economics and into people's private lives.

"Get the pliers yourself."

5   Building a Family

> Marriage is a great institution, but I'm not ready for an institution yet.
>
> —*Mae West*

Most people want a partner, and most want at some time to have children. Are they right, in terms of what will bring them satisfaction and fulfillment? These are important issues for any form of public policy that aims to support people in achieving a good life.

Life-course data provide important evidence on all this. They show decisively the importance of close personal relationships to a satisfying life. When it comes to children, the answer is more nuanced.

Partnering, Separation, and Bereavement

Our surveys provide the following breakdown of people according to their family status:

Married
Living as married
Separated (i.e., married but not living with spouse)
Divorced (but not remarried)
Widowed
Single

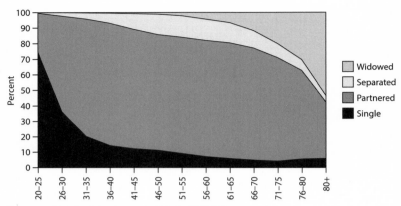

Figure 5.1. Family status by age in Britain (UKHLS, 2010–15)

In earlier times few people "lived as married": they just got married. But in the last fifty years cohabitation has become more and more common, and in Britain a third of children are now born to an unmarried couple who live together.[1] So, from a functional point of view, the first two groups are so similar that we merge them into a single group that we call "partnered."

Similarly, there is no massive difference between being separated and legally divorced, and we combine these two under the generic heading "separated." Separation can occur at any age. But widowhood becomes increasingly common with age, and in this chapter we therefore include adults of all ages. The division of the British population between the different categories is as shown in Figure 5.1.

How much difference does it make whether you are single (our omitted category), partnered, separated, or widowed? We can look at this first using the data from the BCS (see Table 5.1).

Table 5.1. How life-satisfaction (0–10) is affected by family status (British Cohort Study)

Compared with single	Cross-section	Panel
Partnered	**0.77** (.04)	**0.34** (.06)
Separated	−0.11 (.06)	−0.16 (.10)
Widowed	−0.44 (.33)	**−0.97** (.46)

Other things equal, partnered people are (in cross-section) happier than single people by a huge 0.8 points. Widowhood is of course tragic, especially in your 30s and 40s, and the tragedy becomes even more evident when we move to the panel data analysis in the second column. By contrast the coefficient on being partnered is reduced in panel data (so that part of the cross-section correlation reflects inherently happier people being more likely to be with a partner).

Table 5.2. How life-satisfaction (0–10) is affected by family status—compared with single (household panel data)

	Britain	Germany	Australia	USA
Pooled cross-section				
Partnered	**0.59** (.03)	**0.29** (.03)	**0.47** (.03)	**0.49** (.01)
Separated	**−0.15** (.04)	0.03 (.03)	**−0.16** (.05)	−0.04 (.01)
Widowed	0.11 (.08)	0.06 (.07)	**0.18** (.10)	**0.07** (.01)
Panel				
Partnered	**0.28** (.05)	**0.14** (.03)	**0.30** (.03)	
Separated	**−0.12** (.07)	0.01 (.04)	**−0.21** (.04)	NA
Widowed	−0.02 (.12)	**−0.32** (.14)	−0.15 (.13)	

However, we find more comprehensive evidence on family and children from the household panel data, which cover people of all ages. The results are shown in Table 5.2. The cross-sectional effect of partnering here averages around 0.5 points and the panel estimate around 0.2. Separation emerges as very negative—in cross-section about 0.6 points worse than being partnered, and in panel analysis about half that. The effect of losing your partner through death is about 0.4 points.

Adaptation

But do you adapt to the end of a relationship—or indeed to the beginning of one? Figures 5.2–5.4 present our key

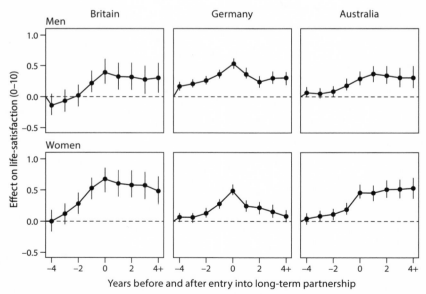

Figure 5.2. Adaptation to partnership (household panel data)

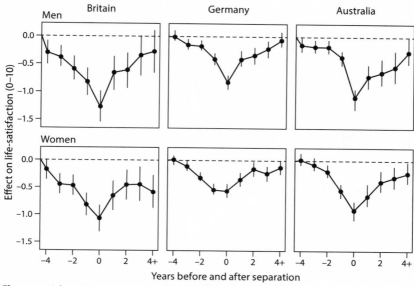

Figure 5.3. Adaptation to separation (household panel data)

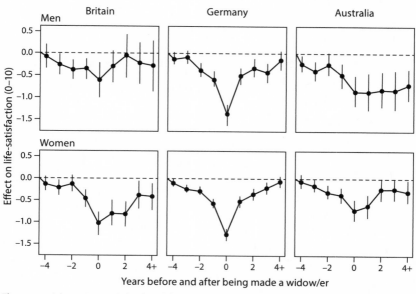

Figure 5.4. Adaptation to widowhood (household panel data)

results. They are estimated in the same way as was described in the case of unemployment in Chapter 4.

The results are striking. On average people who enter a partnership go on enjoying it year after year—see Figure 5.2. In Britain and Australia, there is virtually no habituation either for men or women, though in Germany there appears to be some. In every country there is of course a courtship effect: people are becoming more cheerful as partnership comes in sight.

At first glimpse these results are at odds with most earlier published work on the effects of marriage.[2] But they are not, because here we are focusing on the more relevant variable, which is partnership, including cohabitation. If cohabitation begins first and marriage follows later, all that the earlier research has shown is that the additional marriage premium soon fades. The benefit of the relationship continues.

If relationships bring long-lasting benefits, separation brings pain. Figure 5.3 covers all who were originally partnered but then became separated. It shows the effect of the first separation up to the point when the person becomes repartnered. As the figure shows, the pain is worse to start with, but in no country is there a full return to the original position.[3,4]

There is also some adaptation to losing a partner through death, which earlier research has also shown. As Figure 5.4 shows bereavement is extremely painful, and though substantial recovery generally follows, it is rarely complete.[5,6,7]

But can the social setting help? It surely feels worse to be on your own when everyone else like you is partnered. We find some evidence of this, though it varies between countries. In both Britain and Australia people without partners suffer if more other people are partnered, but the effect is smallish.[8]

Having Children

If partnerships bring joy, what about children? This is complicated to investigate, because people can to a large extent choose whether or not to have children. To a degree people who want children more get more children, just as people who like classical music are more likely to listen to it. So if we compare people with and without children we may be just comparing people with different tastes, without discovering what difference the children made to those who had them.[9] To find that out, we have to follow the same people over time. So we shall focus mainly on that.

In these surveys the only evidence we have is on whether people have children who are still living with them.[10] So we can say nothing about the benefits or otherwise of children who are grown up or of grandchildren. As for having children in the home, we find in our equations that the most effective variable is whether there are any children, not how many there are. So in Figure 5.5 we show for the British household panel, the proportion of people who have any child living at home. After 45 this plunges, and we therefore confine our analysis to people aged 30–45, or in the BCS as usual to people aged 34 and 42.

So what does the evidence show—are children a blessing? In the BCS cohort, the effect of having any child is to raise life-satisfaction by 0.25–0.30 points (in cross-section

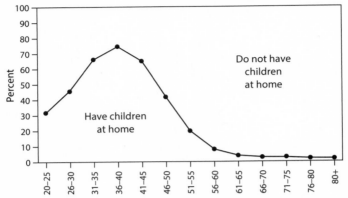

Figure 5.5. Percentage of people with children at home in Britain (BHPS, 2010–15)

and panel respectively). The larger household panel samples give similarly large figures for Germany, but much smaller ones for Britain and Australia.[11]

The effect is also somewhat fleeting, as appears when we look carefully into the pattern of adaptation. Figure 5.6 studies those panel members who ever had a child, over the years before and years after they had their first child. In all three countries there is excitement as the child approaches, joy when the child arrives, and complete adaptation within two years. This is of course an average finding, but it applies to both fathers and to mothers.

This finding—that young children have only small average effects on life-satisfaction—is in line with the findings of previous research.[12] A sensible conclusion is that having young children brings some satisfaction but on average

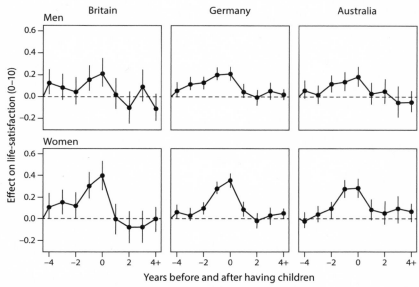

Figure 5.6. Adaptation to parenthood (household panel data)

not a lot (with huge upsides being matched by significant downsides).

Causes of Partnering and Parenting

If being partnered is so desirable while it lasts, what determines who gets partnered? Partnership is not easy to predict, but Table 5.3 provides some interesting insights. Not surprisingly, people whose parents broke up are 4% points less likely to be partnered (in the BCS). And all the different dimensions of child development make equal (but

Table 5.3. How family status and parenthood are determined (British Cohort Study)

	Units	Partnered (1, 0) RH variables standardized	Partnered (1, 0) RH variables unstandardized	Parent (1, 0) RH variables standardized	Parent (1, 0) RH variables unstandardized
Intellectual performance (16)	1, 0	0.00 (.01)	0.01 (.01)	**-0.01** (.01)	**-0.03** (.01)
Behavior (16)	SD (index)	**0.01** (.01)	**0.01** (.01)	0.00 (.00)	0.00 (.00)
Emotional health (16)	SD (index)	**0.01** (.01)	**0.01** (.01)	0.01 (.01)	0.01 (.01)
Family income	Ln	0.01 (.01)	0.02 (.01)	0.00 (.01)	0.01 (.01)
Parents' education	Age	-0.00 (.00)	-0.00 (.00)	-0.00 (.00)	-0.00 (.00)
Father's unemployment	# waves	-0.01 (.01)	-0.04 (.03)	-0.01 (.00)	-0.03 (.03)
Mother's employment	# waves	0.00 (.01)	0.01 (.01)	0.00 (.00)	0.01 (.01)
Parental involvement	SD (index)	**0.01** (.01)	**0.01** (.01)	0.00 (.00)	0.00 (.00)
Family break-up	1, 0	**-0.01** (.01)	**-0.04** (.01)	-0.01 (.00)	-0.02 (.01)
Mother's mental health	SD (index)	-0.00 (.01)	-0.00 (.01)	-0.01 (.00)	-0.01 (.00)
Number of siblings	Number	**0.01** (.01)	**0.01** (.00)	**0.02** (.00)	**0.01** (.00)
Postmarital conception	1, 0	0.00 (.00)	0.00 (.02)	-0.01 (.00)	-0.02 (.02)
Female	1, 0	**0.04** (.01)	**0.07** (.01)	**0.10** (.00)	**0.19** (.01)
Ethnicity: white	1, 0	0.01 (.01)	0.05 (.03)	0.00 (.00)	0.03 (.03)
Low birth weight	1, 0	**-0.01** (.00)	**-0.04** (.02)	**-0.01** (.00)	-0.04 (.02)
Observations		17,803	17,803	17,812	17,812
R²		0.013	0.013	0.044	0.044

small) contributions to explaining whether you become partnered.

Conclusions

As we have seen, human relationships at the most intimate level make a huge difference to a person's happiness. However, family history, in so far as we can measure it, contributes little toward explaining who becomes and remains partnered. This suggests that later interventions to help people's social skills may have as much a role to play as childhood interventions. One obvious issue here is mental health.

"How are the smiling exercises coming along?"

6 Health of Mind and Body

Of all the things that I have lost, I miss my mind
the most.

—*Mark Twain*

"What do you most desire in life?" Many people say physical
and mental health. Physical pain is one of the worst of all
human experiences—bodily torture being an extreme case.
And mental pain is as bad as most physical pain, and very
similar—it is experienced in the same brain areas as the affective components of physical pain.[1] Indeed mental illness
is the most common cause of suicide.[2]

So both mental illness and physical illness are major
causes of human wretchedness. But many existing studies
of life-satisfaction ignore mental illness. Implicitly they assume that misery and mental illness are the same thing. As
we argued in Chapter 1, this is quite wrong. Many things
can cause low life-satisfaction, some of them directly and
others indirectly by causing mental illness. But there are
also sources of mental illness that are uncorrelated with
any of the obvious external causes like poverty, unemployment, separation, or bereavement. We overlook a key part
of human experience if we overlook mental illness of that
type.[3] Multiple regression enables us to study the effects of
that type of mental illness, by holding constant the obvious
external causes.

Causes of Misery

Since only a minority of us are sick at any one time, the distribution of health is not symmetrical—it is highly skewed. For this reason, we begin this chapter by looking at the causes of misery, rather than of life-satisfaction over its full range.

We define those in misery ("les misérables") as all those over 25 who are at the lowest levels of life-satisfaction. For example, in the British BHPS it is those with life-satisfaction of 4 or below, who amount to 8% of the overall population of people over 25.[4] And the first question is, *What changes would do most to reduce the number of people in misery in our society?*

Many people would say "End poverty and unemployment." This would be very desirable, but, as we shall see, it would be even more desirable to eliminate ill health, both physical and mental.

To explore this issue we use data for the United States (BRFSS),[5] Australia (HILDA), and Britain (BCS and BHPS). The first three of these have reasonably objective definitions of mental illness:

The United States and Australia	Has ever been diagnosed for depression or an anxiety disorder.[6]
Britain (BCS)	Has seen a doctor in the last year for emotional problems.

The BHPS uses the GHQ-12, which consists of a set of 12 self-reported diagnostic symptoms. There is a clear danger that transitory mood factors will influence both the GHQ replies and the person's reported life-satisfaction. For the GHQ we therefore always enter the previous year's value.

Physical illness is measured in Britain and the United States by the number of physical illnesses or conditions (like diabetes, angina, stroke, asthma, arthritis, etc.).[7] In Australia it is measured by the physical components of the SF36 questionnaire, entered with a lag.

To answer our original question we can turn all the continuous variables into discrete variables. So in Table 6.1 we examine the effect of eliminating

- Poverty (defined as the lowest 20% of incomes)
- Unemployment
- Physical illness (defined as the lowest 20% of physical health), and
- Mental illness (defined as in the text above, or in the BHPS as the lowest 20% on the GHQ-12).

None of these variables is the same as low life-satisfaction, but all of them contribute to it. Let us see by how much.

The approach in Table 6.1 is simple.[8] In the first column we ask by how much a person's probability of misery is increased if they have each characteristic like poverty or depression, other things equal. The numbers are regression coefficients estimated by OLS with all variables shown being dummy variables (1, 0).[9] In the second column, we record what proportion of the total population have the characteristic in question. In the third column we multiply the effect of the characteristic by its prevalence, which provides the answer to our original question: *How much misery would be eliminated if we eliminated the characteristic in question (ceteris paribus)?*

The results are remarkable. In the United States, a person with diagnosed mental illness is 0.10 points of probability more likely than otherwise to be in misery. Of the total population, 22% have diagnosed mental illness. So if there were

Table 6.1. How would the percentage in misery fall if each problem could be eliminated on its own?

	α-coefficient ×	Prevalence (%) =	α × Prevalence (% points)	Total in misery (% points)
USA (BRFSS)				
Poverty (bottom 20%)	0.052 ×	20 =	1.04	
Unemployed	0.074 ×	4.0 =	0.29	5.6
Physical condition (bottom 20%)	0.025 ×	20 =	0.50	
Depression or anxiety, diagnosed	0.102 ×	22 =	2.24	
Australia (HILDA)				
Poverty (bottom 20%)	0.042 ×	20 =	0.84	
Unemployed	0.094 ×	2.5 =	0.23	7.0
Physical illness lagged (bottom 20%)	0.093 ×	20 =	1.86	
Depression or anxiety, diagnosed	0.092 ×	21 =	1.93	
Britain (BCS)				
Poverty (bottom 20%)	0.011 ×	20 =	0.22	
Unemployed	0.056 ×	3.0 =	0.17	8.0
Physical condition (bottom 20%)	0.019 ×	20 =	0.38	
Has seen a doctor for emotional health problems in last year	0.152 ×	14 =	2.13	

	α-coefficient	×	Prevalence (%)	=	α × Prevalence (% points)	Total in misery (% points)
Britain (BHPS)						
Poverty (bottom 20%)	0.025	×	20	=	0.50	
Unemployed	0.138	×	3.0	=	0.41	9.9
Physical condition (bottom 20%)	0.056	×	20	=	1.12	
Emotional health symptoms lagged (bottom 20%)	0.200	×	20	=	4.00	

no mental illness, all else constant, the percentage of the population in misery would be reduced by 2.2% points—a third of the total in misery (which is 5.6%). Eliminating most physical illness would have a smaller effect. Eliminating unemployment, or raising all incomes above the 20th percentile, would also have much smaller effects than eliminating mental illness.

In Australia and Britain the overwhelming importance of reducing mental illness is equally evident. However a different way to analyze misery is more akin to how we have analyzed most issues in this book. The question now is not how do we eliminate misery, but how do we explain its variance?[10] In other words we calculate β-coefficients. We also allow income and physical illness to be continuous variables, and we do the same for mental illness in the BHPS. The results are in Table 6.2. In all countries, except Australia, mental illness emerges as the most important explanatory factor.[11]

Table 6.2. How misery is affected by adult outcomes
(cross-section) (β-coefficients)

	USA	*Australia*	*Britain BCS*	*Britain BHPS*
Income (log)	**–0.12** (.00)	**–0.09** (.02)	**–0.05** (.01)	**–0.07** (.01)
Unemployed	**0.06** (.00)	**0.06** (.01)	**0.03** (.02)	**0.07** (.00)
Physical illness	**0.05** (.00)	**0.16** (.02)*	**0.05** (.01)	**0.09** (.01)
Mental illness	**0.19** (.00)	**0.14** (.01)	**0.09** (.01)	**0.26** (.00)*

Health and Life-Satisfaction

Does the picture change if, instead of focusing on misery, we analyze everything in terms of its impact on the full range of life-satisfaction, measured 0–10? What role does health play in determining this? Table 6.3 gives the answer. It uses the same definitions of the right-hand variables as in Table 6.2, and the results are essentially the same as when the dependent variable was binary ("miserable" or otherwise).[12] As before, we are looking at the effect of each factor holding all other factors constant. In all the countries differences in mental health explain more of the variance of human experience than differences in income or employment status. Mental illness also explains more of the variation in the quality of human life than does the variation in physical health.

Some people may instinctively feel that income and unemployment must be more important. Don't they, after all, cause a lot of mental illness? To see the effects of poverty and unemployment including their effects via mental illness, we can simply omit mental illness from the equation. The effects of income and unemployment barely increase, because their correlation with mental illness is actually not that high.[13]

Table 6.3. How life-satisfaction is affected by adult outcomes (cross-section) (β-coefficients)

	USA	Australia	Britain BCS	Britain BHPS
Income (log)	**0.16** (.00)	**0.09** (.01)	**0.08** (.01)	**0.09** (.01)
Unemployed	**−0.05** (.00)	**−0.04** (.01)	**−0.03** (.01)	**−0.06** (.00)
Physical illness	**−0.05** (.00)	**−0.17** (.01)*	**−0.06** (.01)	**−0.11** (.01)
Mental illness	**−0.21** (.00)	**−0.18** (.01)	**−0.11** (.01)	**−0.32** (.00)*

The relationships discussed so far are all cross-sectional. They thus include the effect of ongoing differences between people as well as of year-by-year variations in human experience. This gives a broad picture of the full variety of human experience. But, as accounts of the causal effect of specific factors, these estimates are vulnerable to the omission of important unmeasured differences between people. A panel analysis, using a fixed effect for each individual, is less vulnerable to this difficulty. As online Table A6.3 shows, the coefficients measured with individual fixed effects are closer to zero than those in the cross-section, but a part of this may be a failure to allow for longer-term influences on life-satisfaction.[14]

Mental versus Physical Health: The QALY Issue

As is well known, health-care spending in every country is heavily weighted toward physical health. While Britain spends more on mental health than most countries, it still amounts to only 13% of total health-care spending.[15] This partly reflects of course the greater costs of much physical health care and its importance in preserving life. But it partly reflects an underestimate by health-care planners of the suffering caused by mental illness—an underestimate reflected in the British measurement of QALYs (Quality-Adjusted Life Years).

In the QALY system, the impact of a given illness in reducing the quality of life is measured using the replies of patients to a questionnaire known as the EQ5D. Patients with each illness give a score of 1, 2, or 3 to each of five questions (on Mobility, Self-care, Usual Activities, Physical Pain, and Mental Pain). To get an overall aggregate score for each illness a weight has to be attached to each of the scores. For this purpose members of the public are shown 45 cards on each of which an illness is described in terms of the five EQ5D dimensions. For each illness members of the public are then asked, "Suppose you had this illness for ten years. How many years of healthy life would you consider as of equivalent value to you?" The replies to this question provide 45N valuations, where there are N respondents. These valuations can then be regressed on the different EQ5D dimensions.[16] These "Time Trade-Off" valuations measure the proportional Quality of Life Lost (measured by equivalent changes in life expectancy) that results from each EQ5D dimension.

As can be seen, these QALY values reflect how people who have mostly never experienced these illnesses imagine they would feel if they did so. A better alternative is to measure directly how people actually feel when they actually do experience the illness.

The result would be very different. Figure 6.1 contrasts the outcomes from these two different approaches. The existing QALY weights are shown by the shaded bars of Figure 6.1. This scale has been normalized so that the bars can be compared with those from a regression of life-satisfaction on the same variables.[17] This latter regression is shown in the black bars in

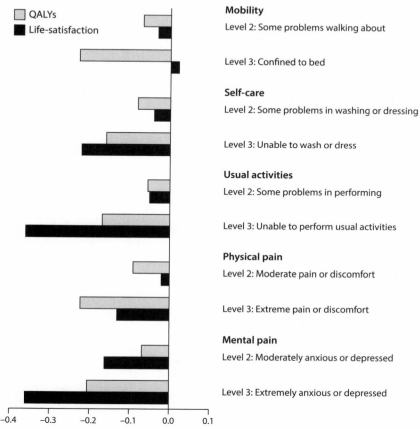

Figure 6.1. How life-satisfaction (0–1) is affected by the EQ5D, compared with weights used in QALYs

the figure—the magnitudes here are not β-statistics but the absolute impact of each variable on life-satisfaction (0–1). As can be seen from the lower part of the figure, the public hugely underestimate by how much mental pain (compared with physical pain) would reduce their satisfaction with life.[18]

External Effects of Ill Health

However, when thinking about the importance of illness, we also have to look at its impact on others in the society as well as the person directly suffering. One of these "external effects" is the economic impact of mental illness on the incomes of other people, since ill people are often receiving working-age disability benefits or sick pay, paid for by other people. As is well known, at least 40% of people on disability benefits have problems of mental rather than physical health, and the same is true of absenteeism.[19] This reflects the fact that mental health problems are as common among people of working age as among retired people, whereas serious physical illnesses are largely illnesses of retirement. This striking difference is illustrated in Figure 6.2—a standard World Health Organisation (WHO) analysis in which the severity of different conditions is based on weights determined by committees of experts. Data from

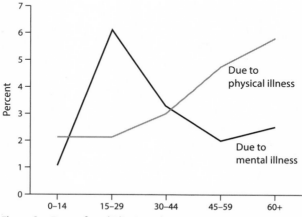

Figure 6.2. Rates of morbidity in each age group

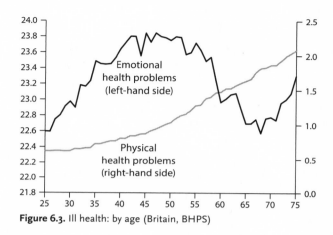

Figure 6.3. Ill health: by age (Britain, BHPS)

the BHPS in Figure 6.3 reveal a similar pattern (though the scales of physical and mental health here are not commensurable). The huge negative external effects of mental illness are much less recognized than they should be.

In Table 6.4 we investigate another key question: How

Table 6.4. How life-satisfaction (0–10) is affected by emotional and physical health of self and others (household panel data) (pooled cross-section)

	Units	Britain (BHPS)	Australia	Germany
Mental illness				
Own	SD	**−0.77** (.01)*	**−0.21** (.02)	**−0.42** (.01)*
Partner's	SD	**−0.13** (.01)*	**−0.04** (.01)	**−0.11** (.01)*
Physical illness				
Own	SD	**−0.22** (.01)	**−0.25** (.02)*	**−0.25** (.01)*
Partner's	SD	−0.02 (.01)	**−0.08** (.02)*	**−0.16** (.01)*

does the illness of a partner affect the other partner? As the table shows, you feel worse when your partner is ill, for whatever reason.[20]

Adaptation to Disability

But do people adapt to being disabled by illness (either physical or mental)? In Britain and Germany we know whether a person is on a disability benefit;[21] in Australia we know if they have a health condition that limits their ability to work. Unfortunately the data do not distinguish between mental and physical disability. As Figure 6.4 suggests, there is little significant adaptation to disability, but this may be

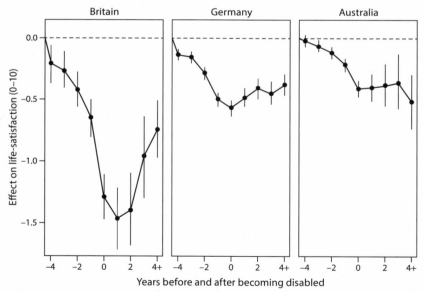

Figure 6.4. Adaptation to disability

mainly true of mental illness. It is widely believed that mental illness is harder to adapt to than physical illness (other than chronic pain) because of the way in which it fills the mind.[22]

Determinants of Ill Health

We turn now to the determinants of ill health, focusing on the middle-aged people in the BCS (see Table 6.5). Interestingly the key determinants are very similar for physical and mental illness. Emotional health in childhood reduces adult illness, physical as well as mental, and so (though less so) does good conduct in childhood. Only intellectual performance has no effect on the number of physical health problems one experiences. (It does reduce the reporting of symptoms of mental illness.)

Turning to the measured influence of parents, neither their education nor their income affect the physical health of their adult offspring. But their mother's mental health has a real effect on both their physical and mental health. Father's unemployment is also a strongly adverse factor. Clearly parents have a large effect through the genes they transmit to their offspring,[23] but we are not able to measure this in these surveys.

More broadly, there is a two-way interaction between happiness and health throughout life. Healthy people are happier, and happy people live longer. This has been known for many years and was made famous through the Nuns Study, which showed that among nuns (who tend to have similar lifestyles) those who were positive in spirit at around age 18 lived much longer than those who were more

Table 6.5. How physical and mental health are affected by childhood outcomes and family (British Cohort Study) (β-coefficients)

	Physical health	Emotional health	Has not seen a doctor for emotional health problems in the last year
Intellectual performance (16)	−0.02 (.01)	**0.05** (.02)	0.03 (.02)
Behavioral skills (16)	0.01 (.01)	**0.04** (.02)	0.02 (.02)
Emotional health (16)	**0.05** (.01)	**0.22** (.02)	**0.13** (.02)
Family income	−0.00 (.01)	0.02 (.02)	−0.01 (.03)
Parents' education	−0.02 (.01)	**0.04** (.02)	0.02 (.02)
Father's unemployment	−0.02 (.01)	**−0.07** (.02)	**−0.09** (.03)
Mother's employment	0.01 (.01)	0.01 (.02)	0.02 (.02)
Parental involvement	0.00 (.01)	0.02 (.02)	**0.06** (.03)
Family break-up	−0.00 (.01)	−0.01 (.02)	−0.03 (.02)
Mother's mental health	**0.03** (.01)	**0.12** (.02)	**0.06** (.02)

negative.[24] More recently, the data from the English Longitudinal Study of Aging provide another striking example. Focusing on people's happiness (measured by a few simple questions), they interviewed a sample of British people aged over 50 and then followed them for the next nine years, recording whether they had died. Those who were least happy to begin with were the most likely to die. The differences were very striking. Even after controlling for age and any illnesses they already had, people in the least happy quarter were three times more likely to die in the next eight years than people in the happiest quarter.[25]

The effect of happiness on physical health is particularly important in later life, but the two-way interaction of physical health and happiness is an important story throughout life. However our analysis focuses mainly on the effect of health on happiness, because happiness is our central outcome.

Conclusion

To conclude, both physical and mental health are hugely important for an enjoyable life. Illnesses of either type can be devastating. But mental illness explains more of the misery in our society than physical illness does, and more than either poverty or unemployment. It also explains more of the variation in life-satisfaction. Moreover, mental illness in one generation is frequently transmitted to the next.

*"My gosh! You remind me so much of your
father when he was in prison."*

7 Crime

Stephen J. Machin

> If poverty is the mother of crime, lack of intelligence is
> its father.
>
> —*Jean de la Bruyère (1688)*

Crime is a problem, both for the criminal and for the community.[1] For the criminal it can lead to social exclusion and a life that fails to satisfy. For the community it reduces the quality of life.

These are the effects of crime. But in this chapter we reverse our usual order and look first at its causes—why in our society some people commit crimes while others don't.

Who Commits Crime?

By the age of 10 we can already predict to some extent who will commit crime later in life.[2] It is those who have behavioral problems in early life, and to a lesser extent those who underperform academically. As we shall show, the pattern is almost identical in Britain and the United States.

Britain

For Britain the evidence comes from the British Cohort Study. From it we can find for each individual whether they had ever been convicted of an offence by the age of 30.[3] We can then estimate what factors affect the probability of having a criminal conviction. The factors we examine are all three dimensions of childhood development, as well as ethnicity, mother's age and education, and whether the father was still present when the child was 10.[4]

Child development is measured at age 10 as follows. Intellectual performance is measured by scores on math and reading; behavioral development by 10 questions answered by the mother; and emotional development by 9 questions answered by the mother. As usual, all the child development variables are measured in standardized form. But in this chapter they are measured in the reverse direction, so that we can see more easily whether bad child development has a positive effect on crime.

The results are in the first column of Table 7.1. They are large effects, given that only 12.5% of the total sample have been convicted. The largest effect is that of behavioral problems at age 10. Someone who is one SD worse-behaved is 3.4 percentage points more likely to become convicted. This means that his or her chance of a conviction has increased by a factor of 27%. Note that this is the effect of behavior measured as early as age 10, and in fact prediction at age 16 is no more accurate than prediction at age 10.[5]

Poor intellectual performance also makes a conviction more likely. By contrast, children who are unhappy are less likely to become criminals—perhaps they lack the desire or energy needed for crime.

Table 7.1. How the probability of conviction is predicted
by childhood problems

	Units	UK (BCS) (Prob. by age 30)	USA (NLSY) (Prob. by age 24–25)
Intellectual problems (age 10)	SD (index)	**0.012** (.004)	**0.030** (.011)
Behavioral problems (age 10)	SD (index)	**0.034** (.004)	**0.062** (.013)
Emotional problems (age 10)	SD (index)	**−0.023** (.004)	**−0.024** (.013)

The United States

Things are remarkably similar in the United States, except
that there is more crime in the United States. By the age of
24/25, 21.9 % of young people have a criminal conviction.
But the pattern of who gets convicted is extraordinarily similar to that in Britain.

Our evidence on the United States comes from the National Longitudinal Survey of Youth's Child and Young
Adult cohort (CNLSY), which provides data on a sample of
people born between 1975 and 1988.[6] For each individual
we know whether they were convicted of a crime by the age
of 24/25, and we also have their childhood outcomes at age
10/11. In addition we know the same detail on the person's
mother as in Britain.

So we can again estimate how childhood outcomes affect

the probability of conviction, other things equal. The estimated coefficients are in the second column of Table 7.1 and (allowing for the greater levels of crime in the US) are broadly similar to those found in Britain. When childhood behavior is worse by one standard deviation, this raises the probability of conviction by 6 percentage points. That is an increase of 28% over the average conviction rate—almost exactly the same as in Britain.

Does Education Reduce Crime?

If early childhood problems tend to produce more crime, can extra years of education offset this? Indeed, is one important by-product of education a reduction in crime? Our BCS data provide a first approach to this issue. In Table 7.2 we regress the number of convictions by age 30 on qualifications obtained, as well as on childhood outcomes at age 10 and family variables.

Table 7.2. How the number of convictions by age 30 is affected by qualifications, childhood outcomes at 10, and family background (British Cohort Study)

	Units	
Qualifications	SD (index)	**−0.06** (.01)
Intellectual performance (age 10)	SD (index)	−0.01 (.01)
Good behavior (age 10)	SD (index)	**−0.13** (.02)
Emotional health (age 10)	SD (index)	**0.07** (.01)
Family characteristics	SD (index)	**−0.17** (.03)

Table 7.3. How the probability of educational failure is predicted by childhood problems at age 10

	Units	UK (BCS) (Prob. of low qualifications)	USA (CNLSY) (Prob. of high school dropout)
Intellectual problems (age 10)	SD (index)	**0.15** (.01)	**0.06** (.01)
Behavioral problems (age 10)	SD (index)	**0.04** (.01)	**0.03** (.01)
Emotional problems (age 10)	SD (index)	**–0.02** (.01)	**–0.01** (.01)

Note: The overall rate of education failure (as measured) is 26% in the UK and 10% in the United States.

This shows that one extra standard deviation of qualifications (equivalent to say 2.5 years of schooling) reduces the number of convictions by 0.06 (or by about 23% of the mean).

This is a useful, though small, addition to the other benefits of education identified in Chapter 3. Online Annex 7 discusses even higher estimates of the effect of education in reducing crime—obtained by exploiting differences in the educational experience of different cohorts.[7]

Educational performance in turn can be explained by early child development. We have already explored this in Chapter 3, but here we focus on educational failure and bring in parallel evidence from the United States. For Britain we identify educational underperformance as equivalent to having no qualifications. As Table 7.3 shows in column (1), bad behavior at 10 makes it more likely that you will end up with poor or no qualifications. Similarly in the United States, data in the CNLSY show whether or not the person was a high school dropout. Again bad behavior at 10 predicts a greater chance of dropping out.

The Effects of Crime

Of course our ultimate reason for studying crime is because of its effects on human well-being. These include effects on the individual criminal *and* effects on everybody else. Let us consider them in turn.

Effects on the Criminal

We have already discussed the effect on the criminal in Chapter 1, and shown that a one standard deviation difference in the number of times arrested by age 34 is associated with a 0.06 standard deviation difference in life-satisfaction at age 34—or 0.12 points of life-satisfaction on the scale 0–10.[8] We do not suggest that this is a directly causal statement. It shows essentially how people who get involved in crime become more isolated or worse treated, and thus become more miserable.

Effects on Others

Crime also affects other people. This brings in a new perspective on well-being, for much well-being research focuses solely on how each individual is affected by his or her own experience, and not at all on how each person affects

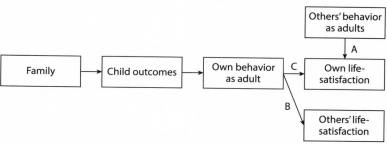

Figure 7.1. How individual experience affects self and others

the experience of others. This is a major shortcoming of much of the empirical literature on well-being, because in the end the well-being of the population depends hugely on how people behave toward each other in their day-to-day behavior—and not just on what they do for others in providing them with income, education, jobs, or health care.

Are other people kind and considerate? Are they encouraging, supportive, and loving? Or are they, in contrast, rough, bullying, oppressive—and in the extreme case criminal in the way they behave? Do we feel that in general other people are on our side or against us?

These things matter to every human being. So we can vary our original diagram of well-being over the life course to show another key set of influences. This is illustrated in Figure 7.1. The person concerned is hugely influenced by how others behave (channel A). By the same token, things that improve an individual's adult behavior derive much of their overall social value from the benefits they confer on *others* (rather than on the individual concerned), that is, through channel B (rather than channel C).

To put numerical values on this influence is not easy, and at this stage we can do no more than give an illustrative example—hopefully, this will become a major area of research. We take our example from an important study of the effect of the local crime rate on local life-satisfaction.[9] This was based on the British Household Panel Survey and included a measure of the quarterly crime rate in the individual's local Police Force Area. It found that individual mental health (0–10) fell by 0.14 points for each unit increase in the log of the local crime rate. This in turn implies that each crime reduces the life-satisfaction (0–10) of the population by roughly 1 point-year, when the effects are cumulated over the whole local population.[10]

Comparing the Two Effects

It would be interesting to compare this *external effect* of 1 point-year (channel B) with the *own effect* on the individual concerned (channel C). On channel C, our data show that each arrest between 16 and 34 reduces the criminal's life-satisfaction (0–10) at 34 by 0.05 points.[11] Thus, supposing the effects of an arrest last 20 years, each arrest reduces the criminal's cumulated life-satisfaction by roughly 1 point-year. Since crimes exceed arrests in the ratio 3.6:1, each crime reduces the criminal's life-satisfaction by 0.3 point-years.[12]

These 0.3 point-years are considerably less than the effect each crime has on the rest of the population, which was approximately 1 point-year. This serves to illustrate why the measured impacts of a policy need to include not only the well-being of those directly affected but also that of others who were not directly affected. The next phase in well-being research needs to pay much more attention to the external effects of people's behavior.

This leads us directly to the issue of social norms. How far do these affect the well-being of a society?

8 Social Norms and Institutions

Please leave your values at the front desk.

—*Paris hotel*

Social norms and institutions are public goods that affect all individuals living in a society. So we can study their effects only by comparing life-satisfaction across societies, rather than across individuals. The simplest thing is to compare different nations.[1]

Countries differ in many ways apart from income and health. Perhaps the most important of these are in their

- ethical norms of behavior (including trustworthiness, generosity, and so on)
- networks of social support ("bonding capital")[2]
- openness and tolerance ("bridging capital")
- personal freedom
- the quality of government (including corruption)
- equality, and
- levels of religiosity.

How do all these features affect the life-satisfaction of citizens in these countries? We can obtain real insight on this from the Gallup World Poll, which covers nearly all countries in the world. It measures satisfaction with your current life by the so-called Cantril ladder.[3] The scale is 0–10, where 0 is the worst possible life you can imagine for yourself and

10 is the best possible life. Countries differ hugely on this scale, showing that there is no set point of happiness dictated by human nature as such. The most satisfied countries are generally those in Scandinavia, as well as the Netherlands and Switzerland. All these have scores above 7. The least happy countries include Syria, Afghanistan, and 17 African states, all scoring below 4.

From this huge spread we can learn a lot about the impact of social norms and institutions on human happiness. Let us begin with a bird's-eye view before looking at each factor in turn. Figure 8.1 and Table 8.1 report a cross-sectional regression across 126 countries in which the average life-satisfaction in each country is the dependent variable. The explanatory factors are as follows (with their definitions).[4]

Trust	Proportion who say Yes to "In general do you think that most people can be trusted (or alternatively that you can't be too careful in dealing with people)?"
Generosity	Proportion who say Yes to "Have you donated money to a charity in the present month?"
Social Support	Proportion who say Yes to "If you were in trouble, do you have relatives or friends you can count on to help you whenever you need them?"
Freedom	Proportion who say Yes to "Are you satisfied or dissatisfied with your freedom to choose what you do with your life?"

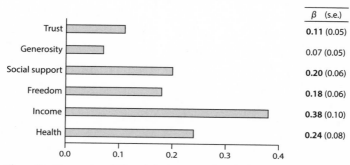

Figure 8.1. How national life-satisfaction is predicted by different national variables

Income	Log GDP per head.
Health	Healthy life expectancy.

We shall look at each of these variables one by one. But first let us look at how they all perform together. Altogether they explain 76% of the variation in life-satisfaction across countries[5] (see Figure 8.1 and Table 8.1). The levels of trust, social support, and freedom are all extremely important.

Table 8.1. How national life-satisfaction (0–10) is predicted by different national variables

	Units	*Coefficient*	*(s.e.)*
Trust	Proportion	**1.08**	(0.45)
Generosity	Proportion	0.54	(0.41)
Social support	Proportion	**2.03**	(0.61)
Freedom	Proportion	**1.41**	(0.49)
Income	Log GDP per head	**0.33**	(0.75)
Health	Years	**0.03**	(0.01)

Trust

For a society to be happy most of its citizens must behave in a trustworthy fashion. It is impossible to measure whether they do so directly. But, indirectly, we can ask the population if they think that other citizens can be trusted. The standard question that has been asked in many surveys over many years in many countries is "In general, do you think that most people can be trusted, or, alternatively that you can't be too careful in dealing with people?"

The proportion of people saying Yes to this question varies astonishingly across countries—from 64% in Norway to 5% in Brazil.[6] One might ask, Do answers to these questions correspond to real differences between countries? Their validity is confirmed by the "lost wallet" experiment, first conducted by the *Reader's Digest Europe* in 1996. This experiment involved dropping 10 cash-bearing wallets (including name and address) in each of 20 cities in 14 western European countries, and in each of a dozen US cities. Researchers later used these data to validate the question on trust.[7] It turned out that, indeed, the actual frequency of return of wallets was highly correlated with national average social trust, as measured in international surveys. In fact in Oslo all 10 wallets were returned, as they were in Copenhagen. But, encouragingly, in the whole experiment two thirds of all the wallets were returned.

The effect of trust revealed in Table 8.1 is truly striking. A move from zero trust to universal trust raises citizen's life-satisfaction by over 1 point (out of 11)—greater than the effect of finding a job.[8] Trust is important for economic growth—as countless studies have shown.[9] But here we are concerned with its direct impact on life-satisfaction, through how people interact with each other. Not surprisingly, levels of trust also have demonstrable effects on suicide, and also, more surprisingly, traffic accidents.[10]

Levels of trust have fallen substantially over time in some countries (like the United States and the UK) and risen in others (such as Denmark and Italy). This may help to explain the fact that life-satisfaction has not risen in the United States and UK, while it has risen in a number of continental European countries. Indeed, for the United States it has been well argued that the main offsets to the private benefits of economic growth include not only comparator incomes but also a decline in the quality of human relationships, as measured by increased solitude, communication difficulties, fear, family infidelity, reduced social engagement, and increased distrust.[11]

In many societies there are of course institutionalized systems of bad behavior. The most common of these is corruption. In this case an official or a business manager does not do what the rulebook says (and what represents the purpose of his or her organization) but rather gives favors in return for a backhander. This hugely undermines trust and is often experienced as a form of personal oppression. If we omit trust in Figure 8.1 and introduce perceived corruption, it has a highly significant effect.[12] The effects of crime are similar and were discussed in the previous chapter.

Generosity

However, good behavior consists of "do's" as well as "don'ts." It is crucially important what positive things we do for each other. We have limited evidence on this at the national level, but a proxy measure is the scale of charitable giving. As Figure 8.1 suggests, this too matters.

Do Good, Feel Good

Thus people are happier in societies where people behave well. But why exactly is this? One obvious reason is that we are happier if *others* treat *us* well (the arrow marked A in Figure 7.1). But are we also happier if *we* treat *others* well (the arrow marked B in Figure 7.1)? Does unselfish behavior bring its own reward?

Sometimes of course it hurts. But in general doing good is internally rewarding to the doer.[13] Here are some experimental examples, beginning with a natural experiment.

When East Germany was united with West Germany, many opportunities for volunteering in East Germany disappeared. At the same time those who had previously volunteered were found to have much larger falls in happiness than those who had not been volunteering. This suggests strongly that volunteering had been a cause of happiness for those who did it.[14] Lab experiments are also convincing. In an experiment on giving, one group were given some money to spend on themselves, and another group were given equal amounts of money to spend on others. At the end of the day the second group reported themselves to be the happier.[15] These effects on happiness can also be observed in the brain's reward centers—when people give money they experience a positive reward.[16] Moreover altruism can be trained. After two weeks' compassion training, the treatment group gave more money than the control group in a laboratory game, and at that time they also showed more neural activity in the reward centers of the brain.[17]

Social Capital

Different from ethical norms are the social structures that give people a sense of belonging, and of having others they can rely on for support. Time use studies show that, apart from sex, what people most enjoy is socializing with friends[18]—there is little worse than being friendless.

Figure 8.1 illustrates the huge importance of this dimension of life—of having people to rely on. Many great books have been written on such "social capital,"[19] and the importance of participation in civil society organizations. It may be enough here to make the key distinction between "bonding capital" and "bridging capital." Bonding capital is what unites like-minded people having similar cultures, experience, and interests, so that they know what to expect from each other. This is reflected, partly at least, in the social support variable in Table 8.1, which suggests that when everyone has someone to rely on (compared with no one), life-satisfaction rises by 2 whole points.

But in any multicultural or multiclass society there is something else that is also critical. That is bridging capital. In most societies, people who belong to minorities, including ethnic minorities and migrants, are on average less happy than the rest of the community.[20] One reason why migrants are unhappy is of course that they are separated from many of their family and friends—they lack bonding capital. But too often they are also second-class citizens in the place they have moved to—they lack bridges.

It is crucial that minorities are treated as equals, so that they have the same sense of belonging as other citizens. Racial tolerance has improved in many countries in recent years, leading to increased happiness in minority groups.[21] But the current upsurge of migration is creating new stresses, for migrants and for natives. It is key for the happiness of all that the circle of sympathy is extended as widely as possible.[22]

Personal Freedom

Closely related to tolerance is the issue of freedom—the willingness of society to let people lead their lives as they wish, provided they do no harm to others.[23] We are not talking here about the organization of government (the next topic) nor about economics, but about the freedom of individuals in their daily lives to choose their own way of life. This includes, for example, the freedom to marry who you want to, to choose where to live, and to speak your mind.[24] More freedom is always better, other things equal. But in practice more freedom may sometimes mean less social cohesion. There is therefore a balance to be struck. But Figure 8.1 shows clearly the importance of freedom in peoples' lives. This helps to explain why so many of the least happy societies documented in the early 1990s were those in the former Soviet bloc (see Figure 8.2). It is not easy to be sure how much of this stemmed from the pains of transition. But we have pretransition data for Hungary and for one district in Russia (the Tambov district) that show that happiness was much lower in both places than in other regions with equal levels of GDP per head.[25]

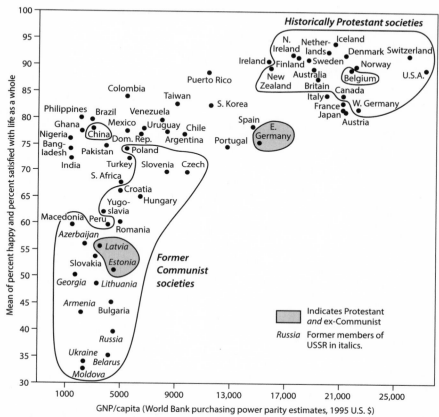

Figure 8.2. Subjective well-being by level of economic development and historical heritage of given societies, ca. 1990

Opponents of the well-being approach to public policy often argue that it would lead to an excessively nanny state where people had lost control over their own lives. Nothing could be further from the truth. For the evidence is overwhelming: people are not happy when they are not free.

Quality of Government

We turn now to the positive role of government. Is it effective in providing services, in regulating economic and social life, and in guaranteeing the rule of law (including the control of corruption)? We can call this the "quality" aspect of government. The complementary issue is the degree of "democracy"— voting rights, media freedom, and political stability.

Much research has shown that for the personal well-being of the population it is the quality of government that is the more important.[26] It is that which impinges on peoples' daily lives. Across countries, democracy is of course correlated with the quality of government. But there are some states that are high on quality but low on democracy. So our analysis here concentrates on quality.

The simplest question is Do you have confidence in your national government? If the measure of trust is dropped and replaced by the proportion saying they have confidence in the government, the coefficient on that proportion is 0.51 (s.e. = 0.17).[27] A more detailed measure is the World Bank's Worldwide Government Indicator of the quality of delivery of government services: when this is added, it also has a significant effect.[28]

Equality

Revolutionaries everywhere have demanded liberty, equality, and fraternity. We have so far discussed fraternity (first) and then liberty. But what of equality?

If we are discussing equality of income, there is one straightforward argument (already referred to in Chapter 2). Extra income is less important, the more income you already have. This is an old conjecture (which used to be called the declining marginal utility of income). But well-being science has shown it to be true.[29] The best relationship between life-satisfaction (0–10) and income is of the form: Life-satisfaction = α Log Income. This means that an extra dollar is x times more valuable (in terms of life-satisfaction) for a poorer person than for a rich person who is x times richer. Thus for a given average income, a more equal society should on average be happier.

But there could also be other reasons why this should be the case. For equality directly influences the quality of interpersonal relations in a society. Wilkinson and Pickett have shown that more equal societies tend to have more trust, better health, and so on—at all levels of society.[30] This implies some kind of atmospheric effect.

But empirical work on the effects of inequality on life-satisfaction has yielded very mixed results. Many studies have failed to find any effect.[31] The most positive results are in an interesting time-series study using both the US General Social Survey and Eurobarometer.[32]

The conclusion should probably be this: an ethos of mutual respect and care is crucial for a happy society. Such an ethos will be highly correlated with trust, low corruption, good social support, effective government—and greater equality of income. The priority is therefore to improve the whole ethos of a society and not simply to equalize income.

Religion

This brings us to the issue of religion, which can play at least three major roles: to instill values, to offer comfort, and to provide valuable social interaction. We began this chapter with the importance of ethical values, be they religious or secular in origin. But what of the specific effects of religion?

The Gallup World Poll provides important evidence.[33] Some 68% of adults in the world say that "religion is important in their daily lives." Religious belief and practice is more common in countries where life is harder (lower income, life expectancy, education, and personal safety). After controlling crudely for those factors, there is no difference in life-satisfaction between more and less religious countries. Nor, within countries where life is less hard, are religious people systematically more satisfied with life than less religious people.

The position is somewhat different if we focus exclusively on the United States, using the Gallup Daily Poll.[34] Here, after allowing for other factors, more religious US states are on average more satisfied with life. And so are more religious people. In comparisons between individuals there is always the problem that people who are naturally happier in given circumstances may be more willing to believe that there is a benevolent deity. However meta-analysis concludes that greater religiosity is mildly associated with fewer depressive symptoms,[35] and 75% of studies find at least some positive effect of religion on well-being.[36] This effect is particularly prevalent in high-loss situations, such as bereavement, and weaker in low-loss situations, such as marital problems. Thus religion can reduce the well-being consequences of stressful events, via its *stress-buffering* role.[37]

A recent large study of individuals in the European Social Survey also found small but statistically significant effects on life-satisfaction of "ever attending religious services" and "ever praying."[38] And interestingly the religiosity of others in the region was also found to have positive benefits both on those who are religious and on those who are not.

This said, the policy implications are not clear. If people cannot believe in an active deity or an afterlife, it is no good recommending that they should. For such people a form of ethics based on satisfying human need may be a more powerful and satisfying source of purpose in life.[39]

Income

Finally we should comment on the large effect of income on happiness when measured by the cross-section of countries. This is greater than the effect within countries, especially when the impact of comparator income is allowed for.[40] It also differs from the weak cross-country relation between economic growth and happiness growth discussed in Chapter 2. One partial explanation could be that all countries are comparing their incomes with a world standard that has risen over time. Only time will tell how far this is true.[41]

Conclusion

In this short chapter we have covered very briefly many of the most important influences on human happiness—those that are common to many members of societies and not just one at a time (as in most of this book). People are not happy where there is distrust, social dislocation, oppression, inequality, and poor government. And ethical movements have an important role to play in every society, in every age.[42]

"You're still the King of the Apes as far as I'm concerned, dear."

9 Happiness at Older Ages

Andrew Steptoe and Camille Lassale

Old age hath yet his honour and his toil.

—*Alfred Tennyson*, Ulysses

As people move from middle into older ages, their circumstances and experiences change in many ways.[1] Most people retire; their children leave home and establish independent lives; physical and cognitive capacities decline; and the experience of the death and loss of loved ones becomes more common. These changes influence financial resources, social relationships, independence, and autonomy. At the same time, people who no longer feel bound by the constraints of middle age may find fresh opportunities as they age, together with relief from many important sources of stress. All these processes mean that the determinants of satisfaction with life may change with ageing, or at least that the relative importance of the various sources of life-satisfaction may shift as we grow older.

Life-Satisfaction at Older Ages

One might think that life-satisfaction would decline progressively as people move from middle to older ages, but this is not the case. Several studies from different countries show that life-satisfaction increases from the early 50s onward, reaching a peak when people are in their early 70s.[2,3] Figure

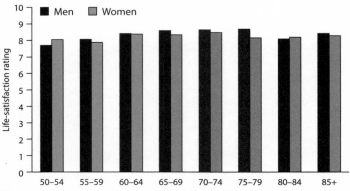

Figure 9.1. Average life-satisfaction (0–10): by age (ELSA)

9.1 outlines this pattern with data from the English Longitudinal Study of Ageing (ELSA). Participants responded to the question "I am satisfied with my life," with ratings that could range from 1 = *strongly disagree* to 7 = *strongly agree*. For comparability purpose with the other chapters, we transposed the responses into a scale of 0–10 and present only these transformed results. It can be seen that mean ratings rose from relatively low levels at age 50–54, reaching a peak around 70–74 years. On average, life-satisfaction levels are slightly higher for men than for women, although this pattern varies with age. Similar results have emerged from the national survey of life-satisfaction conducted by the Office for National Statistics, in which ratings are highest on average at 70–74 years.[4] Various explanations for this pattern have been put forward, including the possibility that older people increasingly focus on a restricted set of positive experiences and social contacts, whereas in middle age people focus on work and other less appealing aspects of life.[5] This highlights the question of what drives life-satisfaction at older ages. There are, of course, very large variations between people, so understanding what factors appear to be associated with greater satisfaction will give us insight into how to tackle issues of low satisfaction.

Sources of Life-Satisfaction at Older Ages

The English Longitudinal Study of Ageing provides a good sample with which to explore the relative importance of different factors in determining life-satisfaction at older ages. The study involves men and women aged 50 and over living in England, recruited to be representative of the population in this age range.[6] There are two particular advantages in analyzing ELSA. First, it is a multidisciplinary study, so it includes detailed measures in many different domains relevant to life-satisfaction, including economic resources, physical and mental health, functional capacity, and social relationships. Second, the longitudinal design with repeated measures over time means that we can look back over several years to see the extent to which changes in experience over earlier years are associated with life-satisfaction later on.

We showed life-satisfaction at different ages in Figure 9.1. These ratings were obtained from 5,413 individuals (55% women) in wave 6 of ELSA, with data collected in 2012. The average age of respondents was 68 years, ranging from 54 to over 90. Beginning with cross-sectional analyses, our strategy is to construct a regression model, including different sets of potential correlates of life-satisfaction in an overall model. We use a Generalized Linear Model (GLM) approach to allow for categorical as well as continuous explanatory variables. Details of the variables included in these analyses can be found in online Annex 9, and description of the sample characteristics is provided in online Table A9.1.

Our model includes age and sex, since it can be seen from Figure 9.1 that there are differences across ages and that men tend to rate their life-satisfaction slightly higher than women do. We also include ethnicity, dividing our sample into white European versus nonwhite groups, education, income, and employment status.[7] Educational attainment, economic resources, and being in paid employment have all been shown in previous chapters and in other work to relate to life-satisfaction, so we investigate the impact of additional factors having taken these into account.[8] In Figure 9.2, we include four sets of factors simultaneously in our analysis and present standardized regression coefficients.

Social relationships and engagement constitute the first set of factors (Figure 9.2, first panel). We include a range of variables such as whether the individual is married, loneliness, the size of their social networks, the social support that they receive from these networks, their involvement in organizations such as social clubs, and their cultural engagement. By cultural engagement, we mean the extent to which respondents go to concerts or the theater, visit museums and galleries, and so on. Respondents who are married compared with never married or divorced have higher life-satisfaction, as do those who are less lonely, and receive more social support. Additionally, respondents who are more engaged with life in terms of participation in organizations and in cultural activities enjoy greater life-satisfaction. Loneliness shows the strongest inverse relationship with life-satisfaction. When it is removed from the model, widowhood becomes significantly associated with lower life-satisfaction.

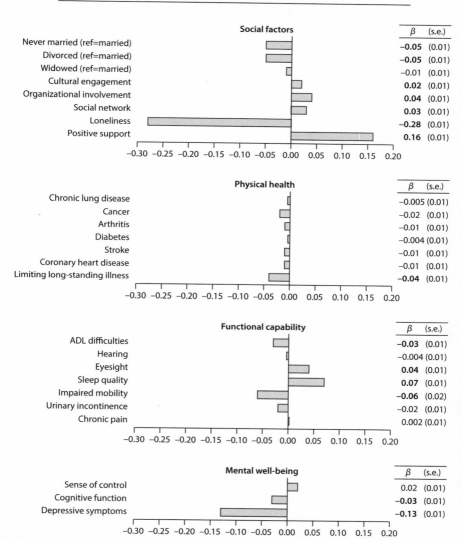

Figure 9.2. What affects life-satisfaction over age 50? (ELSA) (cross-section) (β-coefficients)

The second set of factors we evaluate relates to *physical health*. This is assessed in terms of the presence of doctor-diagnosed serious illness (e.g., cancer, arthritis, and coronary heart disease), together with the presence of long-term limiting illness, as a broader marker of health. Figure 9.2 (second panel) summarizes the standardized regression coefficients (β) for each variable. Positive coefficients indicate that the variable is associated with greater life-satisfaction, and negative scores with lower satisfaction. As we can see, the general question about health was related to life-satisfaction, while the individual illnesses were not. This may be due in part because they are relatively rare, and because a large part of the health status is explained by limiting long-standing illness. For people living with a partner (N = 3,535), we also investigated the effect of the partner's self-rated health, which showed a strong negative relationship with life-satisfaction (β [s.e.] = –0.06 [0.02]) without altering the effects of other factors in the model.

Our next set of factors concerns people's *functional capacity*. As we age, our senses deteriorate, and we may have greater difficulty hearing and seeing. Our sleep may get worse, and our mobility reduced, and we may develop difficulties in carrying out normal activities of daily living such as being able to bathe or shower, or controlling urination. These factors could impair our satisfaction with life. As seen in Figure 9.2 (third panel), they have a sizable impact on life-satisfaction, with independent associations between low life-satisfaction and poorer eyesight, poorer sleep quality, urinary incontinence, and more impairment in mobility.

Finally, *mental well-being* is assessed in terms of depressive symptoms and diagnosed depressive illness, together with people's broader sense of control over their lives, and cognitive capacity. The latter is assessed by aggregating responses on a series of cognitive tests of memory, verbal fluency, attention, and processing speed. All these measures were taken in 2010 in order to avoid direct contamination of the life-satisfaction ratings obtained in 2012. It turns out that mental well-being is a powerful correlate of life-satisfaction at older ages (Figure 9.2, bottom panel), with a large negative association between depressive symptoms and life-satisfaction, and greater satisfaction among individuals who have a stronger sense of control over their lives.

Overall, the four sets of factors combined explain a substantial part (33%) of the variability in life-satisfaction in this sample of English older adults. The largest associations are for mental well-being and social relationships and engagement. What these findings indicate is that targeting efforts at improving mental well-being and increasing social connectedness and social support may provide the best returns in relation to gains in life-satisfaction. We also provide an indication of the absolute size of effects by presenting the unstandardized coefficients on a 0–10 point scale in Table 9.1. It can be seen, for instance, that an increase of 1 unit on the loneliness scale is associated with a decrease of 0.49 points on the life-satisfaction 0–10 scale.

Age Differences

These results were obtained from all participants in the study right across the age spectrum. But it is possible that some of these factors become more important as people move from late middle age to older ages. We therefore repeated the analyses after dividing the sample into those aged 54–64 years (N = 2,028), and 65 years and older (N = 3,385), and

Table 9.1. What affects life-satisfaction (0–10) aged over 50 (ELSA) (cross-section) (unstandardized coefficients)

	Unit	Unstandardized coefficients (s.e.)
Age	years	**0.003** (.002)
Female	1, 0	0.01 (.02)
Ethnicity (nonwhite vs. white)	1, 0	**0.11** (.07)
Education: medium vs. low	1, 0	−0.03 (.03)
Education: high vs. low	1, 0	**−0.09** (.03)
Income (decile)	decile	**0.02** (.004)
Employment: Retired vs. employed	1, 0	**0.07** (.03)
Employment: Unemployed vs. employed	1, 0	−0.05 (.04)
Marital status: never married vs. married	1, 0	**−0.2** (.04)
Marital status: divorced vs. married	1, 0	**−0.13** (.03)
Marital status: widowed vs. married	1, 0	−0.01 (.03)
Cultural engagement	frequency 0–5	0.02 (.01)
Organizational involvement	# membership (0–8)	**0.03** (.01)
Social network	# people	**0.006** (.003)
Short-form UCLA loneliness scale	index (3 items)	**−0.49** (.02)
Positive support	1–4	**0.27** (.02)
Chronic lung disease	1, 0	−0.02 (.05)
Cancer	1, 0	−0.07 (.04)
Arthritis	1, 0	−0.01 (.02)
Diabetes	1, 0	−0.03 (.08)

	Unit	*Unstandardized coefficients (s.e.)*
Stroke	1, 0	−0.07 (.11)
CHD	1, 0	−0.08 (.09)
Limiting long-standing illness	1, 0	**−0.08** (.03)
ADL difficulties	number of difficulties (0–6)	**−0.04** (.02)
Hearing	rating scale 0–4	−0.003 (.01)
Eyesight	rating scale 0–4	**0.04** (.01)
Sleep quality	rating scale 0–3	**0.08** (.01)
Impaired mobility	# of impairments	**−0.02** (.01)
Urinary incontinence	1, 0	−0.04 (.03)
Chronic pain	1, 0	0.004 (.02)
Sense of control W5	index (1–6)	0.01 (.01)
Cognitive function score W5	index	**−0.005** (.002)
Depressive symptom CES-D W5	index (0–8)	**−0.06** (.01)
N		5,413
Adjusted R^2		0.33

these results are summarized in Table 9.2. Overall, the variation in life-satisfaction explained by these factors is greater in the younger than older subsamples (37% versus 30%). The factors in the base model (age, sex, ethnicity, education, income, and employment) have a larger impact among younger participants, which can partly be explained by the greater importance of employment for people of working age. The relative influence of other factors is comparable in the two age groups, with social relationships and engagement and

Table 9.2. What affects life-satisfaction (0–10) over 50: by age range (ELSA) (unstandardized coefficients)

	54–64	*65+*
Age	0.01 (.01)	0.002 (.002)
Female	0.04 (.04)	–0.02 (.03)
Ethnicity (nonwhite vs. white)	**0.18** (.09)	0.01 (.1)
Education: medium vs. low	0.01 (.04)	**–0.05** (.03)
Education: high vs. low	–0.03 (.05)	**–0.13** (.04)
Income (decile)	**0.02** (.01)	0.01 (.01)
Employment: retired vs. employed	**0.11** (.04)	0.03 (.05)
Employment: unemployed/ homemaker vs. employed	**–0.1** (.06)	0.01 (.07)
Marital status: never married vs. married	**–0.26** (.06)	**–0.1** (.06)
Marital status: divorced vs. married	**–0.19** (.05)	–0.07 (.05)
Marital status: widowed vs. married	**–0.29** (.09)	0.04 (.04)
Cultural engagement	0.02 (.02)	0.01 (.01)
Organizational involvement	**0.02** (.01)	**0.03** (.01)
Social network	**0.01** (.005)	0.003 (.003)
Short-form UCLA loneliness scale	**–0.54** (.04)	**–0.45** (.03)
Positive support	**0.25** (.04)	**0.28** (.03)
Chronic lung disease	**–0.18** (.1)	0.04 (.05)
Cancer	**–0.19** (.08)	–0.03 (.05)
Arthritis	0.00 (.04)	–0.01 (.03)
Diabetes	0.06 (.15)	–0.07 (.1)
Stroke	0.26 (.31)	–0.12 (.12)
CHD	–0.05 (.22)	–0.08 (.1)
Limiting long-standing illness	–0.05 (.05)	**–0.09** (.03)

	54–64	*65+*
ADL difficulties	−0.01 (.03)	**−0.05** (.02)
Hearing	−0.001 (.016)	−0.01 (.01)
Eyesight	**0.03** (.02)	**0.04** (.01)
Sleep quality	**0.07** (.02)	**0.08** (.02)
Impaired mobility	**−0.02** (.01)	**−0.02** (.01)
Urinary incontinence	−0.04 (.05)	−0.04 (.03)
Chronic pain	0.02 (.04)	0 (.03)
Sense of control W5	**0.03** (.01)	0 (.01)
Cognitive function score W5	**−0.007** (.003)	−0.004 (.002)
Depressive symptom CES-D W5	**−0.04** (.01)	**−0.07** (.01)
N	2,028	3,385
Adjusted R^2	0.37	0.30

mental well-being being most important. Physical health and functional capacity play a somewhat larger role among the older than younger participants, as problems in these domains such as limiting long-standing illness or diminished eyesight or mobility become more salient.

Gender Differences

Finally, we divided the sample into men and women to investigate potential gender differences (Table 9.3). Interestingly, while retirement has a positive association with life-satisfaction in men, this is not true of women. Instead, older age, higher income, and lower education are related to higher life-satisfaction among women. Social and mental health factors behave similarly in men and women, whereas the influence of physical health (limiting long-standing

Table 9.3. What affects life-satisfaction (0–10) over 50: by gender
(ELSA) (unstandardized coefficients)

	Male	*Female*
Age	0 (.002)	0.006 (.002)
Ethnicity (nonwhite vs. white)	0.15 (.1)	0.08 (.1)
Education: medium vs. low	0.02 (.04)	**−0.06** (.03)
Education: high vs. low	−0.07 (.04)	**−0.09** (.04)
Income (decile)	0.01 (.01)	**0.02** (.01)
Employment: retired vs. employed	**0.11** (.04)	0.04 (.04)
Employment: unemployed/ homemaker vs. employed	−0.01 (.08)	**−0.08** (.05)
Marital status: never married vs. married	**−0.16** (.06)	**−0.24** (.06)
Marital status: divorced vs. married	−0.06 (.05)	**−0.17** (.04)
Marital status: widowed vs. married	0.01 (.06)	−0.03 (.04)
Cultural engagement	0.02 (.02)	0.02 (.02)
Organizational involvement	**0.03** (.01)	**0.03** (.01)
Social network	**0.011** (.004)	0.003 (.004)
Short-form UCLA loneliness scale	**−0.48** (.04)	**−0.49** (.03)
Positive support	**0.22** (.03)	**0.31** (.03)
Chronic lung disease	−0.04 (.07)	0 (.06)
Cancer	−0.07 (.06)	−0.04 (.06)
Arthritis	−0.01 (.03)	−0.02 (.03)
Diabetes	0.01 (.11)	−0.07 (.12)
Stroke	−0.08 (.15)	−0.06 (.18)
CHD	−0.1 (.13)	−0.09 (.13)
Limiting long-standing illness	**−0.09** (.04)	**−0.07** (.04)
Any difficulty with ADL	**−0.05** (.03)	−0.03 (.02)
Hearing	0.001 (.014)	−0.01 (.01)
Eyesight	**0.06** (.02)	**0.03** (.02)

	Male	*Female*
Sleep quality	**0.09** (.02)	**0.07** (.02)
Number of impaired mobilities	−0.01 (.01)	**−0.03** (.01)
Urinary incontinence	**−0.11** (.06)	−0.01 (.03)
Chronic pain	0.01 (.04)	0.005 (.033)
Sense of control W5	**0.02** (.01)	0.001 (.011)
Cognitive function score W5	**−0.006** (.003)	−0.004 (.003)
Depressive symptom CES-D W5	**−0.08** (.01)	**−0.06** (.01)
N	2,438	2,975
Adjusted R^2	0.30	0.34

illness) and functional abilities have a stronger impact on life-satisfaction in men than women. The one exception is impaired mobility, which has a negative effect in women but not in men.

Changes in Life-Satisfaction with Increasing Age

The results described in the last section were based on cross-sectional analyses of life-satisfaction and its correlates, so we don't know the causal sequence. For instance, people may have low life-satisfaction because they are in poor health, or low life-satisfaction may influence health outcomes. One way of exploring this issue is to study the association between changes in the potential determinants and life-satisfaction over time. If, for example, a deterioration in health or decrease in cultural activity predicts changes in life-satisfaction, that would give us insight into the levers that might be used to improve the quality of life and well-being of older men and women. We have therefore tested how changes in economic, social, and personal factors at older age relate to trajectories of life-satisfaction.

We explored these possibilities by studying changes between 2004 and 2012, an eight-year period, in a sample of 3,230 (55% women). The outcome variable in these analyses was the difference between life-satisfaction measured at these two time points, so positive scores indicate an improvement in life-satisfaction. On the scale from 0 to 10, the average life-satisfaction score was 7.28 in 2004 and 6.97 in 2012, so there was a mild decrease over time on average. The changes in characteristics considered as potential factors influencing trajectories of life-satisfaction are described in Table 9.4. The mean change being often quite close to zero, we also present the percentage of people improving (going up) and getting worse (going down), showing that there is substantial movement. For example, a quarter of respondents show a shrinkage in their social networks, while for 20% their networks increase in size. Self-rated hearing or eyesight improve for 21% and 26% of participants respectively, which may be due to starting using a hearing aid or spectacles.

In these analyses, our base model includes not only fixed factors like age in 2004 and sex, but changes in income and employment status. Interestingly, we do not observe any differences in changes in life-satisfaction among people who retired or moved out of paid work compared with those whose situation remained constant; this is probably because retirement can have both positive and negative effects, depending on the individual's circumstances and the measures that are used.[9]

Figure 9.3 and Table 9.5 present estimates of the effects of four sets of factors corresponding broadly to those we

Table 9.4. Changes in characteristics of elderly people over an eight-year interval (ELSA)

	2004		2012		Change 2004–12		% worse	% better
	Mean	(SD)	Mean	(SD)	Mean	(SD)		
Life-satisfaction (0–10)	7.28	1.89	6.97	2.07	-0.31	(2.06)	33	21
Age	62.8	(7.5)	71.1	(7.8)	8.25	(1.05)		
Income (decile)	6.39	(2.79)	5.61	(2.72)	-0.79	(2.66)	53	25
Employed*	0.38	(0.49)	0.14	(0.35)	-0.24	(0.45)	25	1
Married*	0.73	(0.44)	0.68	(0.46)	-0.05	(0.28)	6	2
Cultural engagement	1.57	(1.07)	1.46	(1.08)	-0.11	(0.80)	43	31
Organizational involvement	1.74	(1.47)	1.67	(1.45)	-0.07	(1.29)	32	28
Social network	7.41	(4.18)	7.16	(4.10)	-0.25	(4.12)	25	21
Loneliness scale§	1.31	(0.45)	1.36	(0.49)	-0.05	(0.46)	27	21
Positive support	3.12	(0.56)	3.20	(0.50)	0.08	(0.48)	41	55
Chronic lung disease*	0.01	(0.10)	0.05	(0.23)	0.04	(0.23)	5	0
Cancer*	0.03	(0.16)	0.06	(0.24)	0.04	(0.27)	6	1

continued

143

Table 9.4. *Continued*

	2004		2012		Change 2004–12			
	Mean	(SD)	Mean	(SD)	Mean	(SD)	% worse	% better
Arthritis*	0.32	(0.47)	0.42	(0.49)	0.11	(0.37)	12	2
Diabetes*	0.05	(0.22)	0.01	(0.11)	-0.04	(0.25)	1	5
Stroke*	0.01	(0.11)	0.01	(0.09)	0.00	(0.14)	1	1
CHD*	0.02	(0.15)	0.01	(0.12)	-0.01	(0.19)	1	2
Limiting long-standing illness*	0.27	(0.45)	0.35	(0.48)	0.08	(0.50)	17	9
Number of difficulties with ADL$	0.24	(0.74)	0.31	(0.86)	-0.07	(0.79)	12	8
Hearing	2.54	(1.07)	2.30	(1.07)	-0.24	(1.00)	37	21
Eyesight	2.61	(0.87)	2.51	(0.91)	-0.10	(1.02)	33	26
Number of impaired mobilities$	1.50	(2.15)	1.90	(2.43)	-0.40	(1.79)	35	21
Chronic pain$	0.33	(0.47)	0.42	(0.49)	-0.10	(0.52)	19	9
Sense of control	2.93	(1.44)	2.90	(1.36)	-0.03	(1.56)	33	33
Cognitive function score	31.30	(5.35)	30.90	(5.93)	-0.40	(4.79)	48	43
Depressive symptoms CES-D$	1.25	(1.75)	1.23	(1.74)	0.02	(1.82)	28	29
N								3,230

*Binary variables modeled as categorical
$A negative value of change represents a worse evolution

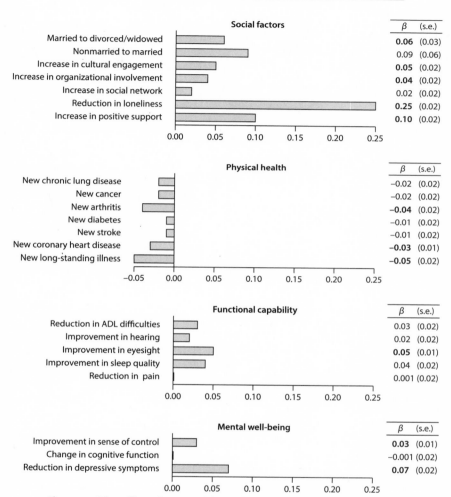

Figure 9.3. What affects changes in life-satisfaction over an eight-year interval (ELSA) (β-coefficients)

Table 9.5. What affects changes in life-satisfaction (0–10) over an eight-year interval (ELSA)

	Unit	*Unstandardized coefficients (s.e.)*
Age in 2004	years	−0.001 (.002)
Female	1, 0	−0.01 (.03)
Ethnicity (nonwhite vs. white)	1, 0	**−0.25** (.13)
Education: medium vs. low	1, 0	0.05 (.04)
Education: high vs. low	1, 0	−0.02 (.04)
Change in income 2004–12	decile	−0.002 (.005)
Change in employment 2004–12 (ref = stable)		
Employed → not employed	1, 0	0.02 (.04)
Not employed → employed	1, 0	0.21 (.14)
Change in marital status 2004–12 (ref = stable)		
Married → divorced/widowed	1, 0	**0.11** (.06)
Nonmarried → married	1, 0	0.17 (.11)
Change in cultural engagement$^{\$}$	frequency 0–5	**0.04** (.02)
Change in organizational involvement$^{\$}$	# membership (0–8)	**0.02** (.01)
Change in social network$^{\$}$	# people	0.004 (.003)
Change in loneliness$^{\$}$	index (3 items)	0.44 (.03)
Change in positive support	index (1–4)	0.17 (.03)
New chronic lung disease	1, 0	−0.07 (.06)
New cancer	1, 0	−0.07 (.06)
New arthritis	1, 0	**−0.07** (.04)
New diabetes	1, 0	−0.03 (.13)
New stroke	1, 0	−0.13 (.16)
New CHD	1, 0	**−0.24** (.12)

	Unit	Unstandardized coefficients (s.e.)
Change in limiting long-standing illness (ref=stable)	1, 0	
New long-standing illness	1, 0	**−0.09** (.04)
No longer report long-standing illness	1, 0	**0.09** (.05)
Change in ADL$^{\$}$	number of difficulties (0–6)	0.04 (.02)
Change in hearing$^{\$}$	rating scale 0–4	0.01 (.01)
Change in eyesight$^{\$}$	rating scale 0–4	**0.05** (.01)
Change in impaired mobility$^{\$}$	# of impairments	0.01 (.01)
Change in pain$^{\$}$	1, 0	0 (.03)
Change in sense of control$^{\$}$	index (1–6)	**0.02** (.01)
Cognitive function score W5$^{\$}$	index	0 (0)
Change in depressive symptom CES-D W5$^{\$}$	index (0–8)	**0.03** (.01)
N		3,230
Adjusted R^2		0.12

$^{\$}$A negative value of change represents a worse evolution

examined before. The *social relationship and engagement* factors are once again the most important. Surprisingly, changes from being married to divorced or widowed do not relate significantly to life-satisfaction, but there is a relatively limited number of people in this category (N = 201, 6.2%). On the other hand, reductions in loneliness, increases in involvement in social and other organizations, increases in positive support, and greater cultural engagement are all linked with increased life-satisfaction over the eight-year period. When loneliness is removed from the model, the association between changes from being married to divorced/widowed and life-satisfaction becomes negative (although remaining nonsignificant).

In the *health* domain, we find that people who developed coronary heart disease or a new long-standing illness over the eight-year period experienced a fall in life-satisfaction. As in the levels analysis (Figure 9.2), individual chronic diseases are not related to life-satisfaction. *Functional* changes were also important, since people whose eyesight improved show a smaller drop in life-satisfaction. Finally, in regard *to mental health*, a decrease in depressive symptoms and an improvement in the sense of control between 2004 and 2010 predict an improvement in life-satisfaction by 2012, while changes in cognitive function have no effect.

Overall, these dynamic processes in people's lives account for 12% of the variation in changes in life-satisfaction. As in the cross-sectional analysis, we wanted to explore any impact of age or gender on the observed associations. These are described in online Tables A9.2 and A9.3 and reveal little difference by age and gender. The main factors related to change in life-satisfaction are changes in loneliness and positive support, improvement in eyesight, and less depressive symptoms. Limiting long-standing illness was associated with life-satisfaction only in men and in people under 65.

Conclusions

In this chapter we explored which factors influence well-being at older ages. In part, our results confirm what is known from analyses of life-satisfaction at earlier stages of life.[10] Economic circumstances play a part, although not a dominant role, and retirement seems to have a positive impact on well-being. Mental and physical ill health are both very important. But at older ages, impairments in our capacity to see, hear, and get around independently become increasingly relevant. Unlike at earlier ages, physical ill health play only a relatively small role in the determinants of life-satisfaction, which may relate to acceptance and adaptation, as declining health is "expected" as we age. Most striking is the crucial role played by social activity and engagement: loneliness stands out as the one factor that most negatively affects life-satisfaction. The strong role played by depressive symptoms is as expected, since depression is related to the measure of life-satisfaction; nevertheless these results also emphasize the importance of mental health in the well-being of older adults. Social interactions and activities have a range of positive consequences, such as coping ability, and feeling respected and recognized. As mental health and social activity also relate to premature mortality, it is a priority to focus on reducing social isolation and the management of depression. Encouragingly, these are modifiable and malleable factors. Among older people, targeting efforts at improving mental well-being and increasing social connectedness and social support may provide the largest gains in life-satisfaction.

PART TWO

What Makes a
Successful Child?

"You can be anything you want to be—no limits."

10 Family Income

One half of the world knows not how the other half lives.

—*Joseph Hall*, Holy Observations *(1607)*

Finally we return to childhood. How does our early experience determine our emotional well-being as a child? And how does it affect the other key dimensions of our development as children—our behavior and our intellectual performance?

To answer these questions we turn to a remarkable survey that has followed children much more frequently and in more detail than most other surveys in the world. This is the Avon Longitudinal Study of Parents and Children (ALSPAC). This survey attempted to cover all children born in and around Bristol (a city of nearly half a million people) and Bath, between April 1991 and December 1992. It achieved about 70% of the total, though there was some subsequent attrition and nonresponse to individual questions.[1]

The survey enables us to study closely the effects of very many childhood influences, all of which are included in the online tables for Part II. But in what follows we focus on five major issues where public policy can have a major impact. These are the effects of

- child poverty
- parents working
- parenting and parents' mental health
- conflict in the family, and
- the quality of schooling.

We have a chapter on each of these five types of experience. The question is how they affect the three main dimensions of child development: emotional, behavioral, and intellectual. We measure these dimensions as shown on the outcome-age-measure grid.

Outcome	Age	Measure
Emotional	16, 11	Short Mood and Feelings Questionnaire, average of replies by mother and child
	5	Strengths and Difficulties Questionnaire, mother-assessed
Behavioral	16, 11, 5	Strengths and Difficulties Questionnaire, mother-assessed
Intellectual	16	General Certificate of Secondary Education (GCSE) points
	11	National curriculum test score (often referred to as SATs)
	5	Local school entry assessment

In the next five chapters we always take the outcomes in this order—beginning with what is intrinsically the most important, which is the emotional well-being of the child. And we look at how, other things equal, it is affected by the specific experience that is the subject of the chapter. Needless to say, outcomes at 5 have to be explained by experiences up to 5; outcomes at 11 by experiences up to 11; and so on. This applies to every table.

Poverty and Child Development

So how are children affected if their parents are poor? We measure income by the log of income per adult-equivalent in the family.[2] The prime issue now, as in the next five chapters, is how this affects children, *all else held constant*. It is important to ask the question this way. For policy makers want to know what they could achieve by directly addressing the problem—in this case the problem of child poverty. What could they achieve by raising financial support for children? To answer this question, we need to hold other things constant, including father's unemployment, mother's work, parenting style, parental separation, family conflict, mother's mental health, father's mental health, and primary and secondary school effects, as well as prebirth variables, like parents' education, mother's age at birth, gender, ethnicity, birth order, birth weight, and being born prematurely.

The Effect of Family Income on Emotional Well-Being

So what does ALSPAC tell us about the effects of child poverty? As we shall see, it confirms the well-known fact that income affects children's academic performance. But ALSPAC also shows that the effect on children's emotional well-being and behavior is much less.

In Table 10.1 the first column shows the β-coefficients— estimates of the explanatory power of income. This suggests that family income explains under 1% of the variance in children's emotional well-being.[3]

However, policy makers would ask a different question, namely: How much happier would our children be if we increased their family's income by say 10%? The second column of the table addresses that question. It shows that, if a child's income were increased by 10% throughout childhood, that

Table 10.1. How children's emotional well-being is affected by log family income (ALSPAC)

Effect on standardized emotional well-being at	β-coefficient	Log income unstandardized
16	**0.07** (.02)	**0.12** (.04)
11	**0.04** (.02)	**0.06** (.03)
5	**0.10** (.01)	**0.17** (.02)

child would be only 0.012 of one standard deviation happier at each age.

Other studies have come to similar conclusions. For example in their book on American children, *Consequences of Growing Up Poor*, published in 1999, Greg Duncan and Jeanne Brooks-Gunn conclude that noncognitive outcomes, such as mental health, physical health, and behavior are less sensitive to family income than are cognitive outcomes.[4] And some studies have even concluded that there is no direct effect at all of family income on children's behavior or emotional health, with the only effect being indirect.[5] Similarly when it comes to the children's physical health, this has been found to be unrelated to the family's income in the ALSPAC sample (holding constant the mother's mental and physical health).[6]

The Effect of Family Income on Behavior

If we turn to behavior in Table 10.2, the findings are very similar. Even the gross correlations (i.e., those that do not control for any other variables) are not high between the family's financial circumstances and the behavior of their children.[7]

Table 10.2. How children's behavior is affected by family income (ALSPAC)

Effect on standardized behavior at	β-coefficient	Log income unstandardized
16	**0.08** (.02)	**0.13** (.04)
11	**0.06** (.02)	**0.10** (.03)
5	**0.02** (.01)	**0.03** (.02)

The Effect of Family Income on Intellectual Performance

By contrast, if we turn to intellectual performance there are effects of a different magnitude, as Table 10.3 shows. The β-coefficient (or partial correlation) between income and intellectual performance is close to 0.14 at every age. And the effect of a 10% rise in family income is a rise of 0.024 standard deviations in intellectual performance. [8]

So suppose one considers a poor family with one child and a total household income of £15,000. This implies that for roughly £10,000 (a 4% increase each year for 16 years) the child's GCSE performance could improve by 0.010 standard deviations.

Table 10.3. How children's intellectual performance is affected by family income (ALSPAC)

Effect on standardized intellectual performance at	β-coefficient	Log income unstandardized
16	**0.14** (.01)	**0.24** (.02)
11	**0.14** (.01)	**0.24** (.02)
5	**0.13** (.01)	**0.21** (.02)

This is quite a high cost. So the policy maker might ask a different question: Is there any other measure by which I could raise the educational performance of a poor child? As online Table A10.1 shows, there is a high correlation between intellectual performance and the quality of secondary schooling. Anticipating Chapter 14, we find that the difference in performance between the best and worst performing three secondary schools in Avon (holding child and parent characteristics constant) is 0.46 standard deviations of GCSE points. Suppose it took £2,000 a year per pupil to lift a school that far—or £10,000 over five years. That would be an increase of 0.46 standard deviations per £10,000—much more than could be achieved by a direct income transfer to parents costing the same amount.

If you are wondering whether these results are too negative about the quantitative impact of income on academic performance, they are in fact consistent with earlier research.[9] For example Jo Blanden and Paul Gregg used three earlier British datasets (BCS; BHPS; and the National Child Development Study, NCDS) to examine how family income at age 16 affected GCSE performance.[10] They concluded that when family income falls by 33% the proportion of children who obtain any GCSE A*-C grades falls by 3–4 percentage points.[11] This corresponds to a β-coefficient of around 0.1—similar to our estimate of 0.15.

For the United States, Daron Acemoglu and Jörn-Steffen Pischke have used three longitudinal studies of school leavers sponsored by the National Center for Education Statistics. These show that a 10% rise in family income leads to a 1.4 percentage point rise in the probability of college attendance, which implies a β-coefficient of around 0.14—again similar.[12] Likewise at the earlier ages of three and five,

Wei-Jun Jean Yeung and colleagues analyze the Panel Study of Income Dynamics and find a β-coefficient of 0.15 for the effect of family income on cognitive skill.[13]

Part of the reason for this is that high-income parents spend a larger proportion of their incomes on children's education than low-income parents. For example, a US study uses two nationally representative expenditure surveys to show that American families in the bottom family expenditure quintile spend 3% of their total expenditure on education enrichment items (e.g., preschool, drama lessons, music lessons); families in the top income quintile spend 9%.[14]

Conclusion

Lack of income is not the only source of financial difficulties.[15] But the family's income as such has a limited effect on the emotional well-being and behavior of the children, other things constant. There is however a stronger relation between the family's income and children's academic achievement.

'A good dog can look after
as many as 30 toddlers'

11 Working Parents

My husband and I have decided to start a family while
my parents are still young enough to look after them.

—*Rita Rudner*

In rich countries few mothers worked outside the house in
1900, except for the very poorest.[1] Today the majority do
(see Figure 11.1). In most advanced countries this is the biggest single social change of the last century. No longer do
most women give birth to large numbers of children, most
of whom die. Instead they have careers and earn money.

But what does this do to their children? There is no more
contentious subject of debate in cafés or around the din-
ner table. But the weight of evidence from ALSPAC is that,
other things held constant (including income), mother's
work has no marked effect, good or bad, on the emotional
health of her children.

In ALSPAC we know at what month after the birth of
the child the mother returned to paid work (which tells us
what fraction of the child's first year of life the mother spent
working). We also know at which of the nine subsequent
times she was questioned she was working.[2] This gives us
two key pieces of information. One is the proportion of the
first year of the child's life for which the mother worked.
The other is the proportion of the remaining years of childhood during which the mother worked. What difference
does it make if the mother worked, and when?

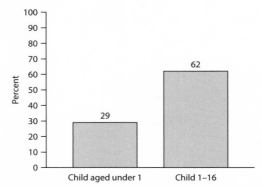

Figure 11.1. Percentage of mothers in work: by age of child

Mother's Work and the Emotional Health of Her Child

Table 11.1 answers the question, holding income constant. As it shows, when the mother worked in the first year of the child's life, there is some negative effect on the child's emotional health, holding income constant. But, when we take into account the relation of mother's work and family income, any negative effect disappears. If the mother works in the subsequent years of childhood, there is no significant negative effect even holding income constant—and the gross effect is positive if enough other factors are taken into account. Online Table A11.1 shows this gross effect, suitably decomposed.[3]

Similar findings to ours appear in the most recent cohort study of children born in the year 2000 (the Millennium

Table 11.1. How children's emotional well-being is affected by mother's work (ALSPAC)

Proportion of time mother worked	*Effect on standardized emotional well-being at*		
	16	11	5
In the 1st year	−0.05 (.04)	**−0.09** (.04)	−0.04 (.03)
Thereafter (up to age shown)	−0.03 (.06)	−0.02 (.04)	**0.07** (.03)

Cohort Study). These children likewise showed no loss of mental health if their mothers went quickly back to work.[4] Equally, in adolescence, children aged 11–15 in the youth section of the BHPS reported higher levels of happiness if their mothers were at work.[5]

Mother's Work and the Behavior of Her Child

But even if the mother's own child fares all right, what about that child's behavior to others? Here there is a long-standing debate about whether being looked after in a nursery or by a child minder makes a child more aggressive. Many surveys have examined the behavioral effects of children's preschool experience both in the United States and UK.[6] US studies tend to find some adverse effects of nursery care while British ones generally do not. Our own ALSPAC results suggest no marked effect of being cared for in a nursery or with a minder in the early years (see Table 11.2). But they do reveal important effects at 11 and 16—where on average

Table 11.2. How children's behavior is affected by mother's work (ALSPAC)

Proportion of time mother worked	*Effect on standardized behavior at*		
	16	11	5
In the 1st year	−0.01 (.05)	0.03 (.04)	0.00 (.03)
Thereafter (up to age shown)	**−0.14** (.06)	**−0.11** (.04)	0.01 (.03)

those whose mothers worked throughout their childhood behaved worse. This effect is significant only for girls—with a coefficient suggesting that, if their mother works throughout (as opposed to never), their average behavior at 16 is worse by 0.18 standard deviations.[7] Even this is not a huge effect, and it is reduced when the effect of work on income is allowed for (see Online Table A.11.1).

Mother's Work and the Intellectual Development of Her Child

So much for effects on the well-being and the behavior of the children. But what about the educator's passion—their intellectual performance? How is this affected if their mother goes out to work?

And when is it affected? This question of when is crucial, because learning is cumulative, and the only thing that matters ultimately is what a person has learned by the end of their education. In this respect intellectual development is quite different from well-being and behavior, which matter every year—it is an outcome every year if a child is happy

Table 11.3. How children's intellectual performance is affected by mother's work (ALSPAC)

Proportion of time mother worked	*Effect on standardized intellectual performance at*		
	16	11	5
In the 1st year	**−0.06** (.02)	**−0.05** (.03)	0.00 (.03)
Thereafter (up to age shown)	**0.11** (.03)	**0.08** (.03)	**0.08** (.03)

that year, or treats other children well that year. But the outcome of academic education is the final state.

By age 16, if we look at Table 11.3, we find an unambiguous picture. The effect is negative if the mother returns to work in the first twelve months. But it is positively beneficial if she works thereafter.[8] The gross effect is even larger, as we can see from the online Table A.11.1.

These findings are broadly in line with other research. UK researchers have generally found that mother's work improves intellectual performance at all ages.[9] In contrast, US work on the National Longitudinal Survey of Youth (NLSY) has suggested that, if the mother goes back to work early, child cognitive performance suffers at ages three and four, but the effect disappears by age six.[10] The broad conclusion has to be "Mothers of the world, relax"—unless working outside of the home makes *you* less happy.

Unemployed Fathers

It is one thing to choose whether you want to work. It is another thing to be able to find work if you want it. As we have seen in Part I, unemployment has a devastating

Table 11.4. How children's outcomes are affected by father's
unemployment (0–1) (ALSPAC)

Effects on standardized outcome at	*Emotional*	*Behavioral*	*Intellectual*
16	−0.29 (.18)	−0.01 (.16)	**−0.23** (.06)
11	**−0.23** (.12)	0.02 (.12)	**−0.15** (.06)
5	−0.03 (.07)	−0.04 (.06)	−0.01 (.05)

effect on both men and women. But how does it affect their
children?

ALSPAC provides clear unemployment data only on the
fathers of the children and shows that this can have a critical effect on children's development. There are many chan-
nels through which this can work—via the parents' mood,
family conflict, reduced aspirations, taunting at school, and
simple loss of income.[11]

In Table 11.4 we look at the effect, holding family conflict
and income constant. One thing is very clear. Like all economic variables, father's unemployment has a substantial
and well-measured effect on academic performance. Its net
effect on behavior and emotional health is less well-defined.[12]
But when we reduce the number of other influences we
hold constant, the gross "effect" of father's unemployment
on behavior (i.e., holding nothing else constant) becomes
negative, owing to the indirect effect of unemployment
through reduced income and increased family conflict. And
the negative effect on emotional well-being also becomes
even more negative, for the same reasons (see online Table
A11.2).

Conclusion

Jawaharlal Nehru wrote "Work is worship." This might be a bit over the top, but work is important for identity as well as for income. So loss of work can wreak havoc in a family. And its acquisition, when a mother goes back to work, can bring benefits, and few costs.

"He's just doing that to get attention."

12 Parenting and Parents' Mental Health

> They fill you with the faults they had,
> And add some extra, just for you.
>
> —*Philip Larkin, "This Be the Verse"*

It is now time to move from the economics of the family to the character of the parents, and how they relate to their child.

Genes

But first a major word of caution is needed, which applies to the book as a whole. All humans are the products of genes and experience, and of how the two interact. So ideally we should include genes among the determinants of child outcomes and of adult well-being. Every parent knows that genes matter—within most families the children differ widely from each other, which must mainly reflect different genes. Moreover, scientifically, there are two types of compelling evidence of the importance of the genes—from twin studies and from studies of adopted children.[1] Twin studies show that identical twins are much more similar to each other in their well-being than are nonidentical twins.[2] This is because identical twins have identical genes, while other twins do not. Similarly when adopted children are raised apart from their biological parents, their well-being is still influenced by that of their biological parents.[3]

At the same time, experience is also incredibly important. Adopted children's well-being also reflects the well-being of their adoptive parents, with whom they share no genes at all. What is more, how they turn out is not just the result of genes and experience added up. Instead it depends on the interaction of the genes with experience.[4] For example, adopted children who grow up in a disturbed home are more likely than other children to become mentally ill, but the effect of their experience is augmented if their biological parents were also mentally ill.[5] Similarly, adopted children who grow up in a criminal home are more likely to become criminals, but the effect of their experience is augmented if their biological parents were also criminal.[6] And this mechanism is beginning to be understood through the science of epigenetics that explains how (for example by methylation) the "expression" of a gene can be silenced as a result of a person's experience.[7] Such gene-experience interaction is pervasive in human life.

The effect of genes can sometimes now be traced to the operation of particular, specific genes. In a few cases it has been possible to identify within the DNA genome specific genes that contribute to well-being.[8] But the number of genes identified so far is only around three, and they account for only 1% of the variance of well-being. So, in studying what causes well-being over the life course, we cannot simply insert the relevant genes in our array of determinants.

But we should be appropriately humble about what we can do. For example, suppose we can show that, if your mother is depressed after you are born, you are *x* percent more likely to grow up depressed (cet. par.). And suppose we could prevent your mother's depression, before you were born. As a result of this intervention, you would indeed have a better childhood. But you would still share your mother's genes. So your chance of growing up depressed would be reduced by less than the full *x* percent. We cannot say how far *x* is an overestimate, and this is true of many of the estimates of effects in this book. Whenever the "cause" being studied is correlated with an omitted measure of the relevant genes, the estimated effect of the cause is biased to be larger than the true effect. On the other hand, since most of these "causes" are measured with error, that biases the estimated effect to be smaller. For both of these reasons the numbers in this book must be treated as a broad first attempt to depict the key environmental determinants of well-being—a first rather than a last word on the subject.[9]

Parents and the Emotional Health of Their Children

So how much does parents' behavior matter for their children's emotional health? A lot, but probably less than some people think. If we take everything we know about parents, it explains only 6 percent of the variance of their children's emotional health at 16.[10] This includes the effect of parents' income and work (already discussed) and family conflict (discussed in the next chapter). In the present chapter we shall look at the main other factors we know in the child's

Table 12.1. How parents affect the emotional well-being of
their children (ALSPAC) (β-coefficients)

| | *Effect on well-being at* | | |
	16	11	5
Mother's mental health	**0.16** (.02)	**0.18** (.02)	**0.22** (.01)
Father's mental health	**0.04** (.02)	**0.04** (.01)	**0.05** (.01)
Mother's involvement (to age 6)	**0.04** (.02)	0.02 (.01)	**0.09** (.01)
Mother's aggression (to age 6)	**−0.03** (.02)	**−0.04** (.01)	**−0.05** (.01)

family background—the mental health of the parents and their style of parenting.

But first we should begin with the situation before the child was born. The following variables have no consistent measurable effect on the child's emotional health at 5, 11, and 16: parents' education, ethnicity (white vs. other), child firstborn, child premature, and low birth weight.[11] But the mental health of both parents (especially the mother) is crucial, and so is the parenting style of both parents.

This can be seen in Table 12.1. The mental health of the mother is measured by the Edinburgh Post-natal Depression Scale (twice in the first year at months 2 and 8, and then at ages 1, 2, 5, 6, 8, and 11). The mental health of the father is measured by the Crown-Crisp Experiential Index (twice in the first year at months 2 and 8, and then at age 1).

As the table shows, the mother's mental health has a powerful influence on her children's well-being, with a partial correlation of 0.15 or more. The effect is especially strong on girls.[12] This is not just an effect of postnatal depression (which affects 10–20% of mothers). In fact, the prevalence of maternal depression is fairly constant throughout the childhood of our sample. The father's mental health also matters, but much less, with a partial correlation of 0.05 or less.[13] This reinforces the view that the effect of the mother's mental health comes largely through the child's experience and not the genes, since fathers' and mothers' genes matter equally.

These findings are consistent with earlier work showing how mental health is transmitted from one generation to another.[14] Even while children are in the womb, their brains are affected by their mother's emotional state, and these effects persist.[15]

So what about the way the parents interact with their children? This is a matter of huge importance, and the evidence from ALSPAC is limited. Standard findings about child development include the following:[16]

- Attachment. It is crucial that a child develops attachment to a parent or parent-surrogate, whom they experience as a source of unconditional love and affection. A related concept is the degree of warmth in the relationship.
- Firmness. The parent needs to set clear boundaries that are implemented with firmness but also affection.

- Involvement. The parent needs to engage with the child: in conversation, in play, in activities of all kinds, and with their life at school.

The first of these three items is especially important for the child's emotional health, the second for behavior, and the third for intellectual development. ALSPAC provides good evidence on the third of these, and less good evidence on the first two.

In ALSPAC, *involvement* is measured by a weighted average of the mother's frequency of conversation with the child, singing to the child, reading to the child, drawing/painting with the child, helping with homework, and preparing for school.[17] This is measured at 6 months and at ages 1, 2, 4, 5, 6, and 7. It is therefore a measure only of early involvement.

On the first two dimensions of good parenting we have evidence only on the degree of the parent's *aggression* to the child: the average of the frequency with which the mother shouts or smacks when the child has a tantrum.[18]

As Table 12.1 shows, the child's emotional health is affected by the mother's involvement with the child, especially when the child is young.[19] However the effect is smaller than is sometimes supposed. As regards parental aggression, this is unsurprisingly bad for a child's emotional health.

Parents and the Behavior of Their Children

Turning to the behavior of children (see Table 12.2), this too is highly influenced by their mother's mental health;

Table 12.2. How parents affect the behavior of their children (ALSPAC) (β-coefficients)

	Effect on behavior at		
	16	11	5
Mother's mental health	**0.17** (.02)	**0.17** (.02)	**0.18** (.01)
Father's mental health	−0.01 (.02)	0.01 (.02)	**0.02** (.01)
Mother's involvement (to age 6)	**0.05** (.02)	**0.10** (.02)	**0.12** (.01)
Mother's aggression (to age 6)	**−0.12** (.02)	**−0.15** (.01)	**−0.20** (.01)

their father's mental health makes little difference. If parents are involved, this improves their children's behavior. By contrast aggressive behavior by mothers is associated with bad behavior from the children. Causality here must surely be in both directions, but clearly bad behavior by mothers can produce bad behavior by children.

Parents and Intellectual Development

When we turn to the cognitive development of children, we expect to find that parental involvement makes a large difference. In net terms (cet. par.) there is a substantial effect at age five (see Table 12.3). This is consistent with arguments for early intervention especially when it comes to the intellectual development of children.[20]

In gross terms there is of course a stronger relationship between involvement and intellectual development. This is

Table 12.3. How parents affect the intellectual development of their children (ALSPAC) (β-coefficients)

	Effect on intellectual performance at		
	16	11	5
Mother's mental health	**0.03** (.01)	**0.03** (.01)	**0.04** (.01)
Father's mental health	–0.00 (.01)	–0.01 (.01)	0.00 (.01)
Mother's involvement (to age 6)	**0.02** (.01)	**0.02** (.01)	**0.07** (.01)
Mother's aggression (to age 6)	–0.01 (.01)	**–0.03** (.01)	0.00 (.01)

shown in the online Table A12.1,[21] which shows that the gross correlation between mother's involvement and GCSE performance at age 16 is 0.05 while the net correlation is 0.02. The difference arises partly because the children of involved parents go to better schools, and partly because involved parents are richer.

When it comes to intellectual development, the net effect of parents' mental health and aggressive parenting is small. But the gross effect is augmented by the types of school their children go to—and by the family's economic resources.

Conclusion

We do not claim that this is the last word on parenting. But some clear conclusions emerge

- A mother's mental health is critical for the happiness and behavior of her children. It deserves high policy priority, for the sake of both mother and child.

- Aggressive parents produce badly behaved children
- Involved parents can help children significantly, especially with their academic development.

"Stanley, we need to talk, so please don't interrupt."

13 Family Conflict

It's just a family that loves each other, and as long as
they do that's a happy family.

—*Eight-year-old girl*

By the time they were 16, one-fifth of the 1970 birth cohort
had experienced the break-up of their family: their parents no
longer lived together.[1] Since then family break-up has become
even more common, and today 40% of British 16-year-olds live
in separated families.[2] In the United States the figure is 50%.

Break-up on this scale is a relatively modern phenomenon
—one of the more important changes over the last forty
years. So what is it doing to our children? ALSPAC provides
good evidence, and the broad answer is this: What matters
is family conflict, rather than family break-up, and, if the
conflict is bad enough, the break-up may help the children.
But the conflict is unambiguously bad, especially for the behavior of the children—parents who fight tend to generate
children who fight.

Measurement

To measure whether there is family conflict the mothers
in ALSPAC were regularly asked: In the past three months
have you or your partner

- argued with each other over 3 times
- been irritable with the other

- not spoken to the other for a long period
- shouted at the other
- hit/slapped the other
- thrown something in anger.

To obtain our measure of conflict we add up these replies. We have measures for ages 2, 3, 6, and 12, and at each age we measure the average conflict up to that age—or up to separation if separation has already occurred.

To measure whether the parents are separated, we have annual reports from the mother on any separation up to age 13, plus the child's report on separations at ages 13–16. So at each age our variable measures whether the original family is no longer intact.

The Effect of Family Conflict

In analyzing the effect of these variables, it is, as so often, difficult to know what to hold constant. There are obvious issues on how to handle mental health in particular, since it is such a powerful determinant of life-satisfaction. Mental illness may cause family conflict, in which case it should be included in the equation if we want to find out the specific effects of conflict without picking up the effect of a confounder. On the other hand conflict may cause mental illness as a mediating variable,[3] in which case if we want to find the effects of conflict we should exclude mental illness from the equation.

In Table 13.1 we look at outcomes at age 16 following both approaches. In the top two rows we do not control for the mental health of the parents. The effects of conflict are

Table 13.1. How family conflict affects children's outcomes at 16 (standardized) (ALSPAC)

	Units	Emotional	Behavioral	Intellectual
Not controlling for mental health				
Effect of conflict	SD	**–0.11** (.02)	**–0.20** (.02)	**–0.02** (.01)
Effect of separation	1, 0	–0.01 (.04)	–0.01 (.04)	**–0.07** (.02)
Controlling for mental health				
Effect of conflict	SD	**–0.04** (.02)	**–0.14** (.02)	–0.01 (.01)
Effect of separation	1, 0	0.01 (.04)	0.00 (.04)	**–0.07** (.02)

large—both on emotional health and behavior (though not academic performance). Separation adds little explanatory power except in explaining academic performance.

By contrast if we control for mental illness all these effects are reduced. To be sure of not overclaiming we proceed from now on to control for mental health and to look at the effects of family conflict throughout a child's life.

We can begin with the effects of the parents' relationship on the children's *emotional well-being*. As Table 13.2 shows, the main issue here is the extent of family conflict. Once the amount of family conflict is given, parental separation is a smaller issue. This is a standard finding in US studies also.[4] Of course if family conflict is omitted (as it is in many studies), separation appears to have a bigger effect; but this is misleading.

The effects on children's *behavior* are more serious, and these effects (as we know) can be carried on into adulthood. Thus the partial correlation of parental conflict and children's behavior is –0.14, a substantial effect. Again separation

Table 13.2. How family conflict affects children's emotional well-being (ALSPAC)

	Effect on standardized well-being at		
	16	*11*	*5*
Parental conflict (standardized)	**−0.04** (.02)	**−0.04** (.02)	−0.02 (.01)
Parental separation (1, 0)	0.01 (.04)	−0.03 (.03)	0.04 (.03)

adds little extra effect, once conflict is allowed for (see Table 13.3).

When it comes to *academic performance*, parental conflict seems to cause much less of a problem, while separation is more disturbing (see Table 13.4). This is consistent with the findings of earlier studies.[5]

When Conflict Is High, Is It Better to Separate?

So far we have examined separately the effects of conflict and of separation (holding the other constant). But what if separation were more beneficial the higher the level of conflict? We investigate this in Table 13.5.[6] In this case, conflict

Table 13.3. How family conflict affects children's behavior (ALSPAC)

	Effect on standardized behavior at		
	16	*11*	*5*
Parental conflict (standardized)	**−0.14** (.02)	**−0.10** (.02)	**−0.04** (.01)
Parental separation (1, 0)	0.00 (.04)	−0.02 (.04)	**−0.06** (.03)

Table 13.4. How family conflict affects children's intellectual development (ALSPAC)

	Effect on standardized intellectual performance at		
	16	*11*	*5*
Parental conflict (standardized)	−0.01 (.01)	0.01 (.01)	0.01 (.01)
Parental separation (1, 0)	**−0.07** (.02)	−0.03 (.02)	−0.02(.03)

Table 13.5. The interacted effect of family conflict and parental separation on children's outcomes (standardized) (ALSPAC)

Emotional health at

	16	*11*	*5*
High Conflict = 1	**−0.08** (.04)	**−0.08** (.03)	**−0.04** (.02)
Separated = 1	−0.01 (.05)	−0.05 (.05)	**0.09** (.04)
Separated*Conflict	0.03 (.07)	0.05 (.06)	−0.07 (.06)

Behavior at

	16	*11*	*5*
High Conflict = 1	**−0.19** (.04)	**−0.17** (.03)	**−0.08** (.02)
Separated = 1	−0.01 (.06)	−0.04 (.05)	−0.07 (.04)
Separated*Conflict	−0.00 (.08)	0.03 (.07)	0.02 (.06)

Intellectual performance at

	16	*11*	*5*
High Conflict = 1	−0.02 (.02)	0.01 (.02)	0.01 (.02)
Separated = 1	**−0.06** (.03)	−0.01 (.03)	−0.02 (.04)
Separated*Conflict	0.00 (.04)	0.00 (.04)	0.01 (.05)

is measured by whether your level of conflict is above the median.

To interpret the analysis we can examine the first row of the table. This says that

Emotional health at 16 = −0.08 High conflict
−0.01 Separated
+0.03 High conflict and separated

In other words, if your parents have high conflict but they separate, your emotional health is improved when they separate by 0.02 points (i.e., 0.03−0.01).

However in the table the interaction term though generally positive is never big enough to be significantly different from zero, given our sample size. It does however confirm an important point that also emerges from the previous tables. This is that children whose parents have high conflict and separate are always worse off emotionally than children whose parents have no conflict and stay together.

Conclusion

In a British survey, teenagers and parents were asked whether they agreed with the statement "Parents getting on well is one of the most important factors in raising happy children." Seven in ten of the teenagers agreed but only a third of the parents did so.[7]

Our analysis suggests the teenagers were right. But if they were right about their well-being, they would have been even more right if they had added that this is also important for their school work and above all for their behavior. Our findings thus confirm the findings of many other studies that parents really do make a difference to their children. Do schools also make a difference, and by how much?

"*Do we have to use our inside voices through clenched teeth, like you, Ms. Baker?*"

14 Schooling

Ask me my three main priorities for government and
I will tell you: education, education, and education

—*Tony Blair (1996)*

In 1966 the US government published the famous Coleman
Report, chaired by the celebrated sociologist James Coleman. It argued that the main cause of children's academic
success was the attitude of their parents. Without a change
in this, the report argued, schools had limited ability to make
a difference. This view was supported by plenty of research
that showed that the measured characteristics of teachers
made little difference to the academic success of their pupils.

The counterattack was rapid and ingenious. A young
researcher called Eric Hanushek asked, What about the
unmeasured characteristics of the teacher? Why not investigate simply how much difference it makes whether you are
taught by Mrs. X, rather than Mr. Y. So he replaced the measured characteristics of teachers in the Coleman analysis
by a string of variables, which simply reflected the name of
the teacher. It turned out that which teacher children were
taught by explained a substantial proportion of the variance
in their test scores.[1]

In this chapter we investigate the impact of the different
schools and teachers in the Avon area on the outcomes of
the children they taught. We begin by investigating the role
of the whole school—what difference does it make which
school you go to? And we start with secondary schools.

The Effects of Individual Secondary Schools

Our aim is to explain child outcomes at age 16: emotional (as measured by reports from parent and child, averaged); behavioral (as measured by the parent); and intellectual (the GCSE score). We control for the child's relevant outcome at age 11 (before they entered the secondary school),[2] as well as for family background. We then estimate the impact of each school by entering a separate dummy for every school. Table 14.1 shows the standard deviation of these school effects.

The effect of the school is remarkable—not only on intellectual performance, as Hanushek found, but also on happiness (emotional health) and behavior. For example, we can take a child of given happiness at age 11 (and given family background) and ask how much happier did that child become at age 16 if in a school at the 83rd percentile of happiness production compared with a school at the 50th percentile of happiness production. The answer, as Table 14.1 shows, is that the child became happier by a massive 0.26 standard deviations of happiness.[3] In other words a child who at 11 was at the median level of happiness would by 16 have been at the 60th percentile. This is a remarkable impact. The effect on behavior is nearly as great, but here we want to stress the effect on happiness—since many

Table 14.1. How children's outcomes at 16 are affected by secondary school attended (ALSPAC) (β-coefficients)

	Emotional	Behavioral	Intellectual
Secondary school	**0.26** (.01)	**0.21** (.01)	**0.29** (.01)

Table 14.2. How children's outcomes at 16 are affected by secondary school characteristics (ALSPAC) (β-coefficients)

	Emotional	*Behavioral*	*Intellectual*
School size	−0.02 (.02)	−0.02 (.02)	**0.03** (.01)
Class size	−0.00 (.02)	−0.01 (.02)	0.01 (.01)
% Free school meals	0.01 (.02)	−0.03 (.03)	**−0.03** (.01)
% English not first language	0.01 (.02)	**0.04** (.02)	**0.02** (.01)

policy makers still question whether that is the business of schools.

We have only limited information on the features of the schools that might explain these huge differences. In Table 14.2 we replace the name of the school by four characteristics reported in the table. We find that these variables have little explanatory power. School size has a small positive effect on GCSE performance. But the average class size in the school has no effect on anything. Clearly the quality of teaching makes much more difference than the size of the class (at least within the existing range of class sizes). This is consistent with findings from earlier research.[4]

The Effects of Individual Primary Schools

Next we look at how primary schools affect their children's outcomes while they are still in primary school (see Table 14.3). We try to explain what children are like at age 11, given how they are at age 8. And we try to explain how they are at age 8, given how they are at age 7. We again control

Table 14.3. How children's outcomes at 8 and 11 are affected by primary school attended (ALSPAC) (β-coefficients)

	Emotional	*Behavioral*	*Intellectual*
At age 11	**0.24** (.01)	**0.19** (.01)	**0.27** (.01)
At age 8	**0.19** (.01)	**0.20** (.01)	**0.30** (.01)

for family background. Once again, the effect of the school is remarkable on all three outcomes and at both ages.

We can again examine the effect of the characteristics of the school (see Table 14.4). At these younger ages, there is no clear advantage intellectually or emotionally from larger schools. And there is absolutely no evidence in favor of smaller class sizes—a clear finding at both age 11 and age 8.

The Effects of Individual Teachers

What can we say about the effect of the individual teacher? In primary schools (unlike secondary) each child has basically only one teacher per year. And that is why our analysis of teachers relates to primary school teachers only.

Researchers and policy makers agree on the fact that teachers are important.[5] The standard approach is to use teacher value-added measures, where children's scores are explained by their previous scores, their parents' characteristics, the school's characteristics, and the name of the teacher. It is then possible to calculate the standard deviation of these value-added teacher scores relative to the overall standard deviation of the outcome across all children. This gives

Table 14.4. How children's outcomes at 8 and 11 are affected by measured primary school characteristics (ALSPAC) (β-coefficients)

Outcomes at age 11

	Emotional	*Behavioral*	*Intellectual*
School size	**−0.06** (.02)	**0.06** (.02)	**−0.14** (.01)
Class size	**0.04** (.02)	−0.01 (.02)	**0.05** (.01)
% Free school meal	−0.02 (.03)	**0.13** (.03)	**−0.11** (.01)
% English not first language	0.04 (.03)	0.02 (.02)	−0.02 (.01)
% SEN statemented	**0.09** (.02)	0.03 (.02)	**−0.05** (.02)
% Home concerns	0.00 (.02)	**0.03** (.02)	−0.02 (.01)

Outcomes at age 8

	Emotional	*Behavioral*	*Intellectual*
School size	**−0.03** (.02)	0.01 (.01)	0.01 (.02)
Class size	**0.04** (.02)	−0.02 (.02)	**0.04** (.02)
% Free school meal	0.01 (.02)	−0.02 (.02)	−0.01 (.02)
% English not first language	**−0.05** (.02)	**−0.04** (.02)	0.01 (.02)
% SEN statemented	**0.05** (.01)	**−0.06** (.01)	−0.03 (.02)
% Home concerns	**−0.06** (.02)	0.01 (.01)	**0.05** (.02)

β-coefficients similar to those we were examining before, but for teachers rather than schools.

Most research on teachers has focused on how they affect their pupils' academic test scores. There is little research on how teachers affect their pupils' emotional health and behavior. However Table 14.5 shows the results of a recent study[6] using information from ALSPAC for primary school teachers of children who ended the school year aged 8 and

Table 14.5. How children's outcomes at 8 and 11 are affected by their teacher (ALSPAC) (β-coefficients)

Outcomes measured by	Emotional	Behavioral	Intellectual
Teacher's reports	**0.23**	**0.12**	**0.14**
Parents' reports	**0.22**	**0.09**	

11 respectively.[7] The first row uses the teacher's own measurement of their children's emotional health and behavior, while the second row uses the parent's measurement of these variables. As can be seen, primary school teachers have more impact on the emotional health of the children than on the children's performance in math.[8]

How well do these measures of the teacher's skills predict their pupils' subsequent academic progress? Looking at the children's academic progress in math over the following years after they were taught by this particular primary school teacher, the same study shows that the teacher's effects on math test scores fade out very rapidly. This has been found elsewhere.[9] By contrast, the teacher's skill in influencing behavior and emotional health has only a small effect on their math performance at the time, but its effect does not fade over time.[10] This shows clearly that helping pupil's well-being does not detract from, but rather adds to, their academic performance.

Conclusion

Primary and secondary schools have major effects on the emotional well-being of their children. The variation across schools in this regard is as large as the variation in their impact on academic performance. There is also a huge variation in the impact of individual primary school teachers on the emotional well-being and academic performance of their children. These effects of primary schools and teachers persist throughout the following five years and longer.

At the same time we find no impact of the (narrow) differences in the size of classes across schools. This would imply that the main target for educational improvement should be the quality of teaching rather than reduction in class sizes.

PART THREE

So What?

"If we're going to prioritize, we're going to need some priorities."

15 Measuring Cost-Effectiveness in Terms of Happiness

> I am afraid there's no money.
>
> —*Liam Byrne in a note to his successor at the UK Treasury (2010)*

So, with all this knowledge, how are policy makers to proceed? The answer is the same whether they run the Ministry of Finance or the smallest NGO: there are four steps.

- First, be absolutely clear that human happiness is the goal of your organization. Build it into its DNA, and hire people who understand it.
- Second, review the evidence on what produces happiness (and what doesn't) and identify areas relevant to your organization where new policies might make a real difference.
- Third, design specific policy changes and then conduct proper controlled trials of their effects. In many cases the trials will have to be relatively brief, showing only the short-run impact of the new policy. But then you can estimate the longer-term effects by using models (from this book or elsewhere) showing the longer-term effects of short-run changes. Simulation of this kind will often be needed.

- Fourth, evaluate the outcome using a method of cost-effectiveness in which the benefits are measured in units of happiness.[1] This last step is the subject of this chapter.

The New Approach

So how would the policy maker evaluate a policy proposal?[2] Whoever we are, we want to see the greatest possible happiness in the community.[3] And let us assume we have a given amount of money to spend. We also have many possible policies we would like to consider. We cannot undertake them all, and we ought obviously to give top priority to those that give the largest happiness-benefits per unit of cost. So we would rank policies according to that criterion and then proceed down the list, commissioning all that we could until the money runs out.[4] Or, which is exactly the same thing, we would rank policies according to their ratio of cost to benefit and adopt only those with low enough cost/benefit ratios.

That is, if you like, the planning approach, but there is also a decentralized approach that is more practical and produces the same result. For, implicit in the planning approach, there is a critical cost-benefit ratio, below which policies are accepted and above which they are rejected. This critical ratio is at the point where the money just runs out. Once this ratio is established, it can be left to decentralized decision makers to evaluate whether any particular policy passes the test. The critical ratio can be adjusted from time to time on the basis of experience.

As we have formulated the approach, it is a form of cost-effectiveness analysis. We measure the costs in one set of units (money) and the benefits in another (happiness-years). And we assume that the total amount of money available is predetermined. By contrast in traditional cost-benefit analysis both benefits and costs are in the same units. So traditional cost-benefit, applied across the board, in principle determines the total scale of public expenditure. As we explain later, this is politically unrealistic. So our form of cost-effectiveness analysis is a sensible way forward for the analysis of public expenditure.

It is similar to what is already meant to happen with National Health Service expenditure in Britain. For all the possible treatments, the government guidelines[5] evaluate the gain in Quality-Adjusted Life Years (QALYs) and the cost. The treatment is then approved if the cost is below a given amount per QALY, with a cut-off of around $35,000 per QALY.[6]

This type of approach makes sense for all aspects of our national life, but using happiness-years rather than QALYs. To be more explicit, we propose that benefits be measured in point-years of happiness, where one happiness point-year corresponds to one individual being one happiness point higher for one year. Since happiness is measured over the range 0–10 and QALYs are measured over the range 0–1, that would make 10 happiness-years "equivalent" to one QALY.[7]

So what cut-off should be used as the maximum cost per happiness point-year? In the end this has to be found by trial and error. But where to start? In Britain it might make sense to start with the same cut-off as for health. This would require that the cost of 1 point-year of happiness be no higher than $3,500.

Why Cost-Effectiveness Analysis Rather Than Cost-Benefit?

As we have said, this approach is a form of cost-effectiveness analysis (CEA). It takes the total available expenditure as given and tries to maximize the effectiveness with which the money is spent. The critical benefit/cost ratio is expressed in point-years of happiness per unit of money.

A quite different approach is that known as cost-benefit analysis (CBA), where costs and benefits are computed in the same metric and total public expenditure is only determined at the end of the process—by the number of policies that pass the test. In this case we could then turn dollar cost into units of happiness by multiplying it by the effect of income on happiness $(\partial.H/\partial.Y)$, which is in traditional language the "marginal utility of income." Clearly this approach is very sensitive to estimates of the marginal utility of income. If marginal utility is estimated by cross-sectional analysis within a country, a typical finding (confirmed in our Chapter 2) is that happiness (on a scale of 0–10) increases by 0.2 points for every unit increase in log household income. In other words the marginal utility of annual income is 0.2/Annual Income. This in Britain would be about 1/125,000 point-years of happiness per $1.[8] So a cost of up to $125,000 would be acceptable if it generated 1 extra point-year of happiness. This test is 40 times less strict than the cut-off of $3,500 that we proposed for cost-effectiveness analysis and would therefore let through much more expenditure.

Moreover, if we were using CBA there could be a case for an even more generous test. This is because happiness depends significantly on relative income, and not just on absolute income.[9] When taxes are raised in order to finance the additional expenditure, relative income may not change much. So the loss of happiness will be less than in the preceding analysis. If this is allowed for, even more projects would pass the test. This would require even more public expenditure.

This shows that cost-benefit analysis is not a politically realistic approach to policy choice. We therefore recommend focusing on cost-effectiveness analysis, with a maximum initial cost of $3,500 per additional point-year of happiness.

Taxes and Regulations

But, for governments, there are other important policy problems as well as how to spend a given budget total. There is the issue of how to raise the taxes. The approach here is more direct. If we envisage a self-financing tax change, we simply evaluate how this alters the happiness of each member of the population and aggregate these changes (if we are, as assumed so far, simply maximizing the sum of happiness across all individuals). Similarly, if we are considering a new regulation, we simply add up its effects on happiness across all members of the population. In practice of course a new regulation may also affect the budget deficit, making possible more (or fewer) opportunities for public expenditure. So we need a way to value such extra money, in units of happiness-years. We already have the answer: the value of the extra money is the extra happiness years that are generated by the marginal public expenditure project.

Why Not Measure Benefits in Units of Money?

Assembling the information needed for the new approach is a real challenge, but so it is with traditional cost-effectiveness analysis where benefits are measured in units of money. So what problems can the new approach handle that cannot be handled when benefits are measured in units of money?

In traditional cost-effectiveness analysis, benefits and costs are measured in money units by estimating what people would be willing to pay for having the benefits and for avoiding the costs. The unit of measurement is money, the idea being that people are willing to pay more for something if it produces more happiness.

But willingness to pay works only when people can show by their choices how much they value different outcomes. Sometimes they can do, this but often they cannot. They can do it for things like transport, industry, education, and some aspects of environment. But many outcomes are not things that people can choose—they are things that just happen to people through outside influences (what economists call external effects). People catch infectious diseases, children get abused, elderly people get abandoned, and people get mugged. Moreover people are often ignorant about key areas of choice, as in health.

We cannot learn about how much people value these issues by observing people's choices. So how are we to evaluate policies like a vaccination program, or child protection, or family courts, or elderly care, or police protection? Measuring benefits in units of happiness is surely the answer.

Even though people can't show their values by choice, couldn't we equally well ask them hypothetical questions about how much they would in principle be willing to pay to promote these public goods? Unfortunately, no. It has been shown repeatedly that asking people hypothetical questions about how they value these things produces nonsensical answers.[10] So data on the happiness effects of these activities offers a better, new method of evidence-based policy making.

Traditional cost-effectiveness analysis can be very informative in some areas, but for the bulk of public or NGO expenditure, it cannot provide much help. In economists' jargon, these are areas bedeviled by externality, public goods, and asymmetric information—which is precisely why the state has become involved in them—in order to produce a more efficient outcome. And in these cases the natural approach is to measure benefits in units of happiness.

But why not, some economists say, then translate them into units of money? From a normal happiness equation, we can after all translate a given change in happiness into an equivalent change in income for the person in question.[11] The method is to divide the person's change in happiness (ΔH) by his or her marginal utility of income ($\partial H_i/\partial Y_i$) (which is of course higher the poorer the person is). We could then, as in standard cost-benefit analysis, add up these equivalent variations across individuals (taking no account of whether the beneficiary is a tramp or a Trump).

There are two overwhelming objections to this approach. First, it automatically makes changes in happiness less important if they occur to poor people. To avoid this, the results could be shown separately for different income groups. But why make it so difficult? Second, we might not in any case want to simply add the ΔH_i but rather to give extra weight to those with low initial happiness. If the monetary valuation procedure is followed, there is no way to do this, since the happiness level of each individual has become invisible.

Equity

The basic inequality in our society is surely between people with different levels of happiness, not different levels of income. So should not policy analysis give more weight to changes in happiness among those who are the least happy? Jeremy Bentham thought not, but modern opinion inclines more in that direction. So how much extra weight?[12] The best approach is probably to ask the population what they think about the weights. When comparing options, one can also use sensitivity analysis to see what difference (if any) the weights make.[13]

The Discount Rate

Another, related, issue is how to add up effects occurring at different points in time. For most individuals the effects of a policy change are spread over a number of years, and indeed some policies affect people not yet born. So what discount rate should we use to combine effects that occur in different years? In traditional cost-benefit analysis the discount rate consists of two elements that are added together. The first element (the "social pure time discount rate") reflects the general uncertainty about the future; the second reflects the fact that future generations are expected to be richer and therefore to have a lower marginal utility of income. In the current UK Treasury Green Book the first element is put at 1.5 percent per annum and the second at 2 percent.[14] There is clearly a case for a pure time discount rate. But, when our measurements are in units of happiness, declining marginal utility of income ceases to be relevant, although there is still the distributional issue of how we should allow for differences in happiness between different generations (or indeed different years of one person's life). There is no neat solution to this problem, and where it is severe it must be shown explicitly in the analysis. Where it is not, the pure time discount rate may suffice.[15]

If this is the approach to discounting happiness, how should we discount future public expenditure? In principle there should be a separate price attached to public expenditure in each period. But in practice, if the path of public expenditure is reasonably smooth, we can probably assume that the price of public expenditure in units of contemporaneous happiness would remain the same from one year to the next. This would mean that the price of future public expenditure in units of today's happiness-years should fall at the same discount rate as is used for future happiness.

The Length of Life and Number of Births

Finally, how should we value changes in the length of life? Most people would agree that a longer life is better, but so is a happier one. So how could we combine these two desirable things into a single objective measure of what we are aiming at for an individual? The most common approach is to multiply the person's length of life by the person's average happiness—so that the result equals the total happiness the person experiences—or in medical parlance the number of Quality-Adjusted Life Years (QALYs).

However for this to make sense we need to assume that there is such a thing as zero happiness—in other words happiness is measured on a ratio scale rather than a cardinal scale.

The typical scale that measures life-satisfaction runs from 0 ("not at all satisfied") to 10 ("extremely satisfied"), and at a stretch one could interpret 0 as equivalent to zero happiness.

But are all years of life after birth equally important? For example is it twice as valuable if we save the life of a new-born infant as if we save the life of a 40-year-old? Any other assumption is bound to be controversial.

Finally there is the issue of the numbers born. Is the world better if more people are born? For most practical purposes we can take the number of births as exogenous. But some policies clearly do affect the number of births, and some countries like France, India, China, and Japan have all tried to influence the fertility of their populations either up (France) or down (the others). How do we evaluate such policies? We can imagine two extreme positions. One position says the only thing that counts is the proportional distribution of QALYs among all those who are born and that the number of people born is immaterial. Thus a world of one million people is as good as one of seven billion who are equally happy and live equally long. The opposite position says that what matters are total QALYs, added up over all the people born.[16] According to that position we should prefer a trebling of births even if it halved the QALYs per person born. Probably most people would prefer policy evaluation that focused on the proportional distribution of well-being, and that is what we recommend.

Some Examples

This is not the place for detailed appraisal of policies to improve well-being. But we can mention just a few examples.

First there are policies involving public expenditure. The simplest cases are when the policy generates so much savings that the net cost to public funds is negative. One example of this is England's new service for Improving Access to Psychological Therapies. It can be convincingly shown that this improves well-being at no net cost to the government.[17]

But we should not of course expect every policy to pay for itself in full. One example of a policy with a positive net cost is the US program called Moving to Opportunity. In this ambitious project, poor families were offered housing vouchers to enable them to live in less disadvantaged areas. The economic effects turned out to be negligible (except on children who moved at a young age).[18] But the well-being effects were significant. After 4–7 years, mental health increased against controls by 0.16 standard deviations. After 15 years, happiness had increased by 0.2 standard deviations for those who used the vouchers. This corresponds to roughly 0.4 points of life-satisfaction (0–10). Cumulated over say 30 years at a real discount rate of 1.5% p.a., this is roughly 10 point-years of life-satisfaction (0–10). The net cost per family was $3,700 (and even less per person).[19] So the cost per additional point-year of happiness was under $300—a real bargain.

Another example is a policy to provide cement floors to peasant houses in Mexico.[20] Treatment households were offered (and all accepted) cement floors; control households were not. After 3 years, mothers were asked Are you satisfied with your quality of life (1 = very satisfied or satisfied; 0 = fair or unsatisfied). The mean for the control was 0.60 and the effect of treatment was +0.11 points—equivalent to an upward shift in mean z-score of roughly 0.22—or 0.4 points of life-satisfaction. The cost was $150 per household. If the gain in life-satisfaction lasted for say 10 years, the gain is 4 point-years of life-satisfaction—another bargain.

Turning to regulation, an obvious issue is "Do smoking bans improve human well-being?" This has been studied using data on more than half a million Europeans since 1990.[21] The conclusion is that the ban increased the life-satisfaction of those smokers who wanted to quit, without significant negative effects on any other group.

Conclusion

To conclude, we believe that policy analysis should be based on happiness as the measure of benefit (except where traditional methods actually work). The approach is developed more formally in online Annex 15. We think it should be generally applied throughout the public services and by NGOs. As the new method took hold, people would become familiar with how many point-years of happiness per dollar were typically acceptable and which were not.

But will policy makers ever use this new-fangled approach? If they want to get reelected, politicians have every reason to do so, for analysis of European elections since 1970 shows that the life-satisfaction of the people is the best predictor of whether a government gets reelected.[22] It is a more powerful predictor than either economic growth, unemployment, or inflation.

Moreover at present policy makers have no clear focus. Most policy proceeds by a series of ad hoc arguments, with no attempt to make one argument commensurate with another. Well-being research offers information of real substance to fill that vacuum. It is early days yet, and the numbers in this book are offered to stimulate further refinement rather than as final answers. But no one can doubt that they offer a significantly different perspective from many that are traditional.

Can they actually be used to evaluate policies? Again the answer is Yes. When existing methods of cost-benefit analysis were first proposed sixty years ago, they seemed impossibly ambitious. But, within the limits to which they apply, they have been constantly refined. As a general approach they are now unquestioned.

The same will happen to policy appraisal based on well-being. It will eventually become totally accepted as the standard way to evaluate social policies, and much else besides. And hopefully experiment will become the standard prelude to policy change. The consequences for good will be massive.

So we have four key proposals.

- The goal of governments should be to increase the happiness of the people and, especially, to reduce misery.
- Where willingness to pay is not a feasible measure of benefit, governments should develop new methods of policy analysis based on point-years of happiness as the measure of benefit.
- All policy change should be evaluated through controlled experiments in which the impact on happiness is routinely measured.
- A major objective of social science (and of its funders) should be to throw light on the causes of happiness, and how it can be enhanced—and at what cost.

Sammy was actually happy, he just didn't know it.

16 The Origins of Happiness

> What matters to people must be the guideline for our policies.
>
> —*Chancellor Angela Merkel (2015)*

So is Angela Merkel right? And is it not time for a fundamental revolution in human thought? Surely the ultimate aim of human endeavor must be to produce flourishing communities of people who are profoundly satisfied with their lives. It cannot be simply the creation of wealth. If people say "We can't do this because it's bad for the economy," do we say "Well of course we can't." Or do we say "Well who actually is the economy? Let us see, instead, whose quality of life is affected and by how much?"

Until recently this approach has not been easy to implement: the knowledge has just not been there. But there is now enough knowledge to shift to the new paradigm. This knowledge has been accumulating over the last thirty years, but in a fragmented way, with many different measures of happiness being used, and one influence being examined after another in isolation. This book is different. We use only one single overarching measure of happiness: life-satisfaction for adults, and emotional well-being for children. And we look at all possible influences simultaneously, so that we can properly compare their influence on happiness.

What we have found is so striking that it calls for a total rethink of the priorities for our society. For it turns out that happiness varies less with income than with other key aspects of our external and internal life. On the external side, the key aspect is the quality of our human relationships—above all with family and loved ones, but also with our colleagues and our boss, and in our local community. There are many cost-effective ways in which the quality of those relationships can be improved in our society.

At the same time the most important internal fact about us is our health, and especially our mental health. Mental health is the biggest single predictor of happiness. So we need a much wider concept of deprivation. People are deprived if they cannot enjoy their life for whatever reason—either external or internal to themselves. Fortunately we now have extremely effective ways of treating mental health problems, many of which save as much money as they cost.[1]

In this chapter, we summarize our main findings on what determines happiness. They are expressed in numerical form because there is no way to compare the importance of different things except by using numbers. Our measure of happiness throughout is life-satisfaction, measured on a scale of 0 to 10. So when for example we examine how unemployment affects happiness, we are asking how many "points" of happiness are lost. The answer is 0.7 points. That is, like all our estimates, an average effect across many people, some of whom will suffer more and others less. But from a policy point of view the average is a good place to start.

In a moment we shall describe how exactly we reach our findings. But, before that, we can illustrate the massive range of issues covered, with a few key findings about what determines our happiness. These are explained more fully in the rest of the chapter.

Some Key Findings

- *Income*. Within most advanced countries income differences explain only 1% of the variation in happiness across people (other things equal),[2] while all the factors we can identify explain 15% of the variation. Doubling a person's income raises their happiness by under 0.2 points (on a scale of 0–10). Moreover people care largely about their income relative to other people. So general increases in income have very small impacts on overall happiness in a society.
- *Unemployment*. By contrast unemployment is in itself an unalloyed bad. It reduces the happiness of each unemployed person by about 0.7 points on average. And it also creates fear and unease among people who are in work: the unemployment of one person reduces the aggregate happiness of the rest of the community by another 2.0 points. So economic policy should give strong priority to the aim of economic stability,[3] and less importance to the aim of long-term economic growth.
- *Family life*. Being partnered rather than single raises happiness by 0.6 points, and losing a partner by separation or death reduces happiness by a roughly equal amount. As with being employed, people need to be needed, and to be in meaningful relationships.
- *Mental health*. The biggest single predictor of individual happiness is mental health. Suffering from depression or anxiety disorders is more common

than unemployment, and it also reduces happiness by 0.7 points. In fact mental health problems are not highly correlated with poverty or unemployment, so we need a much wider concept of what it is to be deprived. This needs to include both mental and physical pain.

- *Education.* An extra year of education has a small direct effect on happiness of 0.03 points and larger indirect effects via income and mental health. These last through life. However people largely value their education relative to that of their peers. So the main overall gains from educational expansion may come from the external effects of a more civilized community of citizens and voters.[4]

- *Child development.* All these adult factors affecting happiness are influenced in turn by the pattern of child development—emotional, behavioral, and intellectual. Here academic qualifications are less effective predictors of a satisfying adult life than a child's emotional health.

- *Parenting.* Your development as a child is in turn determined by your parents and your schooling, The best predictor of a child's emotional development is the mother's mental health. Conflict between parents is also damaging to emotional development, as is child poverty. There is no clear evidence that children suffer emotionally when their mother goes out to work, once the child is over one year of age.

- *Schools.* Differences between schools account for a substantial part of the variation in children's emotional health. The same is true of the variation in their behavior and in their academic performance.

Even at age 16 the influence of the primary school is still nearly as strong as that of the child's secondary school.

- *Loneliness in old age.* In later life a major problem is loneliness. Even controlling for whether they have a partner, people with an extra standard deviation of loneliness have a life-satisfaction that is lower by 0.5 points.
- *Social norms.* Happiness is hugely affected by the ethos of a society, which affects everyone in it. For example, happiness is higher in societies where people trust each other. If those who trust others rises from 0% to 100%, happiness rises by 1 whole point. Freedom is also a crucial determinant of happiness. So no one who favors happiness should favor a totalitarian state.

The Life-Course Approach

The evidence we present in this book comes mainly from studying how people develop over their life course. Chapter 1 gave an outline of our approach, but it can usefully be repeated in stylized form in the following graph. A child grows up in a family and goes to school. These influences (plus the genes) determine the child's "outcomes" at 16. The main dimensions here are the child's intellectual, behavioral, and emotional development, and the emotional dimension is our measure of the happiness of a child.

The child then grows into an adult, with many adult "outcomes" (including income, employment, partnering, and mental and physical health). At the same time the adult's

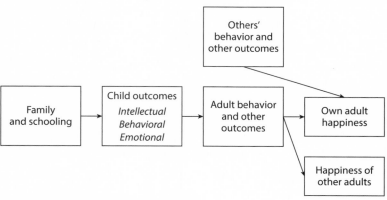

Figure 16.1. The life course of the individual

behavior strongly affects other people, and vice versa. The adult also evaluates many of his or her achievements like income and education in relation to what others have also achieved. So the overall picture of life we try to describe is that shown in Figure 16.1.

So the tables that summarize our findings proceed in the following order. First we look at how adult happiness can be changed by directly changing adult outcomes. Then we look at how it can be changed by changing child outcomes, and then at how these in turn can be changed by altering families or schools.

In this book we have used a multiplicity of data from four main countries (Britain, the United States, Germany, and Australia), which give broadly similar results. In this summary chapter we shall concentrate mainly on three British surveys: the British Household Panel Survey (BHPS),[5] which interviews a sample of adults of all ages every year; the British Cohort Study (BCS) of people born in 1970 and followed up at intervals into their 40s; and the Avon sample (ALSPAC) of people born in 1991–92. The tables that follow are based on the cross-sectional results from these three surveys modified occasionally for reasons we explain.[6] All the numbers are subject to potential margins of error, set out in the preceding chapters.

Our findings are as relevant to every individual as they are to policy makers. But we are particularly keen to see a revolution in policy making—which will only come about if policy makers can find the information in a convenient form. So how would policy makers use these findings?

First, they would want to choose those areas that most called for new policy initiatives. For this purpose they would be interested in the factors that most account for the huge variety in the quality of life in our society—ranging from misery at one end to great fulfillment at the other. The statistic that reflects how much a factor accounts for this variety is the partial correlation coefficient or β-statistic. So in the tables that follow we start with the β-coefficients.

But, having done this, policy makers would want to examine particular policy changes that could improve happiness in the population. Each policy change would have its cost and would produce a specific amount of extra happiness. This requires tables that show how changing one factor by one unit changes the amount of happiness in the community measured in natural units on a scale 0–10. So we also give tables where the effects are measured in this "absolute" way. Like all statistics in this book, these are the best estimates but are subject to quite wide confidence intervals that can be found in the Full Tables online. We are now ready to start.

Which Adults Are Happier Than Others?

People differ hugely in their enjoyment of life. When asked how satisfied people are with their life (on a scale 0–10), 25% of BHPS respondents give a reply of 6 or under, 50% 7 or 8, and 25% 9 or 10.[7] So the first question is what explains this variation and what can we do about it?

We first examine the effect of a person's adult situation, holding constant whatever went before in their life. The results are in the first column of Table 16.1. For each factor they show its influence, when all the other factors are held constant. In Table 16.1 we focus on all adults over 25, while in Figure 1.1 we analyzed this issue only for people aged 34 and 42. The two sets of results are remarkably similar.

Once again we see the enormous importance of mental health and of close personal relationships. Even though we now include the elderly population, mental illness explains more of the variation in happiness than physical illness does. Income explains under 1% of the variation in happiness (as measured by the square of the β-statistic).

However, one obvious question is: What explains the lowest levels of happiness? Is it the same things, or is income for example more important in explaining whether people are really miserable? The second column of the table addresses this question. Those "in misery" are those in the lowest 10% or so of life-satisfaction, and the equation predicts whether an individual is or is not in misery. Income is no better at explaining who is in misery than at explaining overall life-satisfaction. Mental health remains more important than physical health. Similar findings hold in the United States, Australia, and Germany.

Table 16.1. What explains the variation of life-satisfaction and of misery among adults (BHPS) (cross-section) (β-coefficients)

	Life-satisfaction	Misery
Income	0.09	−0.07
Education (years)	0.02	−0.02
Not unemployed	0.06	−0.07
Noncriminality	0.06	−0.04
Partnered	0.11	−0.08
Physical health (no. of conditions)	0.11	−0.09
Mental health (diagnosed depression/ anxiety)	0.19	−0.16
R^2	0.19	0.14

A natural tendency of skeptics is to say "But isn't mental illness caused by poverty or unemployment?" Some of it is. But the equation in the table explicitly measures the impact of that mental illness that is *not* caused by poverty or unemployment. And in any case we have previously shown that most mental illness is in fact not the result of poverty or unemployment.

The Absolute Effects of Experience

As we have said, it is one thing to look at explanatory power and another to show how changing a situation would improve happiness. That is the subject of Table 16.2. It shows how life-satisfaction (0–10) increases as a result of various changes. The scores recorded are points on the scale 0 to 10.

Table 16.2. How adult life-satisfaction (0–10) is affected by current circumstances (BHPS) (cross-section)

	Effect on life-satisfaction (0–10)	*Total effect on the life-satisfaction (0–10) of others*
Income doubles	+0.12	−0.13
One extra year of education (direct effect)	+0.03	−0.09
Unemployed (vs. employed)	−0.70	−2.00
Quality of work (1 SD extra)	+0.40	—
Partnered (vs. single)	+0.59	+0.68
Separated (vs. partnered)	−0.74	—
Widowed (vs. partnered)	−0.48	—
Being a parent	+0.03	—
One physical illness	−0.22	—
Depression or anxiety	−0.72	—
Commit one crime	**−0.30 point-years**	**−1.00 point-year**

The first column shows how the various changes in an individual's life affect that person's *own* happiness. The second column shows how these same changes affect the happiness of *others* in the same region, age group and gender.

We should explain how the second column is obtained, taking income as an example. From our standard regression we know that the happiness of one individual falls by 0.13 points when the average income of her comparators doubles.[8] But for purposes of the table we want to know the opposite: how does the happiness of all the comparators combined fall, when the income of one individual doubles? The effect turns out to be identical in size. There are N comparators. When one individual's income doubles, each comparator finds that her comparison income has risen by a fraction $1/N$, and therefore her happiness has fallen by $0.13/N$. But there are N comparators. So their collective happiness has fallen by 0.13 points. That is the figure in the second column.

The implications are devastating. If the estimates are accurate, increases in income cannot increase the happiness of society. For if one individual increases her income, that person becomes happier, but others become less happy by a roughly equal amount. Similarly, if all individuals increase their income equally, none of them gain. This analysis must help to explain why the huge improvements in living standards in the United States since 1950, West Germany since 1970, and China since 1990 have not been accompanied by increases in happiness. This said, happiness has clearly risen in some other countries, and income growth may have played some role in this. The important conclusion is that social comparisons play an important role in relation to income, which should never be ignored.

Unfortunately the same appears to apply also to years of education, though this has been less well studied in the literature. An extra year of education directly raises your own happiness by 0.03 points on average throughout life—a worthwhile effect. But the evidence for Britain, Germany, and Australia is that education is highly subject to comparison effects—if others have more education, it makes you less happy with whatever you yourself get. Education does of course also raise income, improve mental health, and reduce crime. Even so our estimates imply that educational expansion fails to raise aggregate life-satisfaction, unless this is offset by improved civic behavior. The policy conclusion as we shall see later is to concentrate more on the quality of education and less on its quantity.

By contrast unemployment is unambiguously bad. When one more person becomes unemployed, that person's happiness falls by 0.7 points, on top of the effect of her lost income. And the aggregate loss of happiness in the community is another 2.0 points. The quality of work also matters: if the quality of work index improves by one standard deviation, life-satisfaction rises by 0.4 points.

Partnering is likewise unambiguously good. It brings joy to the individual and on average improves the social environment for others. The coefficients on partnering, separation, and widowhood in the table are cross-sectional, and the panel estimates are about half as large. Even so, this evidence on partnering, separation, widowhood, and unemployment all points strongly to the importance of social relationships for human happiness. With separation and widowhood there is serious loss when these events happen, followed by some adaptation. But on average people do not return to the level of happiness that they had when partnered.

When it comes to having young children, the evidence in panel studies is that, when the child is born, there is great joy. But happiness soon returns almost to its former level. We have little evidence on the effects of older children who have left home, but what there is suggests they are a blessing if they keep in touch.[9]

Illness is of course a major source of unhappiness. Depression or anxiety disorder reduces happiness by 0.72 points, whereas one of a list of physical illnesses costs 0.22 points of happiness.

Finally, we come to crime. From the British Cohort Study we can estimate that a crime committed under the age of 34 reduces the criminal's happiness by 0.30 point-years.[10] But, using data from the British Crime Survey, it reduces the happiness of the rest of the population about 1 point-year.

How the Child Predicts the Adult

The information so far tells us what we could achieve by directly influencing the situation of an adult. But another way to influence adults is through altering their childhood. In Table 16.3 we examine the three main dimensions of child development and ask how well they predict the resulting adult. Column (1) shows the effects on life-satisfaction. The best predictor of how far adults are satisfied with their lives is not their academic performance but their emotional health in childhood. Neither their academic performance nor their behavior—the central focuses for educators—is as important for them as their emotional health.

Table 16.3. How adult life-satisfaction (0–10) and behavior are predicted by child outcomes (British Cohort Study)(cross-section)

	Units	Adult life-satisfaction (0–10)	Number of crimes before 30
Highest qualification	SD (index)	**0.12**	**−0.50**
Good behavior at 16	SD (index)	**0.06**	**−0.50**
Emotional health at 16	SD (index)	**0.18**	**−0.04**

However this is not the end of the story. For, as we have seen, the overall happiness of the population is strongly affected by how people behave to each other. So, when we study individuals, we need to understand not only how their own happiness is determined but also what determines their behavior to others. We have few good measures of behavior. Whether people attract a partner is of course affected by their behavior, but by much else besides. The nearest we have to a measure of behavior is a person's criminal record. So in column (2) we analyze what determines the number of times people have been convicted or cautioned by the age of 30. The best predictors of this are their qualifications, and, not surprisingly, their behavior as a child.

Does allowing for these effects alter the relative ranking of the different dimensions of child development? From other studies we know that on average each crime reduces aggregate life-satisfaction in the population by 1 point-year. So we could compute an aggregate effect of each dimension of child development on human happiness by combining column (1) aggregated (over say sixty years) with the negative of column (2). Aggregating a number over sixty years makes it quite large, even if it is quite small on a per year basis. Given that, the numbers in column (2) would not reverse our previous conclusion that emotional health is the most important dimension of child development for purposes of aggregate human happiness.[11]

How Parents and Schools Form the Child

So what determines how children turn out to be by the age of 16?[12] By far the best evidence on this comes from the Avon study, which records the details of family life and schooling year by year. So in Table 16.4 we look at how family life from birth to age 16 affects how children are at age 16. We also look at the effects of schooling.

We look at the effects on all the three child outcomes. Emotional health at 16 is measured by 32 questions, some

Table 16.4. How children's outcomes at age 16 are affected by family and schooling (ALSPAC) (cross-section) (standardized coefficients)

	Emotional health at 16	Behavior at 16	GCSE score at 16
Family income (log, averaged)	0.07	0.08	0.14
Parents' education (years)	—	0.04	0.17
Father unemployed (% of years)	—	—	−0.03
Mother worked (% of 1st year)	—	—	−0.02
Mother worked (% of other years)	—	−0.05	0.04
Parents' involvement with child	0.04	0.05	0.02
Parents' aggression to child	−0.03	−0.12	—
Mother's mental health	0.16	0.17	0.03
Father's mental health	0.04	—	—
Conflict between parents	−0.04	−0.14	−0.01
Primary school quality	0.27	0.32	0.21
Secondary school quality	0.28	0.31	0.38

answered by the young person and some by the mother. Behavior is measured by 10 questions asked of the mother. And intellectual performance is measured by the number of points scored in the GCSE (General Certificate of Secondary Education) exams, taken mainly at 16.

These three outcomes differ in their ultimate importance. Emotional health is our measure of the well-being of the child—it is a final outcome. Behavior is an intermediate outcome, but an extremely important one for all the other people that the person deals with, either in childhood or as an adult. And academic performance is important mainly as a preparation for adult life.

Until recently the main focus in the policy debate was on academic performance. But what Table 16.4 shows is that academic performance is affected by very different factors from those that affect child well-being. And child behavior has yet another set of determinants.

The biggest single family determinant of a child's well-being is the *mental health* of the mother, and this is also the biggest determinant of a child's behavior. By contrast the biggest family factors affecting academic performance are family *income* and parents' *education*.

Children also gain academically if their *mother goes out to work* (except in the child's first year of life). The children's well-being is unaffected. But there is some evidence of a negative effect on behavior at 16.

Similarly *family conflict* is bad for children's well-being and behavior, but not particularly bad for their academic performance.

After parents, the next major influence on children are their *schools*, both primary and secondary. Because the Avon sample was scattered over many schools with many children in each school, we can ask "How much difference did it make which school your child went to?" The answer is a huge difference.

If we include a dummy variable for each school, we can see how much that school affected the children's outcomes. We can then take the standard deviation of these effects, and this is shown at the bottom of Table 16.4. Even though the outcomes are measured at age 16, the primary school a child went to makes as much difference as the secondary school—when it comes to child well-being and child behavior. Only when it comes to academic performance at 16 is the secondary school more important than the primary school. We can also trace the impact that individual primary school teachers have on their children, which is even larger on their children's emotional health than on their learning of math. The effects of primary school teachers can be detected 10 years later.

Since only one child is studied in each family in the Avon sample we cannot carry out the same analysis for the overall effect of which family you belong to. But we can look at the effect of all the family variables that we can measure. The total of these effects was in each case about the same as the effects of the secondary school.

Public Goods

We have looked so far at what makes one person's happiness different from another's in the same society. But there are many things that affect the well-being of everybody in a society in a similar way, but that differ between societies. These are public goods, and we can study their effects only by comparing societies.

One source of evidence is the differences in well-being between countries.[13] These have been regularly explored by John Helliwell in the World Happiness Report. Each year this report measures the average happiness of every country by the so-called Cantril ladder, where people are asked "Please imagine a ladder, with steps numbered from 0 at the bottom to 10 at the top. The top of the ladder represents the best possible life for you and the bottom of the ladder represents the worst possible life for you. On which step of the ladder would you say you personally feel you stand at this time?" This "life-evaluation" variable has been found to have very similar properties to life-satisfaction. The top country generally is Denmark, with a score of around 7.5. The lowest include Syria (3.4) and the Central African Republic (2.7).[14]

This huge international variation in average happiness can be largely explained by six variables reflecting the income, health, and ethos of the country in question. These variables are

- *Trust*. Proportion saying Yes to "Do you think most other people can be trusted?"
- *Generosity*. Proportion saying Yes to "Have you donated money to a charity in the past month?"
- *Social support*. Proportion saying Yes to "If you were in trouble, do you have relatives or friends you can count on to help whenever you need them?"
- *Freedom*. Proportion saying Yes to "Are you satisfied with your freedom to choose what to do with your life?"

- *Income*. Log GDP per head.
- *Health*. Healthy life expectancy (in years).

As the first column of numbers in Table 16.5 shows, the four social variables explain an important part of the variation of happiness across countries. The difference they can make is substantial. For example if everyone has social support as opposed to none, the average national life-evaluation increases by 2 points. On a scale of 0–10 this is a huge change. Or if we go from the lowest level of trust (7% in Brazil) to the highest (64% in Norway) this raises average life-satisfaction by 57% of 1.08 points—some 0.6 points.

Income also has a substantial effect, with a doubling of average income raising happiness by 0.23 points. This is more than is found in many individual cross-sectional comparisons within countries, but it is not at all consistent with the time-series experience of many countries. For example, average happiness has been flat in the United States, Britain, West Germany, and Australia over many years (see Figure

Table 16.5. How average life-evaluation in a country is affected by country-level variables (Gallup World Poll) (cross-section)

	Units	β-coefficients	Effect on life-evaluation (0–10) of specified changes
Trust	%	0.11	All vs. none: 1.08
Generosity	%	0.07	All vs. none: 0.54
Social support	%	0.20	All vs. none: 2.03
Freedom	%	0.18	All vs. none: 1.41
Income	log	0.38	Doubling: 0.23
Health	years	0.24	One more year: 0.03

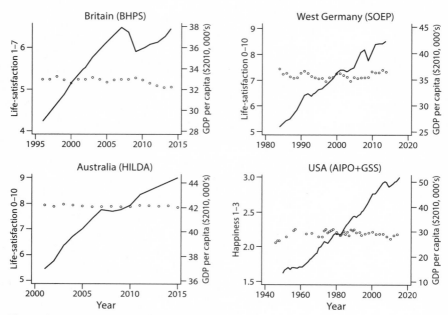

Figure 16.2. Average income and well-being over time

16.2). Even in China, happiness was no higher in 2010 than it was in 1990.[15]

We would be very happy if the cross-section of countries could predict the time-series. But the cross-section surely reflects an element of international comparison, in which case income gains all round the world will have less effect than the table implies. However, we do not think that income gains and losses should be treated as unimportant, and we recommend that a sensible approach to income in project evaluation would be to assume that a doubling of income raises happiness by 0.12 points (as in the first column of Table 16.2).

Policy Evaluation

The purpose of all these numbers (not too many we hope) is to guide decisions—by individuals or by policy makers. Our hope is that policy makers worldwide will in due course adopt the happiness of the people as their overarching policy objective. For this purpose they would be constantly looking for policy changes that would advance that objective. This would be true in the largest Ministry of Finance but also in the smallest NGO.

In each case they would use the science of happiness to select areas for policy development. New policies would then be designed and tested. These new policies could be based on hunch (good or bad), or on previous trials, or on inference from existing science—from all sorts of places. But, wherever they come from, the new policies must be subjected to the acid test of cost-effectiveness, based on a proper controlled trial.

The assumption lying behind any cost-effectiveness analysis is that there is a limited amount of money to be spent. If this money is to produce the greatest amount of happiness, it should be spent on those policies that produce the most happiness-years per dollar spent. So there would be some critical cost/benefit ratio, below which new policies pass the test and above which they fail.

Britain's National Health Service has been operating such a system for the last fifteen years. Any new treatment must produce enough extra Quality-Adjusted Life Years (QALYs) per dollar spent to be recommended for use in the service. At present, at least one extra QALY must result from every $35,000 spent.

So what would be the equivalent cut-off for a policy aimed at maximizing "Happiness-Years" rather than Quality-Adjusted Years? We discussed this in Chapter 15. Clearly in the end the cut-off has to be established by a process of trial and error. But if in doubt an advanced country might choose to start with a similar cut-off to that which has been used in Britain's National Health Service. Since happiness-years are measured on a scale 0–10 and QALYs on a scale 0–1, the maximum allowable cost for one extra happiness-year might be set at $3,500.

In any country there are dozens of initiatives that would pass this test, as well as dozens of existing policies currently in operation that do not. That is not the subject of this book, but to compile such an inventory should be a central aim of happiness research.

There is one other issue on evaluation. As Jeremy Bentham recommended, we have so far simply added up changes in happiness, regardless of who experienced them. But most of us think it is more important to prevent misery than to increase existing happiness. So we would want to give extra weight to changes in happiness among people who were currently miserable. And we would give less weight than average to changes for the happiest people. Those weights are an ethical issue, and policy makers need to choose their weights.

The Way Forward

So we are on the verge of a revolution, not only in human thought but in practical policy making. As Francis Bacon observed, knowledge is power. He was thinking about the physical world. But we have now come, after all these centuries, to where we can quantify the influences on our most basic feelings—of enjoyment and of distress. From the knowledge distilled in this book some overwhelming impressions emerge.

- We have to move "beyond GDP," and we can. The things that matter most for our happiness and for our misery are: our social relationships and our mental and physical health.
- So we need a much wider concept of deprivation than now prevails. You are deprived if you cannot enjoy your life. And the most common cause of deprivation is not poverty or unemployment but mental illness.
- We also need a new role for the state—not wealth creation but well-being creation. In past years the state successively took on poverty, unemployment, education, and physical health. But equally important now are domestic violence, alcoholism, depression and anxiety conditions, alienated youth, exam mania, and much else. These should become center stage.

Angela Merkel was right, and so was Thomas Jefferson. What matters to people must be the guideline for our policy makers—and for all of us as human beings.

OUR THANKS

This has been a long project involving many members of the Wellbeing Programme at the Centre for Economic Performance in the London School of Economics. We are extremely grateful to Nele Warrinnier and Warn Nuarpear Lekfuangfu, who were key members in its earlier phase. We are also grateful to Stephen Machin, Andrew Steptoe, and Camille Lassale for the chapters they have contributed, and to the Centre for Economic Performance, which continues to provide the perfect environment for purposeful research.

Throughout the project Harriet Ogborn has been a superb administrator of the group and a brilliant manager of the manuscript.

We have benefited greatly from advice of all kinds, especially from Tim Besley, Martine Durand, Paul Frijters, Emily Grundy, John Helliwell, Heather Joshi, Martin Knapp, Alan Manning, Gus O'Donnell, Jörn-Steffen Pischke, Jane Waldfogel, and dozens of others who have come to our seminars in London and Paris and to our conferences. We are also grateful to Sarah Caro, our excellent editor at Princeton University Press. Our London Conference in December 2016, where the draft of the book was presented, was part of our valuable cooperation with the OECD and CEPREMAP, as part of the OECD Consortium on Subjective Wellbeing over the Life Course.

This project has been made possible thanks to generous funding from the National Institute on Aging (Grant R01AG040640), the Templeton Foundation, the Department for Work and Pensions, the Economic and Social Research Council, and the What Works Centre for Wellbeing, of which our research group is the Cross-Cutting Capabilities team. We are also extremely grateful for personal contributions from Sushil Wadhwani, Paul Tudor Jones, Andrew Law, Henry and Sara Bedford, Rishi Khosla, Bertrand Kan, and Pavel Teplukhin.

We are enormously indebted to all who have organized the many surveys on which this book depends, and to all who have replied to their questions. Ethical approval for our work on ALSPAC was obtained from the ALSPAC Ethics and Law Committee and the Local Research Ethics Committees. We are extremely grateful to all the families who took part in the ALSPAC study, the midwives for their help in recruiting them, and the whole team, which includes interviewers, computer and laboratory technicians, clerical workers, research scientists, volunteers, managers, receptionists, and nurses. The UK Medical Research Council and the Wellcome Trust (Grant ref: 102215/2/13/2) and the University of Bristol provide core support for ALSPAC. The ALSPAC study website contains details of all the data that are available through a fully searchable data dictionary at http://www.bristol.ac.uk/alspac/researchers/access/. We take full responsibility for their use of all these surveys.

Thank you all.

ANDREW, SARAH, RICHARD, NICK, AND GEORGE

CONTENTS OF ONLINE MATERIALS

Available at http://cep.lse.ac.uk/origins/onlinematerial.pdf

- **Descriptive Statistics (e.g., Table D1)**
  Means, SDs, and Correlations

- **Full Tables**—numbered as in text

- **Additional Tables and Figures (e.g., Table A1.1)**

- **Annexes**
  1 Interpreting the statistics

  2 Income and well-being. Others' findings.

  3a Education and well-being. Others' findings.

  3b Decomposition analysis.

  4 Unemployment and well-being. Others' findings.

  5 Family and well-being. Others' findings.

  6 Data on health of body and mind

  7 Crime and childhood (by Stephen J. Machin)

  9 Definitions of variables in ELSA

  10 Financial difficulties and child development

  15 Cost-effectiveness analysis in terms of happiness

- **Survey Details**
  British Cohort Study (BCS)

  British Household Panel Survey (BHPS)

  German Socio-Economic Panel (SOEP)

Household, Income and Labour Dynamics in Australia (HILDA)
Behavioral Risk Factor Surveillance System (BRFSS)
Avon Longitudinal Study of Parents and Children (ALSPAC)

• **Do Files**

SOURCES AND NOTES FOR TABLES AND FIGURES

Table 0.1. Factors explaining the existing government's vote share (partial correlation coefficients)
Source: Ward (2015).
Notes: Eurobarometer data on life-satisfaction and standard election data for most European countries since the 1970s. The regressors include the government's vote share in the previous election. Life-satisfaction is from the latest survey before the election. Other variables are for the year of the election.

Figure 1.1. How adult life-satisfaction at 34 and 42 is affected by adult outcomes at these ages (British Cohort Study)
Source: Online Full Table for Figure 1.1.
Notes: Robust standard errors in parentheses. Standardized coefficients. Information from BCS respondents at ages 34 and 42. Other controls include child intellectual performance, behavioral, and emotional health outcomes at age 16; parents' education; family income; parental involvement; mother's mental health; family break-up; mother's work; father's unemployment; number of siblings; postmarital conception; gender; ethnicity; low birth weight; and an age dummy (42). Bold: $p < .10$ (2-tailed).

Figure 1.2. How adult life-satisfaction is affected by child outcomes (British Cohort Study)
Source: Online Full Table for Figure 1.2.
Notes: Robust standard errors in parentheses. Standardized coefficients. Information from BCS respondents at ages 34 and 42. For additional controls see the notes to Figure 1.1. Bold: $p < .10$ (2-tailed).

Figure 1.3. How adult life-satisfaction is affected by family background (British Cohort Study)
Source: Online Full Table for Figure 1.3.
Notes: Robust standard errors in parentheses. Standardized coefficients. Information from BCS respondents at ages 34 and 42. For additional controls see the notes to Figure 1.1. Bold: $p < .10$ (2-tailed).

Figure 1.4. How adult outcomes are affected by child outcomes at 16 (British Cohort Study)

Source: Online Full Table for Figure 1.4.

Notes: Intellectual development is measured here at age 16. Robust standard errors in parentheses. Standardized coefficients. Information from BCS respondents at ages 34 and 42. For additional controls see the notes to Figure 1.1. Bold: p < .10 (2-tailed).

Figure 1.5 (a). How the child's outcomes at 16 are affected by family background (Britain, ALSPAC)

Source: Online Full Table for Figure 1.5 (a).

Notes: Robust standard errors in parentheses. Controls for mother's age at birth, parents' marital status at birth, gender, ethnicity, firstborn child, number of siblings, low birth weight, premature baby, and primary school and secondary school fixed effects. Bold: p < .10 (2-tailed).

Figure 1.5 (b). How child outcomes at 16 are affected by family and schooling (Britain, ALSPAC)

Source: Online Full Table for Figure 1.5 (b).

Note: Bold: p < .10 (2-tailed).

Table 2.1. How life-satisfaction (0–10) is affected by adult outcomes (British Cohort Study)

Source: Online Full Table 2.1.

Notes: People aged 34 and 42. Robust standard errors are in parentheses. Controls for child intellectual, behavioral, and emotional health outcomes at age 16; parents' education; family income; parental involvement; mother's mental health; family break-up; mother's work; father's unemployment; number of siblings; postmarital conception; gender; ethnicity; low birth weight; and an age dummy (42). Bold: p < .10 (2-tailed).

Table 2.2. How life-satisfaction (0–10) is affected by log income (household panel data)

Source: Online Full Table 2.2.

Notes: People aged 25+. Robust standard errors are in parentheses. The regression controls for years of education, employment status, partnered, having children, physical and emotional health, comparison income, comparison education, comparison unemployment, comparison partnership, age, age-squared, gender, year, and region fixed effects. Bold: p < .10 (2-tailed).

Table 2.3. How life-satisfaction (0–10) is affected by own income and comparator income (household panel data) (pooled cross-section)
Source: Online Full Table 2.3.
Notes: People aged 25+. Robust standard errors in parentheses. Controls for years of education, employment status, partnered, having children, emotional and physical health, comparison education, comparison unemployment, comparison partnership, age, age-squared, gender, year, and region. Bold: p < .10 (2-tailed).

Table 2.4. How life-satisfaction (0–10) is affected by own income, comparator income, and own previous income (household panel data) (fixed effects)
Source: Online Full Table 2.4.
Notes: People aged 25+. Robust standard errors in parentheses. For additional controls see notes for Table 2.3. Bold: p < .10 (2-tailed).

Table 2.5. How log income is affected by childhood outcomes and family background (British Cohort Study)
Notes: People aged 34 and 42. Robust standard errors in parentheses. Bold: p < .10 (2-tailed).

Figure 3.1. Highest educational attainment of the adult population in advanced countries (%)
Source: Barro and Lee (2012).
Notes: Advanced countries = Australia, Belgium, Canada, Denmark, Finland, France, Iceland, Ireland, Italy, Japan, Luxembourg, Netherlands, New Zealand, Norway, Portugal, Switzerland, Turkey, the United States, and the United Kingdom.

Table 3.1. How life-satisfaction (0–10) is affected by qualifications (British Cohort Study)
Source: Online Full Table 3.1.
Notes: People aged 34 and 42. Robust standard errors in parentheses. Row (2) controls for income; employment status; criminality; marital status; physical health; mental health; child cognitive, behavioral, and emotional health outcomes at age 16; parents' education; family income; parental involvement; mother's mental health; family break-up; mother's work; father's unemployment; number of siblings; postmarital conception; gender; ethnicity; low birth weight; and an age dummy. Bold: p < .10 (2-tailed).

Table 3.2. How life-satisfaction (0–10) is affected by qualifications (British Cohort Study)
Notes: See online Annex 3b for a full description of the "decomposition analysis." For additional controls see online Full Table 3.1.

Table 3.3. How life-satisfaction (0–10) is affected by years of education (household panel data) (pooled cross-section)
Source: Online Full Table 3.3.
Notes: People aged 25–64. Robust standard errors in parentheses. Controls for income, employment status, marital status, having children, physical and emotional health, comparison income, comparison education, comparison unemployment, comparison partnership, age, age-squared, and gender. Bold: $p < .10$ (2-tailed).

Table 3.4. How life-satisfaction (0–10) is affected by years of education (household panel data) (pooled cross-section)
Source: Online Full Table 3.4.
Notes: People aged 25–64. Robust standard errors in parentheses. For additional controls see notes for Table 3.3. Bold: $p < .10$ (2-tailed).

Table 3.5. How highest qualification (standardized) is affected by childhood outcomes and family background (British Cohort Study)
Source: Online Table A3.1.
Notes: People aged 34 and 42. Robust standard errors in parentheses. Highest qualification is measured at age 42. Bold: $p < .10$ (2-tailed).

Table 4.1. How life-satisfaction (0–10) is affected by labor-force status (British Cohort Study)
Source: Online Full Table for Figure 4.1.
Notes: People aged 25–64. Robust standard errors in parentheses. Controls for income; qualifications; noncriminality; partnered; physical health; mental health; child cognitive, behavioral, and emotional health outcomes at age 16; parents' education; family income; parental involvement; mother's mental health; family break-up; mother's work; father's unemployment; number of siblings; postmarital conception; gender; ethnicity; low birth weight; and an age dummy (42). Bold: $p < .10$ (2-tailed).

Table 4.2. How life-satisfaction (0–10) is affected by labor-force status—compared with full-time workers (household panel data)
Source: Online Full Table 4.2.

Notes: People aged 25–64. Robust standard errors in parentheses. Controls for income, years of education, marital status, having children, physical and emotional health, comparison income, comparison education, comparison unemployment, comparison partnership, age, age-squared, gender, year, and region dummies. Bold: p < .10 (2-tailed).

Figure 4.1. Adaptation to unemployment (household panel data) (men)
Source: Online Full Table for Figure 4.1.
Notes: Men aged 25–64. Controls for income, marital status, having children, age, age-squared, year, and region dummies. Vertical bands represent 1.65 times the standard error of each point estimate.

Table 4.3. How life-satisfaction (0–10) is affected by current and previous unemployment (household panel data) (pooled cross-section)
Source: Online Full Table 4.3.
Notes: People aged 25–64. Robust standard errors in parentheses. Controls for income, years of education, marital status, having children, age, age-squared, gender, year, and region dummies. Bold: p < .10 (2-tailed).

Table 4.4. How life-satisfaction (0–10) is affected by your own unemployment and by the regional unemployment rate (household panel data) (pooled cross-section)
Source: Online Full Table 4.4.
Notes: People aged 25–64. Robust standard errors in parentheses. See notes for Table 4.2 for additional controls. Bold: p < .10 (2-tailed).

Table 4.5. How an individual's percentage of time unemployed up to age 30 is affected by childhood factors (British Cohort Study)
Notes: People aged 34 and 42. Robust standard errors in parentheses. Bold: p < .10 (2-tailed).

Table 4.6. Happiness in different activities (sample of Texan women)
Source: Kahneman, Krueger, et al. (2004).
Notes: More than one type of activity is possible at any one time.

Table 4.7. Happiness while interacting with different people (sample of Texan women)
Source: Kahneman, Krueger, et al. (2004).
Notes: More than one type of activity is possible at any one time.

Figure 4.2. How life-satisfaction (0–10) is affected by weekly hours of work—compared with 0–10 hours (household panel data) (pooled cross-section)

Source: Online Full Table for Figure 4.2.

Notes: People aged 25–64. Sample restricted to paid workers. For additional controls see notes for Table 4.2.

Table 4.8. How life-satisfaction (0–10) is affected by various dimensions of workplace quality (European Social Survey)

Source: Online Full Table 4.8. Notes: People aged 25–64. Robust standard errors in parentheses. Controls for gender, age, age-squared, years of education, immigrant status, marital status, and number of children. All right-hand side variables are $(1, 0)$ dummies. Bold: $p < .10$ (2-tailed).

Table 5.1. How life-satisfaction (0–10) is affected by family status (British Cohort Study)

Source: Online Full Table 5.1.

Notes: People aged 34 and 42. Robust standard errors in parentheses. Controls for income; qualifications; noncriminality; employment status; physical health; mental health; child cognitive, behavioral, and emotional health outcomes at age 16; parents' education; family income; parental involvement; mother's mental health; family break-up; mother's work; father's unemployment; number of siblings; postmarital conception; gender; ethnicity; low birth weight; and an age dummy (42). Bold: $p < .10$ (2-tailed).

Table 5.2. How life-satisfaction (0–10) is affected by family status—compared with single (household panel data)

Source: Online Full Table 5.2.

Notes: People aged 25+. Robust standard errors in parentheses. Controls for income, years of education, employment status, having children, physical and emotional health, comparison income, comparison education, comparison unemployment, comparison partnership, age, age-squared, gender, year, and region dummies. Bold: $p < .10$ (2-tailed).

Figure 5.2. Adaptation to partnership (household panel data)

Figure 5.3. Adaptation to separation (household panel data)

Figure 5.4. Adaptation to widowhood (household panel data)

Source to Figures 5.2–5.4: Online Full Tables for Figures 5.2–5.4.

Notes: People aged 25+. All effects are measured relative to the same individual five or more years before entering the new state, holding all else constant. Controls for income, employment status, having children, age, age-squared, year, and region dummies. Vertical bands represent 1.65 times the standard error of each point estimate.

Figure 5.6. Adaptation to parenthood (household panel data)
Source: Online Full Table for Figure 5.6.
Notes: People aged 25+. Controls for income, employment status, marital status, age, age-squared, year, and region dummies. Vertical bands represent 1.65 times the standard error of each point estimate.

Table 5.3. How family status and parenthood are determined (British Cohort Study)
Notes: People aged 34 and 42. Robust standard errors in parentheses. Bold: $p < .10$ (2-tailed).

Table 6.1. How would the percentage in misery fall if each problem could be eliminated on its own?
Source: Online Full Table 6.1.
Notes: People aged 25+, except people aged 34 and 42 for the BCS. The first column consists of regression coefficients.

Table 6.2. How misery is affected by adult outcomes (cross-section) (β-coefficients)
Source: Online Full Table 6.2.
Notes: Robust standard errors are in parentheses. Controls for years of education, marital status, having children, female, age, age-squared, region, and year dummies. In Australia and Britain (BHPS), controls also include comparison income, education, unemployment, and partnership. In Britain (BCS) controls also include noncriminality, child outcomes at 16, and family background. Cross-section regressions using information from BCS respondents at ages 34 and 42, and BHPS, HILDA, and BRFSS respondents at age 25+. Bold: $p < .10$ (2-tailed).
* Lagged by one year.

Table 6.3. How life-satisfaction is affected by adult outcomes (cross-section) (β-coefficients)
Source: Online Full Table 6.3.
Notes: Robust standard errors are in parentheses. Controls for years of education, marital status, having children, female, age, age-squared, region, and year dummies. In Australia and Britain (BHPS), controls

also include comparison income, education, unemployment, and partnership. In Britain (BCS) controls also include noncriminality, child outcomes at 16, and family background. Cross-section regressions using information from BCS respondents at ages 34 and 42, and BHPS, HILDA, and BRFSS respondents at age 25+. Bold: p < .10 (2-tailed).

* Lagged by one year.

Figure 6.1. How life-satisfaction (0–1) is affected by the EQ5D, compared with weights used in QALYs.

Source: Life-satisfaction comes from Dolan and Metcalfe (2012). QALY weights come from Dolan (1997). The QALY weights have been adjusted to have the same mean value as the weights in the life-satisfaction regression. For further discussion, see annex 5.2 of Layard and D. M. Clark (2014).

Notes: The reference case in each domain is no problems at all.

Figure 6.2. Rates of morbidity in each age group

Source: World Health Organisation (WHO) (2008). Western European countries, including UK.

Notes: The units on the vertical axis measure ill health by the average % reduction in the quality of life, spread over the whole population in each age group.

Figure 6.3. Ill health: by age (Britain, BHPS)

Notes: Emotional health is measured using the General Health Questionnaire (left-hand scale); physical health problems are measured using the number of physical health problems (right-hand scale).

Table 6.4. How life-satisfaction (0–10) is affected by emotional and physical health of self and others (household panel data) (pooled cross-section)

Source: Online Full Table 6.4.

Notes: Controls for income, years of education, employment status, marital status, female, age, age-squared, year, and region dummies. Cross-section regressions using information from BHPS, SOEP, and HILDA respondents at age 25+. Bold: p < .10 (2-tailed).

* Lagged by one year.

Figure 6.4. Adaptation to disability

Notes: Controls for age, age-squared, income, qualifications, partnered, children, region, and wave dummies. UK: disabled=1 if respondents report being disabled in answer to the LFS question. Germany:

disabled=1 if registered as legally disabled. Australia: disabled=1 if has health condition that limits ability to work.

Table 6.5. How physical and mental health are affected by childhood outcomes and family (British Cohort Study) (β-coefficients)
Notes: BCS cross-section regressions at age 42 for number of physical health conditions and has seen a doctor for emotional problems in last year; and at age 34 for emotional health symptoms. $R^2 = .0.010$; 0.074; 0.022.

Table 7.1. How the probability of conviction is predicted by childhood problems
Source: Online Annex 7.1.
Notes: Robust standard errors in parentheses. Marginal changes in probability. Probit estimates. Controls for ethnicity, mother's age and education, and whether the father is still present in the household. Bold: $p < .10$ (2-tailed).

Table 7.2. How the number of convictions by age 30 is affected by qualifications, childhood outcomes at 10, and family background (British Cohort Study)
Source: Online Full Table 7.3.
Notes: Robust standard errors in parentheses. OLS estimates. For additional controls see notes for Table 7.1. Bold: $p < .10$ (2-tailed). SD of convictions is 1.0.

Table 7.3. How the probability of educational failure is predicted by childhood problems at age 10
Source: Online Full Table 7.4.
Notes: Robust standard errors in parentheses. Marginal changes in probability. Probit estimates. For additional controls see notes for Table 7.1. Bold: $p < .10$ (2-tailed).

Figure 8.1. How national life-satisfaction is predicted by different national variables
Source: Gallup World Poll.
Notes: Average data for 2009–15 except for trust (mostly 2009). See Helliwell, Huang, and Wang (2016), appendix table 10, column (8), and table 5. $N = 126$, $R^2 = 0.76$.

Table 8.1. How national life-satisfaction (0–10) is predicted by different national variables
Note: See notes for Figure 8.1.

Figure 8.2. Subjective well-being by level of economic development and historical heritage of given societies, ca. 1990
Source: Inglehart and Klingemann (2000).

Figure 9.1. Average life-satisfaction (0–10): by age (ELSA)
Note: Mean life-satisfaction ratings from wave 6 of ELSA (2012) by age and sex.

Figure 9.2. What affects life-satisfaction over age 50? (ELSA) (cross-section) (β-coefficients)
Notes: These charts show the standardized β-coefficient for each variable contributing to the four sets of factors potentially contributing to life-satisfaction. All estimates are mutually adjusted, i.e., all variables are included in a single model. The variables age, sex, ethnicity, education, income, and employment status were also included in the model.
The proportion of variance explained by the model (adjusted R^2) was 33%.
N = 5,413.
Abbreviations: ADL, activity of daily living.

Table 9.1. What affects life-satisfaction (0–10) aged over 50 (ELSA) (cross-section) (unstandardized coefficients)
Notes: These charts show the unstandardized coefficients for each variable. All estimates are mutually adjusted, i.e., all variables are included in a single model. Abbreviations: CHD, coronary heart disease; ADL, activity of daily living; CES-D, Centre for Epidemiologic Studies Depression Scale.

Table 9.2. What affects life-satisfaction (0–10) over 50: by age range (ELSA) (unstandardized coefficients)
Abbreviations: CHD, coronary heart disease; ADL, activity of daily living; CES-D, Centre for Epidemiologic Studies Depression Scale.

Table 9.3. What affects life-satisfaction (0–10) over 50: by gender (ELSA) (unstandardized coefficients)
Coefficients in bold indicate significant associations at the 10% level.

Table 9.4. Changes in characteristics of elderly people over an eight-year interval (ELSA)
Abbreviations: CHD, coronary heart disease; ADL, activity of daily living; CES-D, Centre for Epidemiologic Studies Depression Scale.

Figure 9.3. What affects changes in life-satisfaction over an eight-year interval (ELSA) (β-coefficients)

Notes: These charts show the standardized β-coefficient for each variable contributing to the four sets of factors potentially contributing to life-satisfaction. The standard deviations used for standardization were those measured in 2012, similar to the level analysis. All estimates come from an overall model mutually adjusted, meaning all variables are included in the same model. The variables age, sex, ethnicity, education, changes in income, and employment status were also included in the model.

The proportion of variance explained by the model (adjusted R^2) was 12%.

Abbreviation: ADL, activity of daily living.

N = 3,230.

Table 9.5. What affects changes in life-satisfaction (0–10) over an eight-year interval (ELSA)

Note: These are unstandardized β-coefficients for each variable contributing to the four sets of factors potentially contributing to life-satisfaction. All estimates come from a mutually adjusted overall model.

Table 10.1. How children's emotional well-being is affected by log family income (ALSPAC)

Source: Online Full Table 10.1.

Notes: Robust standard errors in parentheses. Controls for father's unemployment, proportion of time mother worked in 1st year, proportion of time mother worked thereafter (up to age shown), parenting involvement, parenting strictness, family conflict, parental separation, mother's mental health, father's mental health, parents' education, mother's age at birth, parental marital status at birth, child's gender, ethnicity, birth order, number of siblings, birth weight, born prematurely, age in months at testing, and primary and secondary school fixed effects. Emotional well-being: Standardized self- and mother-reported SMFQ at ages 16 and 11; standardized mother-reported internalizing SDQ at age 5. Income: income-per-adult equivalent (£ in constant prices) measured at ages 3, 4, 7, 8, and 11. The log income figure is the log of average income up to the relevant age. Bold: p < .10 (2-tailed).

Table 10.2. How children's behavior is affected by family income (ALSPAC)

Source: Online Full Table 10.2.

Notes: Robust standard errors in parentheses. For additional controls see notes for Table 10.1. Behavior: Standardized mother-reported externalizing SDQ at ages 16, 11, and 5. Income: income-per-adult equivalent (£ in constant prices) measured at ages 3, 4, 7, 8, and 11. The log is the log of average income up to the relevant age. Bold: $p < .10$ (2-tailed).

Table 10.3. How children's intellectual performance is affected by family income (ALSPAC)

Source: Online Full Table 10.3.

Notes: Robust standard errors in parentheses. For additional controls see notes for Table 10.1. Intellectual: standardized GCSE points at age 16; standardized Key Stage 2 points at age 11; and standardized local school entry assessment at age 5. Income: income-per-adult equivalent (£ in constant prices) measured at ages 3, 4, 7, 8, and 11. The log is the log of average income up to the relevant age. Bold: $p < .10$ (2-tailed).

Figure 11.1. Percentage of mothers in work: by age of child

Source: Labour Force Survey, 2015.

Table 11.1. How children's emotional well-being is affected by mother's work (ALSPAC)

Source: Online Full Table 11.1.

Notes: Robust standard errors in parentheses. Controls for family income, father's unemployment, parenting involvement, parenting strictness, family conflict, parental separation, mother's mental health, father's mental health, parents' education, mother's age at birth, parental marital status at birth, child's gender, ethnicity, birth order, number of siblings, birth weight, born prematurely, age in months at testing, and primary and secondary school fixed effects. Emotional well-being: standardized self- and mother-reported SMFQ at ages 16 and 11; standardized mother-reported internalizing SDQ at age 5. Bold: $p < .10$ (2-tailed).

Table 11.2. How children's behavior is affected by mother's work (ALSPAC)

Source: Online Full Table 11.2.

Notes: Robust standard errors in parentheses. For additional controls see notes for Table 11.1. Behavior: standardized mother-reported externalizing SDQ at ages 16, 11, and 5. Bold: p < .10 (2-tailed).

Table 11.3. How children's intellectual performance is affected by mother's work (ALSPAC)

Source: Online Full Table 11.3.

Notes: Robust standard errors in parentheses. For additional controls see notes for Table 11.1. Intellectual: standardized GCSE points at age 16; standardized Key Stage 2 points at age 11; and standardized local school entry assessment at age 5. Bold: p < .10 (2-tailed).

Table 11.4. How children's outcomes are affected by father's unemployment (0–1) (ALSPAC)

Source: Online Full Table 11.4.

Notes: Robust standard errors in parentheses. For additional controls see notes for Table 11.1. Emotional well-being: standardized self- and mother-reported SMFQ at ages 16 and 11; and standardized mother-reported internalizing SDQ at age 5. Behavior: standardized mother-reported externalizing SDQ at ages 16, 11, and 5. Intellectual: standardized GCSE points at age 16; standardized Key Stage 2 points at age 11; and standardized local school entry assessment at age 5. Bold: p < .10 (2-tailed).

Table 12.1. How parents affect the emotional well-being of their children (ALSPAC) (β-coefficients)

Source: Online Full Table 12.1.

Notes: Robust standard errors in parentheses. Controls for family income, proportion of time mother worked in 1st year, proportion of time mother worked thereafter (up to age shown), father's unemployment, family conflict, parental separation, parents' education, mother's age at birth, parental marital status at birth, child's gender, ethnicity, birth order, number of siblings, birth weight, born prematurely, age in months at testing, and primary and secondary school fixed effects. Emotional well-being: standardized self- and mother-reported SMFQ at ages 16 and 11; standardized mother-reported internalizing SDQ at age 5. Bold: p < .10 (2-tailed).

Table 12.2. How parents affect the behavior of their children (ALSPAC) (β-coefficients)

Source: Online Full Table 12.2.

Notes: Robust standard errors in parentheses. For additional controls see notes for Table 12.1. Behavior: standardized mother-reported SDQ externalizing at ages 16, 11, and 5. Bold: p < .10 (2-tailed).

Table 12.3. How parents affect the intellectual development of their children (ALSPAC) (β-coefficients)
Source: Online Full Table 12.3.
Notes: Robust standard errors in parentheses. For additional controls see notes for Table 12.1. Intellectual: standardized GCSE points at age 16; standardized Key Stage 2 points at age 11; and standardized local school entry assessments at age 5. Bold: p < .10 (2-tailed).

Table 13.1. How family conflict affects children's outcomes at 16 (standardized) (ALSPAC)
Source: Online Full Table 13.1.
Notes: Robust standard errors in parentheses. Controls for family income, proportion of time mother worked in 1st year, proportion of time mother worked thereafter (up to age shown), father's unemployment, parental involvement, parental strictness, parents' education, mother's age at birth, parental marital status at birth, child's gender, ethnicity, birth order, number of siblings, birth weight, born prematurely, age in months at testing, and primary and secondary school fixed effects. Emotional well-being: standardized self- and mother-reported SMFQ at 16. Behavior: standardized mother-reported externalizing SDQ at 16. Intellectual: standardized GCSE points at age 16.

Table 13.2. How family conflict affects children's emotional well-being (ALSPAC)
Source: Online Full Table 13.2.
Notes: Robust standard errors in parentheses. Controls for family income, proportion of time mother worked in 1st year, proportion of time mother worked thereafter (up to age shown), father's unemployment, parental involvement, parental strictness, parents' education, mother's age at birth, parental marital status at birth, child's gender, ethnicity, birth order, number of siblings, birth weight, born prematurely, age in months at testing, and primary and secondary school fixed effects. Emotional well-being: standardized self- and mother-reported SMFQ at ages 16 and 11; standardized mother-reported internalizing SDQ at age 5. Bold: p < .10 (2-tailed).

Table 13.3. How family conflict affects children's behavior (ALSPAC)

Source: Online Full Table 13.3.

Notes: Robust standard errors in parentheses. For additional controls see notes for Table 13.1. Behavior: standardized mother-reported externalizing SDQ at ages 16, 11, and 5. Bold: p < .10 (2-tailed).

Table 13.4. How family conflict affects children's intellectual development (ALSPAC)

Source: Online Full Table 13.4.

Notes: Robust standard errors in parentheses. For additional controls see notes for Table 13.1. Intellectual: standardized GCSE points at age 16; standardized Key Stage 2 points at age 11; and standardized local school entry assessments at age 5. Bold: p < .10 (2-tailed).

Table 13.5. The interacted effect of family conflict and parental separation on children's outcomes (standardized) (ALSPAC)

Source: Online Full Table 13.5.

Notes: Robust standard errors in parentheses. For additional controls see notes for Table 13.1. Emotional well-being: standardized self- and mother-reported SMFQ at ages 16 and 11; standardized mother-reported internalizing SDQ at age 5. Behavior: standardized mother-reported externalizing at ages 16, 11, and 5. Intellectual: standardized GCSE points at age 16; standardized Key Stage 2 points SDQ at age 11; and standardized local school entry assessments at age 5. Bold: p < .10 (2-tailed).

Table 14.1. How children's outcomes at 16 are affected by secondary school attended (ALSPAC) (β-coefficients)

Source: Online Full Table 14.1.

Notes: Robust standard errors in parentheses. Controls for family income, proportion of time mother worked in the 1st year, proportion of time mother worked thereafter, father's unemployment, mother's mental health, father's mental health, involvement, aggression, family conflict, parental separation, parents' education, mother's age at birth, parents' marital status at birth, female child, ethnicity, first-born child, number of siblings, low birth weight, premature baby, Special Educational Needs (SEN) statement, free school meal eligibility, English not first language, and the lagged dependent variable (at 11). Bold: p < .10 (2-tailed).

Table 14.2. How children's outcomes at 16 are affected by secondary school characteristics (ALSPAC) (β-coefficients)
Source: Online Full Table 14.2.
Notes: Robust standard errors in parentheses. Controls for child's Special Educational Needs (SEN) statement, free school meal eligibility, whether English is not the first language, and lagged dependent variables (at 11). For additional controls see notes for Table 14.1. Bold: p < .10 (2-tailed).

Table 14.3. How children's outcomes at 8 and 11 are affected by primary school attended (ALSPAC) (β-coefficients)
Source: Online Full Table 14.3.
Notes: Robust standard errors in parentheses. Lagged dependent variables for the age 11 (8) are measured at age 8 (7). For additional controls, see notes for Table 14.1. Bold: p < .10 (2-tailed).

Table 14.4. How children's outcomes at 8 and 11 are affected by measured primary school characteristics (ALSPAC) (β-coefficients)
Source: Online Full Table 14.4.
Notes: Robust standard errors in parentheses. Controls for family background, child's Special Educational Needs (SEN) statement, free school meal eligibility, whether English is not the first language, lagged dependent variables, and primary school teacher dummies. Lagged dependent variables for the age 11 (8) are measured at age 8 (5). For a complete list of controls see notes for Table 14.1. Bold: p < .10 (2-tailed).

Table 14.5. How children's outcomes at 8 and 11 are affected by their teacher (ALSPAC) (β-coefficients)
Source: Flèche (2017).
Notes: Teacher value-added are estimated in regressions that include controls for school characteristics, pupil characteristics, family background, school-cohort effects, grade dummies, and lagged pupil dependent variables. All three outcomes are measured at ages 8 and 11.

Table 16.1. What explains the variation of life-satisfaction and of misery among adults (BHPS) (cross-section) (β-coefficients)
Source: Online Full Table 16.1.
Note: Based on BHPS, with the following exceptions: Crime from BCS (see notes for Figure 1.1); for depression/anxiety we use the average of the US and the Australian figures in Tables 6.2 and 6.3. Controls for comparison income, education, unemployment, partnership,

age, age-squared, women, having children, year, and region dummies. Bold: p < .10 (2-tailed). Misery is defined as the bottom 9.9% in the BHPS.

Table 16.2. How adult life-satisfaction (0–10) is affected by current circumstances (BHPS) (cross-section)

Source: Online Full Table 16.2 shows the basic regression.

Notes: Based on BHPS. However, for the coefficients on education and unemployment we focus on people aged 25–64; see Chapters 3 and 4. For quality of work (from ESS) see Chapter 4. For crime see Chapter 7. For depression and anxiety we use the average coefficients for the United States and Australia, which can be obtained from Table 6.3 and online Descriptive Statistics. Bold: p < .10 (2-tailed). — means "not studied."

Table 16.3. How adult life-satisfaction (0–10) and behavior are predicted by child outcomes at 16 (British Cohort Study) (cross-section)

Source: Online Full Table 16.3.

Notes: Based on BCS. Controls for family background, gender, and age dummy. Bold: p < .10 (2-tailed). Crimes are assumed to be arrests × 3.6.

Table 16.4. How children's outcomes at age 16 are affected by family and schooling (ALSPAC) (cross-section) (standardized coefficients)

Source: Online Full Table 16.4.

Note: Controls for mother's age at birth, parental marital status at birth, child's gender, ethnicity, birth order, number of siblings, birth weight, born prematurely, and age in months at testing Bold: p < .10 (2-tailed). — means not significant at p < .10 (2-tailed).

SD (family income) = 0.57; SD (parents' education) = 0.41; SD (father unemployed) = 0.14; SD (mother work—1 year) = 0.37; SD (mother work—other years) = 0.37.

Table 16.5. How average life-evaluation in a country is affected by country-level variables (Gallup World Poll) (cross-section)

Source: See sources and notes for Figure 8.1 and Table 8.1.

NOTES

Introduction: The New Paradigm

1. Bentham ([1789] 1996); Layard (2011).

2. Jefferson (1809).

3. Layard, Mayraz, and Nickell (2010), Easterlin (2016).

4. O'Donnell et al. (2014).

5. See the publications of the National Institute for Health and Care Excellence (NICE).

6. This is called a visual analogue scale.

7. OECD (2013a).

8. It is also not clear whether the experience of dreaming should be included or not. On average dreaming takes up over 10% of all time spent on mental activity (NIH National Institute of Neurological Disorders and Stroke, "Brain Basics: Understanding Sleep"). https://www.ninds.nih.gov/Disorders/Patient-Caregiver-Education/Understanding-Sleep.

9. Kahneman (2011).

10. Ward (2015). The partial correlation coefficients are sometimes called the standardized regression coefficients. They are the βs in a regression where all variables are divided by their standard deviation. The overall explanatory power of the equation is given by $R^2 = \Sigma_i \beta_i^2 + \Sigma_i \Sigma_j \beta_i \beta_j r_{ij}$ $(i \neq j)$.

11. Replies to questions on subjective well-being are also quite well correlated with measurements of brain activity (Davidson [1992]).

12. Steptoe and Wardle (2012). Contrary findings are in Liu et al. (2015), but this study is flawed (see Diener, Pressman, and Lyubormirsky [2015]). On the effects of life-satisfaction, see De Neve, Diener, Tay, and Xuereb (2013). On validity, see also OECD (2013a).

13. We use the Short Mood and Feelings Questionnaires (SMFQ).

14. For the history of these studies, see Pearson (2016).

15. British Household Panel Survey (BHPS); German Socio-Economic Panel (SOEP); Household, Income and Labour Dynamics in Australia (HILDA).

16. The Behavioral Risk Factor Surveillance System (BRFSS), Gallup World Poll (GWP), Eurobarometer, and European Social Survey (ESS). These are repeated surveys but use different samples each time. We also use the English Longitudinal Study of Ageing (ELSA). The Panel Study of Income Dynamics (PSID) also now includes measures of well-being, but we do not use it because the series is short. For the United States we use the BRFSS in preference to the PSID because it has good data on mental health. We also use the US National Longitudinal Survey of Youth.

17. For contents, see Contents of Online Materials in this book. The online materials are available at http://cep.lse.ac.uk/origins/online material.pdf.

18. OECD (2016). For France, see https://www.legifrance.gouv.fr/af fichTexte.do?cidTexte=JORFTEXT000030478182&dateTexte=20150809, and for Italy http://www.senato.it/leg/17/BGT/Schede/FascicoloSchede DDL/ebook/46876.pdf.

19. On launching the National Dialogue on Wellbeing, April 2015.

Chapter 1. Happiness over the Life Course: What Matters Most?

1. The Avon Longitudinal Study of Parents and Children (ALSPAC). For Survey Details, see online materials.

2. In the Gallup World Poll 78% of the variance of life-evaluation across the human adult population is within countries, and 22% between countries (Helliwell, Layard, and Sachs [2012], chapter 2).

3. For each individual there are two observations, at 34 and 42. These are the only ages we include as they are the only ages where health was measured by the number of health conditions. Apart from that the equations for ages 30 and 26 are very similar to those for ages 34 and 42—see Flèche, Lekfuangfu, and Clark (2017).

4. The standard deviation of X in a population is $\sqrt{\dfrac{\Sigma(X_i - \bar{X})}{N}}$ where N is the size of the population.

5. These standardized variables thus all have a standard deviation of 1.

6. The share of the variance of the dependent variable that is explained by the independent variables is

$$R^2 = \sum_i \beta_i^2 + \sum_i \sum_j \beta_i \beta_j r_{ij} \ (i \neq j)$$

where rij is the correlation coefficient.

7. The corresponding α-coefficients can be calculated from the β-coefficients using the standard deviations provided in online Descriptive Statistics.

8. In a 2-tailed test. This is of course equivalent to a 95% probability using a 1-tailed test. Each regression uses data on all subjects who give data on the dependent variable. Where data are missing for a right-hand variable, we use instead the average value of all replies to that variable. We also include a variable-specific dummy to reflect that the value is missing. (Multiple Imputation methods give very similar results.)

9. Apart from mental health, we do not in this book examine the effects of personality on happiness since these are largely captured in the effects of mental health. Nor do we examine the hugely important issue of the individual's philosophy of life, which cannot be easily studied using large surveys, but is well covered in positive psychology and in ancient wisdom.

10. We do not measure intellectual performance at 16 because the BCS offers only a binary variable—whether the individual obtained any O-level or equivalent grade A*–C at GCSE.

11. The "malaise" score.

12. Emotional health remains the best predictor if we measure child development over the whole course of childhood; see Layard, A. E. Clark, et al. (2014).

13. Measured separately as the mother's and father's highest educational qualification at the time of the pregnancy.

14. Our analysis relates to any work, full-time or part-time.

15. In other words we include a school dummy, and Figure 5 (b) therefore reports the influence of the whole set of school dummies. (This influence equals the standard deviation of the coefficients on the school dummies.) In Chapter 14 we look separately at the effect of primary schools on outcomes in primary schools and the effect of secondary schools, given the measured outcomes of the children when they leave primary school.

Chapter 2. Income

1. Basically a measure of real hourly wages times working hours *plus* income from wealth (Becker [1964]).

2. See Layard (2011), chapter 9.

3. http://www.cls.ioe.ac.uk/page.aspx?&sitesectionid=795&sitesectiontitle=Welcome+to+the+1970+British+Cohort+Study+(BCS70).

4. Life-satisfaction as a broad measure of subjective well-being has been subject to a number of validity tests, via its relations to physiological and neurological measures, and its predictive power regarding future observed behaviors. Some of this validation work is described in Clark, Frijters, and Shields (2008). The BCS life-satisfaction question is a little different from that found in some other general-purpose surveys, although we believe that this question behaves similarly to the more standard question.

5. See Chapter 1, n. 3.

6. See, for example, Layard, Nickell, and Mayraz (2008).

7. We calculate equivalized household income using the OECD equivalence scale. This scale gives the first adult a weight of one, any extra adults a weight of 0.7, and children a weight of 0.5. A household consisting of one single adult earning 50,000 a year would thus have an equivalent income of $50,000. The same income for a two-adult household produces an equivalent income of 29,400 (= 50,000/1.7), and for a two-adult two-child household an equivalent income of 18,500 (= 50,000/2.7).

8. The results are very similar if children are treated as a choice variable and income is therefore measured as income per adult.

9. In 2012 pounds sterling the mean is £18,089, and the standard deviation £14,728.

10. See online Annex 2.

11. $\alpha_1 \Delta$ log Income = 0.20 × 0.7.

12. 0.20 × 0.10. We have also examined whether this effect would be larger at the lowest level of income and found no evidence of non-linearity in the effect of log income (see Chapter 6 and Layard, Nickell, and Mayraz [2008]).

13. Now known as Understanding Society.

14. All report disposable household income.

15. Online Table A2.1 repeats the analysis for 30-to-45-year-olds (the ages of the BCS), and the fixed effects estimates remain small.

16. For other data using Eurobarometer, see online Figure A2.1. The Eurobarometer samples are much smaller than those in Figure 2.3. For Britain, we also have the large ONS survey, which shows a steady mild increase in life-satisfaction from 2011 to 2016.

17. Easterlin (1974).

18. For No, see Easterlin, Angelescu-McVey, Switek, et al. (2010), chapter 5; and Easterlin (2016). For Yes, see Sacks, Stevenson, and Wolfers (2012). For a summary of the debate, see Layard, A. E. Clark, and Senik (2012).

19. Easterlin, Wang, and Wang (2017).

20. For an attempt to marshal all the possible factors see Bartolini, Bilancini, and Sarracino (2016)—also discussed in Chapter 8. Another factor limiting the benefits of national income growth is boom and bust. As De Neve, Ward, De Keulenaer, et al. (forthcoming) show, the losses in happiness when income falls exceed the gain in happiness from an equal rise in income.

21. The key table on social comparisons is the pooled cross-sectional table shown in online Full Table 2.3. This table includes all comparisons simultaneously.

22. Card et al. (2012).

23. One issue is the relevant reference group. Two common choices are neighbors (broadly defined, as here) or coworkers (or those similar to the individual on the labor market). See Clark and Senik (2010), and Layard, Mayraz, and Nickell (2010). As regards neighbors, well-being has been found to fall with average incomes in the local area (Ferrer-i-Carbonell [2005]; Luttmer [2005]; Kingdon and Knight [2007]). As regards coworkers, a number of papers have shown that well-being is negatively correlated with others' earnings (G. Brown et al. [2008]; Cappelli and Sherer [1988]; Card et al. [2012]; and Godechot and Senik [2015]). See also evidence from neuroeconomics (Fließbach et al. [2007]) and hypothetical preference questions (Solnick and Hemenway [2005]).

However in some studies well-being has been found to rise with others' income. This could be for reasons related to local public goods, to the tunnel effect (whereby others' good fortune informs you about your own future prospects), or altruism: see, for example, Clark, Kristensen, and Westergård-Nielsen (2009), Dunn, Aknin, and Norton (2008), Senik (2004), and see also Clark and D'Ambrosio (2015).

24. For comparator effects we focus on the results using pooled cross-sections. The reason is that in a fixed-effects analysis, the effect of comparator incomes (as measured) depends heavily in our sample on information for people who move between regions—a quite small number of people.

25. This assumes that average comparator income is measured by absolute mean income rather than the mean of log income. To check on this we estimated an equation that included simultaneously $\log \bar{Y}$ and $\overline{\log Y}$. The effects of $\log \bar{Y}$ far exceeded that of $\overline{\log Y}$, which was in three out of four countries insignificant.

26. See online Table A2.2, second column for each country.

27. See also Clark and D'Ambrosio (2015). In many ways experimental data involve fewer problems than naturalistic data. In this case the work is not based on happiness regressions, but rather stated preferences over hypothetical scenarios involving income distributions that an imaginary grandchild will face (in Johannsson-Stenman, Carlsson, and Daruvala [2002]) or leaky-bucket experiments where individuals are asked to indicate the amount of "lost money" that they are willing to accept for a transfer of money from a richer to a poorer individual (see for example Amiel, Creedy, and Hurn [1999]). The conclusion from this work is that individuals do seem to have preferences over income inequality, and not only because their own income or their relative income is affected. However it does seem to be difficult to quantify exactly how much this income inequality matters.

28. See full results in online Table A2.3.

29. If we add highest qualification, the R^2 of the equation rises from 0.26 to 0.31; see online Table A2.3.

30. If $H = \alpha \log Y$ where H is happiness and Y income, $dH/dY = \alpha/Y$.

31. See also Layard (2006).

Chapter 3. Education

1. For earlier work on this issue, see online Annex 3a. On the issue of credentialism, note that measured IQ has risen sharply over time (Pietschnig and Voracek [2015]).

2. On the United States see Oreopoulos and Petronijevic (2013). On the UK, see Blundell, Green, and Jin (2016) and Walker and Zhu (2008).

3. It may also lead to more enjoyable jobs (which are therefore less well paid). The surveys provide no data on this.

4. No qualifications, Level 1 (CSE and O-level equivalent [grades (D–G)]), Level 2 (O-level equivalent [grades A*–C]), Level 3 (A-level equivalent), and degree or above.

5. We first run the following equation:

$$\text{Log } Y = \alpha + \Sigma_{j=1}^{5} \beta_j \text{Educ}_j + \text{etc.}$$

where Y is income and Educ_j are education dummies for each level of qualification. We then use the coefficients on each education dummy to create a simple continuous education variable.

6. This is the standard deviation of years of schooling in the BHPS.

7. See also Oreopoulos and Salvanes (2011).

8. $0.08 = (0.03 + 0.05 - 0.01 + 0.07)/4 + 0.06/2.5$. It could be turned into a rate of return as follows. The monetary equivalent of 0.07 points of life-satisfaction per year is a change in income of 0.07/0.2 or 33%. This is a good annual return on the sacrifice of one year's income in order to obtain the extra education—plus of course the cost of tuition.

9. See also Nikolaev (2016).

10. Suppose the individual's income rises by 10%. Taxes could increase by one-half of this, and the social value of an extra 5% of income is 0.01 (i.e., 0.05×0.2).

11. 1 SD of qualification reduces the number of convictions by age 30 by 0.064. Since the SD of years of education is 2.5, this means that one extra year of education reduces the number of convictions by 0.026. But Home Office data show that crimes/arrests = 3.6 and BCS data show that arrests/convictions = 1.5. So one extra year of education reduces crimes by 0.14. As Chapter 7 shows, each crime reduces population well-being by one point-year.

12. A lot is often claimed for the effects of educated parents on their children. But, as we show, parents' education mainly affects their children's academic performance; it appears to have little effect on the children's emotional health.

13. The ALSPAC cohort data are not yet able to provide evidence on the subjects' final highest qualification.

14. Only 2% of the sample were nonwhite.

15. See online Table A3.1.

16. See Barro and Lee (2015). On individuals, the so-called screening hypothesis argues that more educated people receive higher incomes because education is simply a signal of higher preceding ability; but there is much evidence against this view (see, for example, Layard and Psacharopoulos [1974] and the evidence at national level provided by Barro and Lee [2015] and others).

Chapter 4. Work and Unemployment

1. Say 1,600 hours a year in advanced countries out of 6,000 hours.

2. Kahneman, Krueger, et al. (2004), Krueger, Kahneman, Schkade, et al. (2009).

3. For two early demonstrations of this by economists see Clark and Oswald (1994) and Winkelmann and Winkelmann (1998). See also online Annex 4.

4. Thus to some extent the unemployment was "involuntary" since in a frictionless economy they would have chosen to return at

once. However the duration of unemployment is also influenced by the income replacement ratio for the unemployed and the conditions attached to the receipt of benefit. On these issues, see Layard, Nickell, and Jackman (2005) and Pissarides (2000).

5. On self-employment, see Blanchflower and Oswald (1998) and Colombier and Masclet (2008).

6. For 30-to-45-year-olds, see online Table A4.1.

7. The results in the existing literature broadly find no evidence of any such adaptation to unemployment. This holds for the analysis of data from the SOEP (Clark, Diener, Georgellis, and Lucas 2008), BHPS (Clark and Georgellis, 2013), Russian Longitudinal Monitoring Survey (RLMS) (Clark and Uglanova, 2012), the Korean Labor and Income Panel Study (KLIPS) for men (there are insufficient data points for women to reach a conclusion) in Rudolf and Kang (2015), and HILDA (Frijters, Johnston, and Shields [2011]). The research in Lucas et al. (2004) suggests only partial adaptation to unemployment in SOEP data, as does that on Swiss Household Panel (SHP) survey in Anusic, Yap, and Lucas (2014), although these latter two papers use parametric rather than nonparametric statistical methods. See also online Annex 4.

8. The regression is the same as that in Clark, Flèche, and Senik (2014).

9. We exclude everyone for whom we lack any of this knowledge.

10. The controls were marital status, children, income, age, age squared, and regional and time dummies.

11. Strictly the variable is the proportion of waves when this occurred. We also tried including this variable in panel regressions, but it did not vary sufficiently for each individual for the analysis to produce sensible results. (It is also of course somewhat arbitrary to take just five years of previous experience.)

12. See Clark, Georgellis, and Sanfey (2001); Ruhm (1991).

13. See online Full Table A2.2.

14. See Clark (2003); Clark, Knabe, and Rätzel (2010); Powdthavee (2007). It also of course expands the competition for jobs.

15. 0.138/0.70. This assumes that the labor-force participation rate of the population under 65 is 70%. Di Tella, MacCulloch, and Oswald (2003) also estimate that the employed bear three-fourths of the cost—see online Annex 4.

16. The overall unemployment rate is determined by many other factors that affect the level of the equation for individuals. See, for example, Layard, Nickell, and Jackman (2005).

17. The simple correlation is 0.12.

18. Kahneman, Krueger, et al. (2004).

19. Krueger (2007), Krueger, Kahneman, Fischler, et al. (2009). See also Krueger, Kahneman, Schkade, et al. (2009), tables 1.3, 1.6 and 1.9; and Bryson and MacKerron (2017).

20. Krueger, Kahneman, Schkade, et al. (2009), table 1.10.

21. Edmans (2011), Edmans (2012).

22. See for example Clark (2001), Clark (2010), OECD (2013b), Clark (2011), Lundberg and Cooper (2011), Robertson and Cooper (2011).

23. The effect of hours is swamped by the question on family life.

24. These actual effects are fairly consistent with what people in the BHPS say about what matters to them in a job—see Clark (2011).

Chapter 5. Building a Family

1. Office for National Statistics (2015).

2. Previous work on marriage suggested broadly complete adaptation in the SOEP (Clark, Diener, Georgellis, and Lucas 2008) and Lucas et al. [2003], BHPS (Clark and Georgellis [2013]), HILDA (Frijters, Johnston, and Shields [2011]) and Swiss Household Panel (Anusic, Yap, and Lucas [2014]). Adaptation is however only partial at best in Russia (Clark and Uglanova [2012]) and Korea (Rudolf and Kang [2015]). See also Qari (2014).

3. The small coefficients in Table 5.1 are an average of the big onset coefficient and subsequent adaptation.

4. There is a large literature on divorce, but this often happens some years after the worst period of separation. The existing literature finds full adaptation to divorce in the SOEP, BHPS, and HILDA, but only partial adaptation in the Swiss Household Panel (Anusic, Yap, and Lucas [2014]) and for Korean men (Rudolf and Kang [2015]).

5. See also online Annex 5.

6. See Clark, Diener, Georgellis, and Lucas (2008), Lucas et al. (2003).

7. See Frijters, Johnston, and Shields (2011).

8. See online Table A5.1. This shows that the happiness of those who are not partnered is lower by 0.27 points, when everyone else is partnered, compared to the situation when only 50% of other people are partnered.

9. People can also choose whether to partner. But not everyone who would like a partner gets one, while some 90% of people who want children get them.

10. We do of course know whether some people in the sample have had children who have left home, but we do not know this for those who joined the sample after their children had left.

11. For BCS see Online Table A5.1, and for the household panels, see Online Table A5.2.

12. See Myrskyla and Margolis (2014); Cetre, Clark, and Senik (2016); online Annex 5. The numbers in Figure 5.6 include controls.

Chapter 6. Health of Mind and Body

1. The anterior cingulate cortex and anterior insula; see Layard and Clark (2014), 274n37.

2. Layard and D. M. Clark (2014).

3. For a classic analysis of how external events can cause mental illness, see G. W. Brown and Harris (1978), and on the general causes of mental illness, see Layard and D. M. Clark (2014), chapter 7.

4. Life-satisfaction is an integer variable, so it is not possible to define the same percentage of the population as miserable in every country. In addition the number of categories of life-satisfaction is 11 in the BCS and HILDA, 7 in the BHPS, and 4 in the BRFSS. The percentages defined as in misery are shown in Table 6.1.

5. Behavioral Risk Factor Surveillance System.

6. They also ask whether you are currently in treatment (which of course understates prevalence). The questions used in all the surveys appear in Annex 6.

7. The distribution of conditions is as follows (%):

	0	1	2	3	4	5+
BCS	37	34	17	7	2	1
BHPS	38	30	17	8	4	3

8. For a simple description of the characteristics of the most miserable people, see online Table A6.1.

9. Logit analysis produces very similar results.

10. The relation between Tables 6.1 col. 3 and Table 6.2 for any discontinuous variable is as follows. In Table 6.1 we estimate an equation that implies $p_M = \Sigma \propto_i p_i + etc.$ where p_M is the proportion in misery and p_i is the proportion with characteristic i. Column 3 is $\propto_i p_i$. By contrast for each characteristic Table 6.2 shows $\propto_i \sqrt{\dfrac{p_i(1-p_i)}{p_M(1-p_M)}} \cdot$

11. In online Table A6.2 we show, for those surveys where the data permit, a fixed-effects analysis.

12. See online Table A6.2.

13. See online Descriptive Statistics.

14. In Australia, the results here confirm that mental health has the largest single impact. For Britain mental health has to be entered with a lag, and its effects are therefore understated.

15. Layard and D. M. Clark (2014).

16. See Dolan (1997).

17. In other words the average of the shaded bars has been made equal to the average of the black bars. For the life-satisfaction regression, see Dolan and Metcalfe (2012).

18. To get the full QALY impact of a condition we also of course have to add its impact on longevity, but that is not our concern in this book.

19. Layard and D. M. Clark (2014).

20. On the negative impact of partner's illness on the caregiver in Australia, see van den Berg, Fiebig, and Hall (2014).

21. In Britain this is in measured by "is disabled"; in Germany it is measured by "registered as disabled." For earlier work on the BHPS, see Oswald and Powdthavee (2008).

22. Dolan and Metcalfe (2012).

23. Plomin et al. (2013). On the issue of genes, see Chapter 12.

24. Danner, Snowdon, and Friesen (2001).

25. Steptoe, Deaton, and Stone (2015).

Chapter 7. Crime

1. For the full version of the paper on which this chapter is based, see online Annex 7.

2. The predictive power of the equation is not huge. In Figure 1.4 the equation for crime has an R^2 of 0.10.

3. This is a different dependent variable for that in Figure 1.4, where the dependent variable was the number of times arrested by the age of 34. The convictions variable is measured at age 30 so as to facilitate comparison with the US data.

4. The controls are more limited than those in the rest of the book to facilitate the UK/US comparison that follows.

5. At both ages one standard deviation extra of bad behavior raises the probability of arrest by nearly five percentage points—a 33% increase in risk. See online Annex 7.

6. For details of the study, including variable definitions, see online Annex 7.

7. See Lochner and Moretti (2004), Machin, Marie, and Vujic (2011), Bell, Costa, and Machin (2016). See also Anderson (2014).

8. The standard deviation of life-satisfaction is 1.9.

9. Dustmann and Fasani (2016). There have been many efforts to put money values on the effects of crime; for a survey, see Soares (2010).

10. From Dustmann and Fasani's (2016) table 3 column (1), $GHQ = .14 \, log \left(\frac{C}{PY} \right) + etc.$ where C is the number of crimes, P is the population, and Y is the number of years. Thus $\Delta GHQ = \frac{.14}{C/PY} \, \frac{1}{PY} \, \Delta C$. Using an average annual rate for C/PY of 0.09, this gives $PY.\Delta GHQ \simeq 1.5\Delta C$. To convert a change in GHQ (0–10) to one in life-satisfaction (LS) we note from Mukuria et al. (2016) that when GHQ is measured 0–10, $\frac{\partial LS}{\partial GHQ} = -0.21(3.6) = -0.75$. So $PY\Delta LS = -0.75 \, PY.\Delta GHQ \simeq -1.1\Delta C$. Note that since their table 3 uses panel data with a fixed effect, any effect of crime on house prices (which is spread over many years) is largely removed.

11. The SD of arrests is 3.8. Interestingly adding a quadratic term in arrests adds no explanatory power.

12. The ratio of 3.6/1 is for 2006/7 from Crime Survey for England and Wales and Arrests Collection, Home Office.

Chapter 8. Social Norms and Institutions

1. This chapter draws heavily on the great work done by John Helliwell, Haifang Huang, and Shun Wang in each World Happiness Report.

2. See Putnam (2000).

3. The question is "Please imagine a ladder/mountain with steps numbered from zero at the bottom to ten at the top. Suppose we say that the top of the ladder/mountain represents the best possible life for you and the bottom of the ladder/mountain represents the worst possible life for you. If the top step is 10 and the bottom step is 0, on which step of the ladder/mountain do you feel you personally stand at the present time?" The corresponding response categories range from 0 (Worst possible life) to 10 (Best possible life).

4. The ranges of values for these variables are: Trust 0.07–0.64; Generosity 0.16–0.54; Social support 0.29–0.99; and Freedom 0.26–0.98. See Helliwell, Huang, and Wang (2016), appendix table 5.

5. In each World Happiness Report you can see how each variable contributes to life-satisfaction in each individual country. Note that if we take the worldwide variance of the Cantril ladder across all

individuals, only 22% is across countries and 78% within countries (Helliwell, Layard, and Sachs [2012], 12).

6. World Values Survey.

7. Knack (2001).

8. Similar size effects are found in the World Values Survey and even larger ones in the European Social Survey—see table 2 of Helliwell, Huang, and Wang (2016). For the effect of unemployment, see our Chapter 3.

9. Summarized in Helliwell and Wang (2011).

10. Helliwell (2007).

11. Bartolini, Bilancini, and Sarracino (2016), Sarracino (2010).

12. See Helliwell, Layard, and Sachs (2016), 16.

13. See for example, T. Singer and Ricard (2016), Ricard (2015), S. L. Brown et al. (2003), and Thoits and Hewitt (2001).

14. Meier and Stutzer (2008).

15. Anik et al. (2010). See also Dunn, Aknin, and Norton (2008).

16. Harbaugh, Mayr, and Burghart (2007). See also Zaki and Mitchell (2011), who also show that inequitable behavior causes activity in brain regions associated with subjective disutility.

17. Davidson and Begley (2012), 220–23.

18. Kahneman, Krueger, et al. (2004), table 1; Krueger, Kahneman, Schkade, et al. (2009), chapter 2; and Bryson and MacKerron (2017).

19. For example, Putnam (2000) and Halpern (2004).

20. Nguyen and Benet-Martínez (2012), Knight and Gunatilaka (2010), Knight, Song, and Gunatilaka (2010), and Easterlin, Morgan, Switek, and Wang (2012). For a different view of Chinese migration, see Easterlin, Wang, and Wang (2017).

21. Stevenson and Wolfers (2008).

22. P. Singer (1981), Pinker (2011).

23. For an analysis of the importance of freedom, see Sen (1999).

24. Clearly freedom to speak your mind and to participate in political life spans this topic and the next.

25. Inglehart and Klingemann (2000).

26. Helliwell, Grover, and Wang (2014).

27. Helliwell, Grover, and Wang (2014), table 10, column (6).

28. Helliwell, Grover, and Wang (2014).

29. Layard, Mayraz, and Nickell (2010).

30. Wilkinson and Pickett (2009). They do not examine the relationship between equality and life-satisfaction.

31. Stevenson and Wolfers (2010), Blanchflower and Oswald (2004), Helliwell (2003), 351, and Clark and D'Ambrosio (2015). But for positive results see Morawetz (1977) and Schwarze and Härpfer (2007).

32. Alesina, Di Tella, and MacCulloch (2004).

33. See Diener, Tay, and Myers (2011). In this context Buddhists normally report themselves as religious, even if others question this use of words.

34. Diener, Tay, and Myers (2011).

35. Smith, McCullough, and Poll (2003).

36. Pargament (2002).

37. Ellison (1991).

38. Clark and Lelkes (2009).

39. Helliwell, Layard, and Sachs (2016), chapter 3.

40. Note that incomes here do not include the benefits from public services, which are better in richer countries.

41. On this issue, see Becchetti et al. (2013).

42. A modern example is Action for Happiness, www.actionforhap piness.org.

Chapter 9. Happiness at Older Ages

1. Definitions of older age vary across agencies and in different parts of the world. The ages of 60 and 65 are often used, but the World Health Organisation used age 50 to define an older person in the Minimum Data Set project. We do not adopt a strict definition in this chapter.

2. E.g., Stone et al. (2010).

3. Cheng, Powdthavee, and Oswald (2017).

4. Office for National Statistics. http://www.ons.gov.uk/peoplepop ulationandcommunity/wellbeing/datasets/measuringnationalwellbe inglifesatisfaction.

5. Steptoe, Deaton, and Stone (2015).

6. Steptoe, Breeze, et al. (2013).

7. The proportion of nonwhite participants in ELSA is very small (2.1%).

8. Kahneman and Deaton (2010); Pinquart and Sorensen (2000).

9. Westerlund et al. (2009), Olesen et al. (2014).

10. Lamu and Olsen (2016).

Chapter 10. Family Income

1. See online Survey Details.

2. Income was measured at ages 3, 4, 7, 8 and 11. The log figure is the log of average income up to the relevant age.

3. This is true for both boys and girls. See online Table A10.1.

4. Duncan and Brooks-Gunn (1999).

5. For the United States see Yeung, Linver, and Brooks-Gunn (2002) and Mistry et al. (2002). For the UK see Washbrook, Gregg, and Propper (2014). Using the national survey of the Mental Health of Children and Young People in Britain, 2004, Ford, Goodman, and Meltzer (2004) showed that, cet. par., family income had no effect on child mental health either on a cross-section of children or in explaining changes over time.

6. Burgess, Propper, and Rigg (2004). Also income and self-esteem are uncorrelated (Axinn, Duncan, and Thornton [1997]).

7. See online Descriptive Statistics, Table D.10.

8. For the gross effect and its breakdown see online Table A10.2, which covers emotional, behavioral, and intellectual outcomes.

9. Blanden and Gregg (2004). The basic controls include the child's sex, ethnicity, separate dummies for the number of siblings in the household, and controls for parents' age group. For the effect of financial problems in the NCDS (not holding income constant), see Gregg and Machin (2000), who show significant effects on school attendance and staying on at school.

10. See, for example, Blau (1999), Shea (2000), Maurin (2002), and Hardy (2014) for evidence on the direct effects, and Guo and Harris (2000), Yeung, Linver, and Brooks-Gunn (2002), and Washbrook, Gregg, and Propper (2014) for the indirect effects of income on children's achievements. See Haveman and Wolfe (1995) for an excellent summary of the multidisciplinary approaches taken in this context.

11. Related work has considered measures of economic conditions other than income as determinants of child achievements. Variables such as wealth or financial assets reflect economic security that can reduce family stress and financial anxiety and promote child development. Using data on family wealth—represented by the total assets values for the family in the past five years—and black-white test-score gaps in children aged 3 and 12 in PSID data, the sociologists and demographers Wei-Jun Jean Yeung of the National University of Singapore and Dalton Conley find that wealth plays no role in the test-score gaps of preschool children but does so for in-school children (Yeung and Conley [2008]). They also show wealth to be significantly correlated with mediating factors such as parental warmth, parental activities with the child, and the learning resources available at home. In another study by the sociologists Youngmi Kim and Michael Sherraden, family assets

are found to be strongly predictive of children's educational outcomes that include completion of high school and attainment of a college degree (Kim and Sherraden [2011]). Including family assets into the estimation of children's educational outcomes also reduces the size of the income effect and, in some cases, even renders it statistically insignificantly different from zero.

12. Acemoglu and Pischke (2001).

13. Yeung, Linver, and Brooks-Gunn (2002).

14. Waldfogel, Han, and Brooks-Gunn (2002).

15. See Online Annex 10 on financial problems.

Chapter 11. Working Parents

1. This whole chapter is about work outside the home—referred to for convenience as "work."

2. Questionnaires at months 21, 33, 47, 61, 73, 97, 110, 122, and 134. The surveys at these ages ask whether the mother is currently working or not. Unfortunately, for those who are not working we do not know whether they are out of the labor force or are unemployed. This means the analysis must follow the somewhat anachronistic logic of working mothers and unemployed fathers.

3. It doesn't. For explanation of decomposition, see Online Annex 3b.

4. McMunn et al. (2010). Mental health is measured by total SDQ. The statement in the article relates to two-parent families.

5. Powdthavee and Vernoit (2013).

6. For a brief summary, see Layard and Dunn (2009), 20–21. In the UK see Sammons et al. (2014). In the United States see also Cooksey, Joshi, and Verropoulou (2009) and Berger, Hill, and Waldfogel (2005).

7. This is also true at 11.

8. In future work we shall look at the effects when we do not control for income.

9. Using the BCS, see P. Gregg et al. (2005), and using EPE, Sylva et al. (2004), and Sammons et al. (2014). By contrast for intellectual development up to age 5, Ermisch and Francesconi (2013), using BHPS linked data on parents and children, found a negative and statistically significant maternal employment effect on intellectual problems up to age five. One possible explanation is that they were able to take into account both the unobserved heterogeneity that is common across siblings and the endogeneity of mother's choice to return to employment.

In other words, they correct for the fact that some mothers who decided to return to work early did so because of their preferences for work and/or their children were well developed enough to allow them to go back to work. With fixed effects and IV estimation, Ermisch and Francesconi (2013) basically estimated the effect of an *exogenous* effect of maternal employment (induced by regional and time variation in aggregate female unemployment rates) on child's outcome. In other words, there will be mothers who returned to work not because they are ready to, but because the opportunity cost of not going back is simply just too high for them.

10. Ruhm (2004) building on Waldfogel, Han, and Brooks-Gunn (2002). See also Joshi and Verropoulou (2000) for the UK.

11. Becker and Tomes (1986); Duncan and Brooks-Gunn (1999); Clark and Oswald (1994); Goldsmith, Veum, and Darity (1996); Powdthavee and Vignoles (2008); Gruber (2004); McLoyd (1989); Christoffersen (1994); and S. Brown and Taylor (2008).

12. The standard errors in columns (1) and (2) exceed those in (3) because we have GCSE scores for all children, from the National Pupil Database, whereas there are a significant number of missing observations on emotional and behavioral outcomes at age 16.

Chapter 12. Parenting and Parents' Mental Health

1. See Plomin et al. (2013).
2. Lykken (1999) and Caprara et al. (2009).
3. Tellegen et al. (1988).
4. See Plomin et al. (2013).
5. Tienari et al. (1994).
6. Bohman (1996) and Cadoret et al. (1995).
7. See Plomin et al. (2013).
8. Pluess (2015) and Okbay et al. (2016).
9. The same applies to all claims about the role of genes. In particular we should be wary of estimates offered of the "heritability" of a trait. There are two problems here:

(i) These estimates assume that gene and environment effects are additive (no gene/environment interaction). The trait (T) is thus determined by $T = G + E$ and $VarT = VarG + VarE + 2Cov(G, E)$.
(ii) These estimates assume that the covariance term $Cov(G, E)$ reflects a causal impact of G on E and therefore heritability is measured as $(VarG + 2Cov[G, E])/VarT$. However this implies a

fixity in the correlation of genes and environment that it is the specific aim of policy to unfix.

10. See Figure 1.5 (b).

11. Two exceptions are that premature children are recorded as (cet. par.) happier at 11 and firstborn children as less happy at 5.

12. See online Full Table 10.1, p. 4.

13. Presumably the mother matters more since she interacts more. However the mother's mental health is measured eight times up to when the child is 11, while the father's is measured only three times until the child is 2. To see if this matters, we also focused on explaining the child's emotional health at 5, using three observations on both parents' mental health. The difference between the effect of mother and father remained as large as it is in Table 12.1. The same occurred if we focused on explaining the child's emotional health at 16, but using only the first three observations on each parent's mental health.

The mother's mental health was measured using the Edinburgh Post-natal Depression Scale (EDPS), and the father's was tested using the Crown-Crisp Experiential Index.

14. Johnston, Schurer, and Shields (2013) show this in the BCS. Powdthavee and Vignoles (2008) use BHPS data to show how parent's emotional distress in year t produces a fall in the life-satisfaction of their children aged 11–15 between years t and $t + 1$.

15. O'Connor et al. (2002). See also Talge, Neal, and Glover (2007) for a review on this issue. On the temporal effects of parents' mood on the mood of children, see Larson and Gillman (1999) and Downey, Purdie, and Schaffer-Neitz (1999).

16. Aunola, Stattin, and Nurmi (2000); Dornbusch et al. (1987); Lamborn et al. (1991); Steinberg et al. (1992).

17. The weights come from a principal component analysis.

18. There are no data on fathers' behavior to the child, nor fathers' involvement.

19. For results using the Millennium Cohort see Kiernan and Huerta (2008). Age: three years old.

20. Heckman and Carneiro (2003) and Cunha and Heckman (2007).

21. The table is for intellectual performance only, since for emotional health and behavior the gross correlations are hardly any bigger than the partial correlations shown in Tables 12.1 and 12.2.

Chapter 13. Family Conflict

1. Epigraph quoted in Layard and Dunn (2009).

2. Office for National Statistics. http://www.ons.gov.uk/peoplepop ulationandcommunity/birthsdeathsandmarriages/divorce/datasets/di vorcesinenglandandwaleschildrenofdivorcedcouples.

Note that in the ALSPAC sample almost all the children lived initially with both biological parents. This is no longer the case, but in our sample we are unable to study the impact of being born to a single mother.

3. Duncan and Hoffman (1985); Weitzman (1985).

4. See Amato and Keith (1991) and Amato, Loomis, and Booth (1995) for the United States. Cherlin et al. (1991) also look at the UK.

5. See for example, Antecol and Bedard (2007); Bratberg, Elseth Rieck, and Vaage (2014); Cooper et al. (2011); Ermisch, Francesconi, and Pevalin (2004); Fronstin, Greenberg, and Robins (2001); Kiernan (1997); and Prevoo and ter Weel (2015).

6. On this issue, see also Amato, Loomis, and Booth (1995); Hanson (1999); and Jekielek (1998). We also reran Table 13.5 omitting as controls both mother's and father's mental health—since these could be affected by conflict and/or separation and thus act as mediating variables. When this was done the coefficients in the bottom line rose to

0.08 (.07)   0.11 (.08)   0.05 (04)

This interaction affect was thus larger but still not significant, given the sample size.

7. NFPI (2000).

Chapter 14. Schooling

1. Hanushek (1970).

2. One could do a value-added calculation for each child characteristic—by subtracting the score at 11 from the score at 16. But we prefer to estimate a freely determined coefficient, rather than imposing a coefficient of unity on the lagged dependent variable.

3. This estimate is an underestimate due to measurement error in emotional health but an overestimate due to the omission of variables, such as neighborhood effects.

4. (i) On class size and academic performance, using Tennessee's Project STAR, Hanushek (1999) found no effect of class size while

Krueger (2003) found that the internal rate of return from reducing class size from 22 to 15 students is around 6%. Using other data Hoxby (2000) found no effect, while Angrist and Levy (1999) showed that reducing class size induces a significant and substantial increase in test scores for fourth and fifth graders (although not for third graders) using the effects of Maimonides' Rule.

(ii) On class size and noncognitive development, Fredriksson, Ockert, and Oosterbeek (2013) and Dee and West (2011) discover some beneficial effects of smaller classes in primary schools (often rural), which persist over time, while Jakobsson, Persson, and Svensson (2013) found none using data on mental health problems and well-being among adolescents in Swedish schools.

5. Rockoff (2004), Aaronson, Barrow, and Sander (2007), Rivkin, Hanushek, and Kain (2005), Kane and Staiger (2008), Chetty, Friedman, and Rockoff (2014).

6. Flèche (2017).

7. See also Jackson (2012) and Araujo et al. (2016) for teacher effects on non-test-score outcomes.

8. In online Table A14.1 we replace the teacher's name by the measured characteristics and teaching practices of the teacher. These have almost no explanatory power, except in the case of academic performance, which is shown to respond to teachers' emotional health, self-esteem, and confidence in teaching their subject. There is however no effect of teacher's experience on academic performance (in line with most other research, e.g., Hanushek [1971], but also see Rockoff [2004]).

9. Chetty, Friedman, and Rockoff (2014); Rothstein (2010); Jacob, Lefgren, and Sims (2010).

10. See Flèche (2017).

Chapter 15. Measuring Cost-Effectiveness in Terms of Happiness

1. This assumes cardinality and comparability across people. For evidence on comparability across people, see Layard (2010). On cardinality, if a variable is cardinal, this means that the difference between a score of x and $(x + 1)$ is the same as the difference between a score of y and $(y + 1)$, whatever the values of x and y. The evidence on whether happiness measures are truly cardinal is limited, but Krueger and Schkade (2008) found that test-retest differences were independent of

the level of reported happiness, which if generally true would support cardinality.

2. For a more formal exposition, see online Annex 15.

3. We come later to the issue of what weight to give to the happiness of different individuals. For the moment we can assume that we simply add them up.

4. The position is more complicated when there are large mutually exclusive projects.

5. Produced by the National Institute for Health and Care Excellence (NICE).

6. NICE has used a cut-off between £20,000 and £30,000—say $35,000. This is the cut-off for a healthy life year. It is broadly in line with the Department of Transport's estimate of the human cost of a fatality, which in 2008 was £1.65 million (see Deloitte LLP [2009], table 1). This value, though based on willingness to pay, presumably reflects the discounted value of the remaining years of life of the typical traffic accident victim. The US Department of Transportation uses a somewhat higher figure.

7. For the present we assume that one unit of LS equals 0.1 QALYs. By questionnaires to the public, a team at Sheffield has established that people are willing to sacrifice approximately ten units of life-satisfaction for one more year of life at LS = 10.

8. Disposable income is about £20,000 per head, or say $20,000 × 1.5. Thus $\partial H / \partial Y = 0.2/(20,000 \times 1.25) = 1/125,000$.

9. See Chapter 2.

10. Kahneman, Ritov, and Schkade (2000).

11. We obtain the monetary value of some nonmonetary experience X by running a happiness equation (where H is happiness and Y income), $H = a_1 log Y + a_2 X$. Then the equivalent variation of income when X changes is given by $\Delta Y = \frac{a_2 Y}{a_1} \Delta X$.

12. According to Rawls (1971) we should simply focus on the very bottom.

13. We ought to mention some other more data-intensive approaches that focus directly on misery. One approach is to focus specifically on negative emotion as measured by replies to questions like "How sad/worried/frustrated/angry were you yesterday?" (For data on replies to these questions see Helliwell, Layard, and Sachs [2012], chapters 2 and 3.) Alternatively we could use time-use data, where individuals are asked about each episode in the previous day, with questions for each episode about the extent of various positive and negative emotions. As

Krueger and colleagues have proposed, we could then rate an episode as miserable if the most powerful negative emotion was more powerful than the most positive emotion (Krueger, Kahneman, Schkade, et al. [2009]). From this we could find what fraction of the day each person spent being miserable—what they called the person's "misery" index or U-index. And we could make the average misery index into our measure of social welfare. Such an exercise, however, is very data intensive and requires the collection of time-use data.

14. These are real amounts (inflation adjusted).

15. Stern (2007) argues that 1.5% is too high.

16. See Broome (2004).

17. Layard and D. M. Clark (2014).

18. Ludwig et al. (2012); Ludwig et al. (2013); Kling, Ludwig, and Katz (2005); Chetty, Hendren, and Katz (2016).

19. Data from Lawrence Katz of Harvard University.

20. Cattaneo et al. (2009).

21. Odermatt and Stutzer (2015).

22. Ward (2015).

Chapter 16. The Origins of Happiness

1. Layard and D. M. Clark (2014).

2. The figure is roughly 2% in the United States; see Table 2.2 and online Descriptive Statistics. See also the Gallup Daily Poll.

3. Since the Phillips curve is nonlinear, economic fluctuations lead to higher average unemployment rates over the cycle, if the inflation rate is not to increase. In addition, income growth adds less to happiness than falls in income decrease happiness, De Neve, Ward, De Keulenaer, et al. (forthcoming).

4. For a discussion of this complicated issue, see Chapter 3.

5. Now known as Understanding Society.

6. We use the cross-sections because the results of panel studies are more biased toward zero by measurement error and by problems of exact timing. The cross-sectional data are also somewhat biased toward zero by measurement error but are biased away from zero by the omission of key variables.

7. The BHPS uses a range of 1–7, but these figures have been transformed to a scale of 0–10. For the distribution of life-satisfaction in the BCS, see Chapter 1.

8. 0.18 (0.7). See online Full Table 16.2.

9. White and Edwards (1990). Buddelmeyer, Hamermesh, and Wooden (forthcoming) show how stress is reduced when children leave home.

10. A reduction of one point-year means one point less of life-satisfaction for one year. From Figure 9.2, $(\partial LS/\partial LON)$. $\sigma_{LON} = 0.28\sigma_{LS.}$

11. For example the impact of highest qualification over 60 years would be $(7.2–0.87)$ point-years while that of emotional health would be $(10.8–0.04)$ point-years.

12. On the role of genes, see Chapter 12.

13. Of the worldwide variance of life-satisfaction across persons, only 22% is between countries and 78% within countries (Helliwell, Layard, and Sachs [2012], 12).

14. See Helliwell, Layard, and Sachs (2017), figure 2.2. Other "top" countries include Norway, Iceland, and Switzerland, and other "low" countries include Tanzania and Burundi.

15. Easterlin, Morgan, Switek, and Wang (2012), and Easterlin, Wang, and Wang (2017).

REFERENCES

Aaronson, D., L. Barrow, and W. Sander. 2007. "Teachers and Student Achievement in the Chicago Public High Schools." *Journal of Labor Economics* 25 (1):95–135.

Acemoglu, D., and J.-S. Pischke. 2001. "Changes in the Wage Structure, Family Income, and Children's Education." *European Economic Review* 45 (4–6):890–904.

Alesina, A., R. Di Tella, and R. MacCulloch. 2004. "Inequality and Happiness: Are Europeans and Americans different?" *Journal of Public Economics* 88 (9):2009–42. doi: 10.1016/j.jpubeco.20033.07.006.

Amato, P. R., and B. Keith. 1991. "Parental Divorce and the Well-Being of Children: A Meta-analysis." *Psychological Bulletin* 110 (1):26–46.

Amato, P. R., L. S. Loomis, and A. Booth. 1995. "Parental Divorce, Marital Conflict, and Offspring Well-Being during Early Adulthood." *Social Forces* 73 (3):895–915.

Amiel, Y., J. Creedy, and S. Hurn. 1999. "Measuring Attitudes towards Inequality." *Scandinavian Journal of Economics* 101 (1):83–96.

Anderson, D. M. 2014. "In School and Out of Trouble? The Minimum Dropout Age and Juvenile Crime." *Review of Economics and Statistics* 96 (2):318–31.

Angrist, J. D., and V. Levy. 1999. "Using Maimonides' Rule to Estimate the Effect of Class Size on Scholastic Achievement." *Quarterly Journal of Economics* 114 (2):533–75.

Anik, L., L. B. Aknin, M. I. Norton, and E. W. Dunn. 2010. "Feeling Good about Giving: The Benefits (and Costs) of Self-Interested Charitable Behavior." *Harvard Business School Discussion Paper No. 10–012.*

Antecol, H., and K. Bedard. 2007. "Does Single Parenthood Increase the Probability of Teenage Promiscuity, Substance Use, and Crime?" *Journal of Population Economics* 20 (1):55–71.

Anusic, I., S. Yap, and R. Lucas. 2014. "Testing Set-Point Theory in a Swiss National Sample: Reaction and Adaptation to Major Life Events." *Social Indicators Research* 119 (3):1265–88.

Araujo, M. C., P. M. Carneiro, Y. Cruz-Aguayo, and N. Schady. 2016. "Teacher Quality and Learning Outcomes in Kindergarten." *Quarterly Journal of Economics* 131 (3):1415–53. doi: 10.1093/qje/qjw016.

Aunola, K., H. Stattin, and J. E. Nurmi. 2000. "Parenting Styles and Adolescents' Achievement Strategies." *Journal of Adolescence* 23 (2):205–22.

Axinn, W. G., G. J. Duncan, and A. Thornton. 1997. "The Effects of Parents' Income, Wealth, and Attitudes on Children's Completed Schooling and Self-Esteem." In *Consequences of Growing Up Poor*, edited by G. J. Duncan and J. Brooks-Gunn, 518–40. New York: Russell Sage Foundation.

Barro, R., and J.-W. Lee. 2012. *A New Data Set of Educational Attainment in the World, 1950–2010*. Harvard University mimeo.

———. 2015. *Education Matters*. Oxford: Oxford University Press.

Bartolini, S., Bilancini, E., and Sarracino, F. 2016. "Social Capital Predicts Happiness over Time: World-Wide Evidence from Time Series." In *Policies for Happiness*, edited by S. Bartolini, E. Bilancini, L. Bruni, and P. L. Porta. Oxford: Oxford University Press, 175–98.

Becchetti, L., S. Castriota, L. Corrado, and E. Ricca. 2013. "Beyond the Joneses: Inter-country Income Comparisons and Happiness." *Journal of Behavioral and Experimental Economics* 45 (C):187–95.

Becker, G. S. 1964. *Human Capital*. New York: Columbia University Press for the National Bureau of Economic Research.

Becker, G. S., and N. Tomes. 1986. "Human Capital and the Rise and Fall of Families." *Journal of Labor Economics* 4 (3):S1–S39.

Bell, B., R. Costa, and S. Machin. 2016. "Crime, Compulsory Schooling Laws and Education." *Economics of Education Review* 54:214–26.

Bentham, J. [1789] 1996. *An Introduction to the Principles of Morals and Legislation*. Oxford: Clarendon.

Berger, L. M., J. Hill, and J. Waldfogel. 2005. "Maternity Leave, Early Maternal Employment and Child Health and Development in the US." *Economic Journal* 115 (501):F29–F47.

Blanchflower, D. G., and A. J. Oswald. 1998. "What Makes an Entrepreneur?" *Journal of Labor Economics* 16 (1):26–60.

———. 2004. "Well-Being over Time in Britain and the USA." *Journal of Public Economics* 88 (7–8):1359–86. doi: 10.1016/S0047-2727 (02)00168-8.

Blanden, J., and P. Gregg. 2004. "Family Income and Educational Attainment: A Review of Approaches and Evidence for Britain." *Oxford Review of Economic Policy* 20 (2):245–63.

Blau, D. M. 1999. "The Effect of Income on Child Development." *Review of Economics and Statistics* 81 (2):261–76.

Blundell, R., D. Green, and W. Jin. 2016. *The UK Wage Premium Puzzle: How Did a Large Increase in University Graduates Leave the Education*

Premium Unchanged? IFS Working Paper (W16/01). Institute for Fiscal Studies. doi: 10.1920/wp.ifs.2016.1601.

Bohman, M. 1996. "Predisposition to Criminality: Swedish Adoption Studies in Retrospect." In *Genetics of Criminal and Antisocial Behaviour*, edited by G. Bock and J. Goode, 99–114. Chichester, UK: John Wiley.

Bratberg, E., K. M. Elseth Rieck, and K. Vaage. 2014. "Intergenerational Earnings Mobility and Divorce." *Journal of Population Economics* 27 (4):1107–26.

Broome, J. 2004. *Weighing Lives*. Oxford: Oxford University Press.

Brown, G., J. Gardner, A. J. Oswald, and J. Qian. 2008. "Does Wage Rank Affect Employees' Wellbeing?" *Industrial Relations* 47 (3):355–89.

Brown, G. W., and T. O. Harris. 1978. *Social Origins of Depression: A Study of Psychiatric Disorder in Women*. London: Tavistock.

Brown, S., and K. Taylor. 2008. "Bullying, Education and Earnings: Evidence from the National Child Development Study." *Economics of Education Review* 27 (4):387–401.

Brown, S. L., R. M. Nesse, A. D. Vinokur, and D. M. Smith. 2003. "Providing Social Support May Be More Beneficial Than Receiving It: Results from a Prospective Study of Mortality." *Psychological Science* 14 (4):320–27.

Bryson, A., and G. MacKerron. 2017. "Are You Happy While You Work?" *Economic Journal* 127 (599):106–25. doi: 10.1111/ecoj.12269.

Buddelmeyer, H., D. S. Hamermesh, and M. Wooden. Forthcoming. "The Stress Cost of Children on Moms and Dads." *European Economic Review*.

Burgess, S. M., C. Propper, and J. Rigg. 2004. "The Impact of Low Income on Child Health: Evidence from a Birth Cohort Study." *LSE STICERD Research Paper No. CASE085*.

Cadoret, R. J., W. R. Yates, E. Troughton, G. Woodworth, and M. A. Stewart. 1995. "Genetic-Environmental Interaction in the Genesis of Aggressivity and Conduct Disorders." *Archives of General Psychiatry* 52 (11):916–24. doi: 10.1001/archpsyc.1995.03950230030006.

Cappelli, P., and P. Sherer. 1988. "Satisfaction, Market Wages and Labor Relations: An Airline Study." *Industrial Relations* 27 (1):56–73.

Caprara, G., C. Fagnani, G. Alessandri, P. Steca, A. Gigantesco, L. Cavalli Sforza, and M. Stazi. 2009. "Human Optimal Functioning: The Genetics of Positive Orientation towards Self, Life, and the Future." *Behavioural Genetics* 39 (3):277–84.

Card, D., A. Mas, E. Moretti, and E. Saez. 2012. "Inequality at Work: The Effect of Peer Salaries on Job Satisfaction." *American Economic Review* 102 (6):2981–3003.

Cattaneo, M. D., S. Galiani, P. J. Gertler, S. Martinez, and R. Titiunik. 2009. "Housing, Health, and Happiness." *American Economic Journal: Economic Policy* 1 (1):75–105.

Cetre, S., A. E. Clark, and C. Senik. 2016. "Happy People Have Children: Choice and Self-Selection into Parenthood." *European Journal of Population* 32:445–73.

Cheng, T. C., N. Powdthavee, and A. J. Oswald. 2017. "Longitudinal Evidence for a Midlife Nadir in Human Well-Being: Results from Four Data Sets." *Economic Journal* 127 (599):126–42.

Cherlin, A. J., F. F. Furstenberg, L. Chase-Lansdale, K. E. Kiernan, P. K. Robins, D. R. Morrison, and J. O. Teitler. 1991. "Longitudinal Studies of Effects of Divorce on Children in Great Britain and the United States." *Science* 252 (5011):1386–89.

Chetty, R., J. Friedman, and J. Rockoff. 2014. "Measuring the Impacts of Teachers I: Evaluating Bias in Teacher Value-Added Estimates." *American Economic Review* 104 (9):2593–632.

Chetty, R., N. Hendren, and L. F. Katz. 2016. "The Effects of Exposure to Better Neighborhoods on Children: New Evidence from the Moving to Opportunity Experiment." *American Economic Review* 106 (4):855–902.

Christoffersen, M. N. 1994. "A Follow-Up Study of Longterm Effects of Unemployment on Children: Loss of Self-Esteem and Self-Destructive Behavior among Adolescents." *Childhood* 2 (4):212–20.

Clark, A. E. 2001. "What Really Matters in a Job? Hedonic Measurement Using Quit Data." *Labour Economics* 8 (2):223–42.

———. 2003. "Unemployment as a Social Norm: Psychological Evidence from Panel Data." *Journal of Labor Economics* 21 (2):323–51.

———. 2010. "Work, Jobs and Well-Being across the Millennium." In *International Differences in Well-Being*, edited by E. Diener, J. Helliwell and D. Kahneman, 436–68. Oxford: Oxford University Press.

———. 2011. "Worker Well-Being in Booms and Busts." In *The Labour Market in Winter: The State of Working Britain*, edited by J. Wadsworth and P. Gregg, 128–43. Oxford: Oxford University Press.

Clark, A. E., and C. D'Ambrosio. 2015. "Attitudes to Income Inequality: Experimental and Survey Evidence." In *Handbook of Income Distribution*, edited by A. Atkinson and F. Bourguignon, 1147–208. Amsterdam: Elsevier.

Clark, A. E., E. Diener, Y. Georgellis, and R. Lucas. 2008. "Lags and Leads in Life Satisfaction: A Test of the Baseline Hypothesis." *Economic Journal* 118 (529):F222–F243.

Clark, A. E., S. Flèche, and C. Senik. 2014. "The Great Happiness Moderation." In *Happiness and Economic Growth: Lessons from Developing Countries*, edited by Andrew E. Clark and Claudia Senik. Oxford: Oxford University Press.

Clark, A. E., P. Frijters, and M. Shields. 2008. "Relative Income, Happiness and Utility: An Explanation for the Easterlin Paradox and Other Puzzles." *Journal of Economic Literature* 46 (1):95–144.

Clark, A. E., and Y. Georgellis. 2013. "Back to Baseline in Britain: Adaptation in the BHPS." *Economica* 80 (319):496–512.

Clark, A. E., Y. Georgellis, and P. Sanfey. 2001. "Scarring: The Psychological Impact of Past Unemployment." *Economica* 68 (270):221–41.

Clark, A. E., A. Knabe, and S. Rätzel. 2010. "Boon or Bane? Others' Unemployment, Well-Being and Job Insecurity." *Labour Economics* 17 (1):52–61.

Clark, A. E., N. Kristensen, and N. Westergård-Nielsen. 2009. "Economic Satisfaction and Income Rank in Small Neighbourhoods." *Journal of the European Economic Association* 7 (2–3):519–27.

Clark, A. E., and O. Lelkes. 2009. *Let Us Pray: Religious Interactions in Life Satisfaction*. PSE Working Paper No. 2009-01. Paris School of Economics.

Clark, A. E., and A. J. Oswald. 1994. "Unhappiness and Unemployment." *Economic Journal* 104 (424):648–59.

Clark, A. E., and C. Senik. 2010. "Who Compares to Whom? The Anatomy of Income Comparisons in Europe." *Economic Journal* 120 (544):573–94.

Clark, A. E., and E. Uglanova. 2012. "Adaptation in the East: Does Context Matter?" PSE mimeo.

Colombier, N., and D. Masclet. 2008. "Intergenerational Correlation in Self-Employment: Some Further Evidence from ECHP Data." *Small Business Economics* 30 (4):423–37.

Cooksey, E., H. Joshi, and G. Verropoulou. 2009. "Does Mothers' Employment Affect Children's Development? Evidence from the Children of the British 1970 Birth Cohort and the American NLSY79." *Longitudinal and Life Course Studies* 1 (1):95–115.

Cooper, C. E., C. A. Osborne, A. N. Beck, and S. S. McLanahan. 2011. "Partnership Instability, School Readiness, and Gender Disparities." *Sociology of Education* 84 (3):246–59.

Cunha, F., and J. Heckman. 2007. "The Technology of Skill Formation." *American Economic Review* 97 (2):31–47.

Danner, D., D. Snowdon, and W. Friesen. 2001. "Positive Emotions in Early Life and Longevity: Findings from the Nun Study." *Journal of Personality and Social Psychology* 80 (5):804–13.

Davidson, R. J. 1992. "Emotion and Affective Style: Hemispheric Substrates." *Psychological Science* 3 (1):39–43.

Davidson, R. J., and S. Begley. 2012. *The Emotional Life of Your Brain*. London: Penguin.

Dee, T. S., and M. R. West. 2011. "The Non-cognitive Returns to Class Size." *Educational Evaluation and Policy Analysis* 33 (1):23–46.

Deloitte LLP. 2009. Review of the Highways Agency Value of Life Estimates for the Purpose of Project Appraisal: A Report to the NAO. National Audit Office.

De Neve, J.-E., E. Diener, L. Tay, and C. Xuereb. 2013. "The Objective Benefits of Subjective Well-Being." In *World Happiness Report 2013*, edited by J. Helliwell, R. Layard and J. Sachs, 58–89. New York: Columbia Earth Institute.

De Neve, J., G. Ward, F. De Keulenaer, B. Van Landeghem, G. Kavestos, and M. Norton. Forthcoming. "The Asymmetric Experience of Positive and Negative Economic Growth: Global Evidence Using Subjective Wellbeing Data." *Review of Economics and Statistics*.

Diener, E., S. D. Pressman, and S. Lyubormirsky. 2015. "Can 1 Million Women Be Wrong about Happiness and Health?" *LA Times*. 17 December. http://www.latimes.com/opinion/op-ed/la-oe-lyubomirsky-et-al-happiness-affects-health-20151217-story.html.

Diener, E., L. Tay, and D. G. Myers. 2011. "The Religion Paradox: If Religion Makes People Happy, Why Are So Many Dropping Out?" *Journal of Personality and Social Psychology* 101 (6):1278–90. doi: 10.1037/a0024402.

Di Tella, R., R. J. MacCulloch, and A. J. Oswald. 2003. "The Macroeconomics of Happiness." *Review of Economics and Statistics* 85 (4):809–27.

Dolan, P. 1997. "Modeling Valuations for EuroQol Health States." *Medical Care* 35 (11):1095–108.

Dolan, P., and R. Metcalfe. 2012. "Valuing Health: A Brief Report on Subjective Well-Being versus Preferences." *Medical Decision Making* 32 (4):578–82.

Dornbusch, S. M., P. L. Ritter, P. H. Leiderman, D. F. Roberts, and M. J. Fraleigh. 1987. "The Relation of Parenting Style to Adolescent School Performance." *Child Development* 58 (5):1244–57.

Downey, G., V. Purdie, and R. Schaffer-Neitz. 1999. "Anger Transmission from Mother to Child: A Comparison of Mothers in Chronic Pain and Well Mothers." *Journal of Marriage and the Family* 61 (1):62–73.

Duncan, G. J., and J. Brooks-Gunn, eds. 1999. *Consequences of Growing Up Poor*. New York: Russell Sage Foundation.

Duncan, G. J., and S. D. Hoffman. 1985. "A Reconsideration of the Economic Consequences of Marital Dissolution." *Demography* 22 (4):485–97.

Dunn, E., L. Aknin, and M. Norton. 2008. "Spending Money on Others Promotes Happiness." *Science* 319:1687–88.

Dustmann, C., and F. Fasani. 2016. "The Effect of Local Area Crime on Mental Health." *Economic Journal* 126 (593):978–1017. doi: 10.1111/ecoj.12205.

Easterlin, R. 1974. "Does Economic Growth Improve the Human Lot?" In *Nations and Households in Economic Growth*, edited by P. A. David and W. B. Melvin, 89–125. Palo Alto, CA: Stanford University Press.

———. 2016. "Paradox Lost?" *IZA Discussion Paper 9676*. Institute for the Study of Labor (IZA).

Easterlin, R., L. Angelescu-McVey, M. Switek, O. Sawangfa, and J. Zweig. 2010. "The Happiness—Income Paradox Revisited." *Proceedings of the National Academy of Sciences* 107 (52):22463–68.

Easterlin, R. A., R. Morgan, M. Switek, and F. Wang. 2012. "China's Life Satisfaction, 1990–2010." *PNAS* 109 (25):9775–80.

Easterlin, R. A., F. Wang, and S. Wang. 2017. "Growth and Happiness in China, 1990–2015." In *World Happiness Report 2017*, edited by J. F. Helliwell, R. Layard, and J. Sachs, 48–83. New York: Sustainable Development Solutions Network.

Edmans, A. 2011. "Does the Stock Market Fully Value Intangibles? Employee Satisfaction and Equity Prices." *Journal of Financial Economics* 101:621–40. doi: 10.1016/j.jfineco.2011.03.021.

———. 2012. "The Link between Job Satisfaction and Firm Value, with Implications for Corporate Social Responsibility." *Academy of Management Perspectives* 26 (4):1–19.

Ellison, C. G. 1991. "Religious Involvement and Subjective Well-Being." *Journal of Health and Social Behavior* 32 (1):80–99.

Ermisch, J., and M. Francesconi. 2013. "The Effect of Parental Employment on Child Schooling." *Journal of Applied Econometrics* 28 (5):796–822.

Ermisch, J., M. Francesconi, and D. J. Pevalin. 2004. "Parental Partnership and Joblessness in Childhood and Their Influence on Young People's Outcomes." *Journal of the Royal Statistical Society. Series A (Statistics in Society)* 167 (1):69–101.

Ferrer-i-Carbonell, A. 2005. "Income and Well-Being: An Empirical Analysis of the Comparison Income Effect." *Journal of Public Economics* 89:997–1019.

Flèche, S. 2017. "Teacher Quality, Test Scores and Non-cognitive Skills: Evidence from Primary School Teachers in the UK." *CEP Discussion Paper 1472*. LSE Centre for Economic Performance.

Flèche, S., W. Lekfuangfu, and A. E. Clark. 2017. "The Long-Lasting Effects of Childhood on Adult Life-Satisfaction: Evidence from Cohort Data." *CEP Discussion Paper 1493*. LSE Centre for Economic Performance.

Fließbach, K., B. Weber, P. Trautner, T. Dohmen, U. Sunde, C. Elger, and A. Falk. 2007. "Social Comparison Affects Reward-Related Brain Activity in the Human Ventral Striatum." *Science* 318 (5854):1305–8.

Ford, T., R. Goodman, and H. Meltzer. 2004. "The Relative Importance of Child, Family, School and Neighbourhood Correlates of Childhood Psychiatric Disorder." *Social Psychiatry and Psychiatric Epidemiology* 39 (6):487–96.

Fredriksson, P., B. Ockert, and H. Oosterbeek. 2013. "Long-Term Effects of Class Size." *Quarterly Journal of Economics* 128 (1):249–85.

Frijters, P., D. Johnston, and M. Shields. 2011. "Happiness Dynamics with Quarterly Life Event Data." *Scandinavian Journal of Economics* 113 (1):190–211.

Fronstin, P., D. H. Greenberg, and P. K. Robins. 2001. "Parental Disruption and Labour Market Performance of Children When They Reach Adulthood." *Journal of Population Economics* 14 (1):137–72.

Godechot, O., and C. Senik. 2015. "Wage Comparisons in and out of the Firm: Evidence from a Matched Employer-Employee French Database." *Journal of Economic Behavior and Organization* 117:395–410.

Goldsmith, A. H., J. R. Veum, and W. Darity. 1996. "The Psychological Impact of Unemployment and Joblessness." *Journal of Socioeconomics* 25 (3):333–58.

Gregg, P., and S. Machin. 2000. "Child Development and Success or Failure in the Youth Labour Market." In *Youth Unemployment and Joblessness in Advanced Countries*, edited by D. Blanchflower and R. Freeman, 247–88. NBER Comparative Labour Market Series. Chicago: University of Chicago Press.

Gregg, P., E. Washbrook, C. Propper, and S. Burgess. 2005. "The Effects of a Mother's Return to Work Decision on Child Development in the UK." *Economic Journal* 115 (501):F48–F80.

Gruber, J. 2004. "Is Making Divorce Easier Bad for Children? The Long-Run Implications of Unilateral Divorce." *Journal of Labor Economics* 22 (4):799–833.

Guo, G., and K. M. Harris. 2000. "The Mechanisms Mediating the Effects of Poverty on Children's Intellectual Development." *Demography* 37 (4):431–47.

Halpern, D. 2004. *Social Capital.* Cambridge: Polity.

Hanson, T. L. 1999. "Does Parental Conflict Explain Why Divorce Is Negatively Associated with Child Welfare?" *Social Forces* 77:1283–316.

Hanushek, E. A. 1970. "The Production of Education, Teacher Quality, and Efficiency." In *Do Teachers Make a Difference?*, edited by U.S. Office of Education, 79–99. Washington, DC: Government Printing Office.

———. 1971. "Teacher Characteristics and Gains in Student Achievement." *American Economic Review* 61 (2):208–88.

———. 1999. "Some Findings from an Independent Investigation of the Tennessee STAR Experiment and from Other Investigations of Class Size Effects." *Educational Evaluation and Policy Analysis* 21 (2):143–63.

Harbaugh, W. T., U. Mayr, and D. R. Burghart. 2007. "Neural Responses to Taxation and Voluntary Giving Reveal Motives for Charitable Donations." *Science* 316:1622–25.

Hardy, B. L. 2014. "Childhood Income Volatility and Adult Outcomes." *Demography* 51 (5):1641–65.

Haveman, R., and B. Wolfe. 1995. "The Determinants of Children's Attainments: A Review of Methods and Findings." *Journal of Economic Literature* 33 (4):1829–78.

Heckman, J., and P. Carneiro. 2003. "Human Capital Policy." In *Inequality in America: What Role for Human Capital Policy?*, edited by J. J. Heckman and A. B. Krueger. Cambridge, MA: MIT Press.

Helliwell, J. F. 2003. "How's Life? Combining Individual and National Variables to Explain Subjective Well-Being." *Economic Modelling* 20 (2):331–60. doi: http://dx.doi.org/10.1016/S0264–9993(02)00057–3.

———. 2007. "Well-Being and Social Capital: Does Suicide Pose a Puzzle?" *Social Indicators Research* 81 (3):455–96. doi: 10.1007/s11205–006–0022-y.

Helliwell, J. F., H. Huang, S. Grover, and S. Wang. 2014. *Good Governance and National Well-Being: What Are the Linkages?* OECD Working Papers on Public Governance No. 25. OECD.

Helliwell, J. F., H. Huang, and S. Wang. 2016. *New Evidence on Trust and Wellbeing.* NBER Working Paper No. 22450.

Helliwell, J. F., R. Layard, and J. Sachs, eds. 2012. *World Happiness Report.* New York: Earth Institute, Columbia University.

———, eds. 2016. *World Happiness Report Update 2016.* New York: UN Sustainable Development Solutions Network.

———, eds. 2017. *World Happiness Report 2017.* New York: UN Sustainable Development Solutions Network.

Helliwell, J. F., and S. Wang. 2011. "Trust and Wellbeing." *International Journal of Wellbeing* 1 (1):42–78. doi: 10.5502/ijw.v1i1.9.

Hoxby, C. M. 2000. "The Effects of Class Size on Student Achievement: New Evidence from Population Variation." *Quarterly Journal of Economics* 115 (4):1239–85.

Inglehart, R., and H.-D. Klingemann. 2000. "Genes, Culture, Democracy and Happiness." In *Culture and Subjective Wellbeing,* edited by Ed Diener and Eunkook M. Suh. Cambridge, MA: MIT Press.

Jackson, K. 2012. *Non-cognitive Ability, Test Scores and Teacher Quality: Evidence from 9th Grade Teachers in North Carolina.* NBER Working Paper No. 18624.

Jacob, B. A., L. Lefgren, and D. Sims. 2010. "The Persistence of Teacher-Induced Learning Gains." *Journal of Human Resources* 45 (4):915–43.

Jakobsson, N., M. Persson, and M. Svensson. 2013. "Class-Size Effects on Adolescents' Mental Health And Well-Being in Swedish Schools." *Education Economics* 21 (3):248–63.

Jefferson, T. 1809. Letter to the Maryland Republicans." In *The Writings of Thomas Jefferson.* Memorial edition, edited by A. A. Lipscomb and A. E. Bergh, 16:359. Washington, DC: Thomas Jefferson Memorial Association of the United States.

Jekielek, S. M. 1998. "Parental Conflict, Marital Disruption, and Children's Emotional Well-being." *Social Forces* 76:905–36.

Johannsson-Stenman, O., F. Carlsson, and D. Daruvala. 2002. "Measuring Future Grandparents' Preferences for Equality and Relative Standing." *Economic Journal* 112:362–83.

Johnston, D. W., S. Schurer, and M. A. Shields. 2013. "Exploring the Intergenerational Persistence of Mental Health: Evidence from Three Generations." *Journal of Health Economics* 32 (6):1077–89.

Joshi, H., and G. Verropoulou. 2000. Maternal Employment and Child Outcomes. London: Smith Institute Report.

Kahneman, D. 2011. *Thinking, Fast and Slow.* London: Allen Lane.

Kahneman, D., and A. Deaton. 2010. "High Income Improves Evaluation of Life but Not Emotional Well-Being." *Proceedings of the National Academy of Science* 107 (38):16489–93.

Kahneman, D., A. B. Krueger, D. A. Schkade, N. Schwarz, and A. A. Stone. 2004. "A survey method for characterizing daily life experience: the day reconstruction method (DRM)." *Science* 306:1776–1780. doi: 10.1126/science.1103572.

Kahneman, D., I. Ritov, and D. A. Schkade. 2000. "Economic Preferences or Attitude Expressions? An Analysis of Dollar Responses to Public Issues." In *Choices, Values and Frames*, edited by D. Kahneman and A. Tversky. Cambridge: Cambridge University Press and Russell Sage Foundation.

Kane, T., and D. Staiger. 2008. *Estimating Teacher Impacts on Student Achievement: An Experimental Evaluation.* NBER Working Paper No. 14607.

Kiernan, K. E. 1997. *The Legacy of Parental Divorce: Social, Economic and Demographic Experiences in Adulthood.* Centre for Analysis of Social Exclusion, London School of Economics and Political Science.

Kiernan, K. E., and M. C. Huerta. 2008. "Economic Deprivation, Maternal Depression, Parenting and Children's Cognitive and Emotional Development in Early Childhood." *British Journal of Sociology* 59 (4):783–806.

Kim, Y., and M. Sherraden. 2011. "Do Parental Assets Matter for Children's Educational Attainment? Evidence from Mediation Tests." *Children and Youth Services Review* 33 (6):969–79.

Kingdon, G., and J. Knight. 2007. "Community, Comparisons and Subjective Well-Being in a Divided Society." *Journal of Economic Behavior and Organization* 64 (1):69–90.

Kling, J., J. Ludwig, and L. Katz. 2005. "Neighborhood Effects on Crime for Female and Male Youth: Evidence from a Randomized Housing Voucher Experiment." *Quarterly Journal of Economics* 120 (1):87–130.

Knack, S. 2001. "Trust, Associational Life and Economic Performance." In *The Contribution of Human and Social Capital to Sustained Economic Growth and Well-Being*, edited by J. Helliwell and A. Bonikowska. Ottawa: HRDC and OECD.

Knight, J., and R. Gunatilaka. 2010. "Great Expectations? The Subjective Well-Being of Rural-Urban Migrants to China." *World Development* 38 (1):113–24.

Knight, J., L. Song, and R. Gunatilaka. 2010. "The Determinants of Subjective Well-Being in China." *China Economic Review* 20 (4):635–49.

Krueger, A. B. 2003. "Economic Considerations and Class Size." *Economic Journal* 113 (485):F34–F63.

———. 2007. "Are We Having Fun Yet? Categorizing and Evaluating Changes in Time Allocation." *Brookings Papers on Economic Activity* 2:193–217.

Krueger, A. B., D. Kahneman, C. Fischler, D. A. Schkade, N. Schwarz, and A. A. Stone. 2009. "Comparing Time Use and Subjective Well-being in France and the US." *Social Indicators Research* 93:7–18.

Krueger, A. B., D. Kahneman, D. A. Schkade, N. Schwarz, and A. A. Stone. 2009. "National Time Accounting: The Currency of Life." In *Measuring the Subjective Well-Being of Nations: National Accounts of Time Use and Well-Being*, edited by A. B Krueger, 9–86. Chicago: University of Chicago Press.

Krueger, A. B., and D. A. Schkade. 2008. "The Reliability of Subjective Well-Being Measures." *Journal of Public Economics* 92 (8–9):1833–45.

Lamborn, S. D., N. S. Mounts, L. Steinberg, and S. M. Dornbusch. 1991. "Patterns of Competence and Adjustment among Adolescents from Authoritative, Authoritarian, Indulgent, and Neglectful Families." *Child Development* 62 (5):1049–65.

Lamu, A. N., and J. A. Olsen. 2016. "The Relative Importance of Health, Income and Social Relations for Subjective Well-Being: An Integrative Analysis." *Social Science and Medicine* 152:176–85.

Larson, R. W., and S. Gillman. 1999. "Transmission of Emotions in the Daily Interactions of Single-Mother Families." *Journal of Marriage and the Family* 61 (1):21–37.

Layard, R. 2006. "Happiness and Public Policy: A Challenge to the Profession." *Economic Journal* 116 (March):C24–C33.

———. 2010. "Measuring Subjective Well-Being." *Science* 327 (5965): 534–35.

———. 2011. *Happiness: Lessons from a New Science.* 2nd ed. London: Penguin.

Layard, R., A. E. Clark, F. Cornaglia, N. Powdthavee, and J. Vernoit. 2014. "What Predicts a Successful Life? A Life-Course Model of Well-Being." *Economic Journal* 124:F720–38.

Layard, R., A. E. Clark, and C. Senik. 2012. "The Causes of Happiness and Misery." In *World Happiness Report*, edited by J. F Helliwell, R. Layard and J. Sachs, 58–89. New York: Earth Institute, Columbia University.

Layard, R., and D. M. Clark. 2014. *Thrive: The Power of Evidence-Based Psychological Therapies.* London: Penguin.

Layard, R., and J. Dunn. 2009. *A Good Childhood: Searching for Values in a Competitive Age, Report for the Children's Society.* London: Penguin.

Layard, R., G. Mayraz, and S. J. Nickell. 2010. "Does Relative Income Matter? Are the Critics Right?" In *International Differences in Well-Being*, edited by E. Diener, J. F. Helliwell, and D. Kahneman, 139–65. New York: Oxford University Press.

Layard, R., S. Nickell, and R. Jackman. 2005. *Unemployment: Macroeconomic Performance and the Labour Market.* 2nd ed. Oxford: Oxford University Press.

Layard, R., S. J. Nickell, and G. Mayraz. 2008. "The Marginal Utility of Income." In "Happiness and Public Economics," special issue, *Journal of Public Economics* 92 (8–9):1846–57.

Layard, R., and G. Psacharopoulos. 1974. "The Screening Hypothesis and Returns to Education." *Journal of Political Economy* 82 (5):985–98.

Liu, B., S. Floud, K. Pirie, J. Green, R. Peto, and V. Beral. 2015. "Does Happiness Itself Directly Affect Mortality? The Prospective UK Million Women Study." *Lancet* 387 (10021):874–81. doi: http://dx.doi.org/10.1016/S0140-6736(15)01087-9.

Lochner, L., and E. Moretti. 2004. "The Effect of Education on Crime: Evidence from Prison Inmates, Arrests and Self-Reports." *American Economic Review* 94:155–89.

Lucas, R., A. E. Clark, Y. Georgellis, and E. Diener. 2003. "Re-examining Adaptation and the Setpoint Model of Happiness: Reaction to Changes in Marital Status." *Journal of Personality and Social Psychology* 84 (3):527–39.

———. 2004. "Unemployment Alters the Set-Point for Life Satisfaction." *Psychological Science* 15 (1):8–13.

Ludwig, J., G. J. Duncan, L. A. Gennetian, L. F. Katz, R. C. Kessler, J. R. Kling, and L. Sanbonmatsu. 2012. "Neighborhood Effects on the Long-Term Well-Being of Low-Income Adults." *Science* 337 (6101):1505–10. doi: 10.1126/science.1224648.

———. 2013. "Long-Term Neighborhood Effects on Low-Income Families: Evidence from Moving to Opportunity." *American Economic Review* 103 (3):226–31.

Lundberg, U., and C. L. Cooper. 2011. *The Science of Occupational Health: Stress, Psychobiology and the New World of Work.* Oxford: Wiley-Blackwell.

Luttmer, E. 2005. "Neighbors as Negatives: Relative Earnings and Well-Being." *Quarterly Journal of Economics* 120 (3):963–1002.

Lykken, D. 1999. *Happiness: The Nature and Nurture of Joy and Contentment.* New York: St Martin's Griffin.

Machin, S., O. Marie, and S. Vujic. 2011. "The Crime Reducing Effect of Education." *Economic Journal* 121:463–84.

Maurin, E. 2002. "The Impact of Parental Income on Early Schooling Transitions: A Re-examination Using Data over Three Generations." *Journal of Public Economics* 85 (3):301–32.

References

McLoyd, V. C. 1989. "Socialization and Development in a Changing Economy: The Effects of Paternal Job and Income Loss on Children." *American Psychologist* 44 (2):293–302.

McMunn, A., Y. Kelly, N. Cable, and M. Bartley. 2010. "Maternal Employment and Child Socio-emotional Behavior in the UK: Longitudinal Evidence from the Cohort Study." *Journal of Epidemiology and Community Health* 66 (7): e19.

Meier, S., and A. Stutzer. 2008. "Is Volunteering Rewarding in Itself?" *Economica* 75 (1):39–59.

Mistry, R. S., E. A. Vandewater, A. C. Huston, and V. C. McLoyd. 2002. "Economic Well-Being and Children's Social Adjustment: The Role of Family Process in an Ethnically Diverse Low-Income Sample." *Child Development* 73 (3):935–51.

Morawetz, D. 1977. " Income Distribution and Self-Rated Happiness: Some Empirical Evidence." *Economic Journal* 87:511–22.

Mukuria, C., T. Peasgood, D. Rowen, and J. Brazier. 2016. "An Empirical Comparison of Well-Being Measures Used in UK." Research Interim Report RR0048. Policy Research Unit in Economic Evaluation of Health and Social Care Interventions, University of Sheffield and University of York. http://www.eepru.org.uk/EEPRU%20Report%20-%20Empirical%20comparison%20of%20well-being%20measures%20version%20final%20November%2016.pdf.

Myrskyla, M., and R. Margolis. 2014. "Happiness: Before and after the Kids." *Demography* 51 (5):1843–66.

NFPI (National Family and Parenting Institute). 2000. "Teenagers' Attitudes to Parenting: A Survey of Young People's Experiences of Being Parented, and Their Views on How to Bring Up Children." *NFPI Survey Conducted by MORI*. London: National Family and Parenting Institute.

Nguyen, A.-M. D., and V. Benet-Martínez. 2012. "Biculturalism and Adjustment: A Meta-analysis." *Journal of Cross-Cultural Psychology* 20 (10):1–38.

Nikolaev, B. 2016. "Does Other People's Education Make Us Less Happy?" *Economics of Education Review* 52:176–91.

O'Connor, T. G., J. Heron, J. Golding, M. Beveridge, and V. Glover. 2002. "Maternal Antenatal Anxiety and Children's Behavioral/Emotional Problems at 4 Years: Report from the Avon Longitudinal Study of Parents and Children." *British Journal of Psychiatry* 180 (6):502–8.

Odermatt, R., and A. Stutzer. 2015. "Smoking Bans, Cigarette Prices and Life Satisfaction." *Journal of Health Economics* 44:176–94.

O'Donnell, G., A. Deaton, M. Durand, D. Halpern, and R. Layard. 2014. *Wellbeing and Policy*. London: Legatum Institute.

OECD. 2013a. *OECD Guidelines on Measuring Subjective Well-Being*. Paris: OECD.

———. 2013b. "Well-Being in the Workplace: Measuring Job Quality." In *How's Life? 2013: Measuring Well-Being*, 147–74. Paris: OECD.

———. 2016. Strategic Orientations of the Secretary-General: For 2016 and Beyond. Meeting of the OECD Council at Ministerial Level Paris, 1–2 June 2016. https://www.oecd.org/mcm/documents/strate gic-orientations-of-the-secretary-general-2016.pdf.

Office for National Statistics. 2015. "Births by Parents' Characteristics in England and Wales: 2014." *Statistical Bulletin*. https://www.ons.gov .uk/peoplepopulationandcommunity/birthsdeathsandmarriages/ livebirths/bulletins/birthsbyparentscharacteristicsinenglandand wales/2014.

Okbay, A., B.M.L. Baselmans, J.-E. De Neve, P. Turley, M. G. Nivard, M. A. Fontana, . . . and D. Cesarini. 2016. "Genetic Variants Associated with Subjective Well-Being, Depressive Symptoms, and Neuroticism Identified through Genome-Wide Analyses." *Nature Genetics* 48 (6):624–33. doi: 10.1038/ng.3552 http://www.nature.com/ng/ journal/v48/n6/abs/ng.3552.html#supplementary-information.

Olesen, K., R. Rugulies, N. Rod, and J. Bonde. 2014. "Does Retirement Reduce the Risk of Myocardial Infarction? A Prospective Registry Linkage Study of 617 511 Danish Workers." *International Journal of Epidemiology* 43 (1):160–67.

Oreopoulos, P., and U. Petronijevic. 2013. "Making College Worth It: A Review of the Returns to Higher Education." *Future of Children* 23:41–65.

Oreopoulos, P., and K. Salvanes. 2011. "Priceless: The Nonpecuniary Benefits of Schooling." *Journal of Economic Perspectives* 25 (1):159–84.

Oswald, A. J., and N. Powdthavee. 2008. "Does Happiness Adapt? A Longitudinal Study of Disability with Implications for Economists and Judges." *Journal of Public Economics* 92:1061–77.

Pargament, K. I. 2002. "The Bitter and the Sweet: An Evaluation of the Costs and Benefits of Religiousness." *Psychological Inquiry* 13:168–81.

Pearson, H. 2016. *The Life Project: The Extraordinary Story of Our Ordinary Lives*. London: Allen Lane.

Pietschnig, J., and M. Voracek. 2015. "One Century of Global IQ Gains: A Formal Meta-analysis of the Flynn Effect (1909–2013)." *Perspectives on Psychological Science* 10 (3):282–306.

Pinker, S. 2011. *The Better Angels of Our Nature: The Decline of Violence in History and Its Causes.* London: Allen Lane.

Pinquart, M., and S. Sorensen. 2000. "Influences of Socioeconomic Status, Social Network, and Competence on Subjective Well-Being in Later Life: A Meta-analysis." *Psychological Aging* 15 (2):187–224.

Pissarides, C. 2000. *Equilibrium Unemployment Theory.* Cambridge, MA: MIT Press.

Plomin, R., J. C. DeFries, V. S. Knopik, and J. M. Neiderhiser, eds. 2013. *Behavioral Genetics,* 6th ed. New York: Worth.

Pluess, M., ed. 2015. *Genetics of Psychological Well-Being: The Role of Heritability and Genetics in Positive Psychology.* Oxford: Oxford University Press.

Powdthavee, N. 2007. "Are There Geographical Variations in the Psychological Cost of Unemployment in South Africa?" *Social Indicators Research* 80:629–52.

Powdthavee, N., and J. Vernoit. 2013. "Parental Unemployment and Children's Happiness: A Longitudinal Study of Young People's Well-Being in Unemployed Households." *Labour Economics* 24:253–63.

Powdthavee, N., and A. Vignoles. 2008. "Mental Health of Parents and Life Satisfaction of Children: A Within-Family Analysis of Intergenerational Transmission of Well-Being." *Social Indicators Research* 88 (3):397–422.

Prevoo, T., and B. ter Weel. 2015. "The Effect of Family Disruption on Children's Personality Development: Evidence from British Longitudinal Data." *De Economist* 163 (1):61–93.

Putnam, R. 2000. *Bowling Alone: The Collapse and Revival of American Community.* New York: Simon and Schuster.

Qari, S. 2014. "Marriage, Adaptation and Happiness: Are There Long-Lasting Gains to Marriage?" *Journal of Behavioral and Experimental Economics* 50:29–39.

Rawls, J. 1971. *A Theory of Justice.* Cambridge, MA: Harvard University Press.

Ricard, M. 2015. *Altruism: The Power of Compassion to Change Yourself and the World*: Little, Brown.

Rivkin, S. G., E. A. Hanushek, and J. F. Kain. 2005. "Teachers, Schools, and Academic Achievement." *Econometrica* 73 (2):417–58.

Robertson, I., and C. L. Cooper. 2011. *Well-Being: Productivity and Happiness at Work.* London: Palgrave Macmillan.

Rockoff, J. E. 2004. "The Impact of Individual Teachers on Student Achievement: Evidence from Panel Data." *American Economic Review* 94 (2):247–52.

Rothstein, J. 2010. "Teacher Quality in Educational Production: Tracking, Decay and Student Achievement." *Quarterly Journal of Economics* 125 (1):175–214.

Rudolf, R., and S.-J. Kang. 2015. "Lags and Leads in Life Satisfaction in Korea: When Gender Matters." *Feminist Economics* 21 (1):136–63.

Ruhm, C. J. 1991. "Are Workers Permanently Scarred by Job Displacements?" *American Economic Review* 81:319–24.

———. 2004. "Parental Employment and Child Cognitive Development." *Journal of Human Resources* 39 (1):155–92.

Sacks, D. W., W. Stevenson, and J. Wolfers. 2012. "The New Stylized Facts about Income and Subjective Wellbeing." *Emotion* 12 (6):1181–87.

Sammons, P., K. Sylva, E. Melhuish, I. Siraj-Blatchford, B. Taggart, K. Toth, and R. Smees. 2014. *"Effective Pre-school, Primary and Secondary Education 3–16 (EPPSE 3–16): Influences on Students' GCSE Attainment and Progress at Age 16."* Research Report DFE-RR202. London: Department for Education. http://eppe.ioe.ac.uk/eppse3-14/eppse3-14pdfs/DFE-RR202.pdf.

Sarracino, F. 2010. "Social Capital and Subjective Well-Being Trends: Comparing 11 Western European Countries." *Journal of Socio-economics* 39:482–517.

Schwarze, J., and M. Härpfer. 2007. "Are People Inequality Averse, and Do They Prefer Redistribution by The State? Evidence from German Longitudinal Data on Life Satisfaction." *Journal of Socio-economics* 36 (2):233–49.

Sen, A. 1999. *Development as Freedom*. New York: Knopf.

Senik, C. 2004. "When Information Dominates Comparison: A Panel Data Analysis Using Russian Subjective Data." *Journal of Public Economics* 88:2099–123.

Shea, J. 2000. "Does Parents' Money Matter?" *Journal of Public Economics* 77 (2):155–84.

Singer, P. 1981. *The Expanding Circle: Ethics and Sociobiology*. Oxford: Oxford University Press.

Singer, T., and M. Ricard, eds. 2016. *Caring Economics*. Picador USA.

Smith, T. B., M. E. McCullough, and J. Poll. 2003. "Religiousness and Depression: Evidence for a Main Effect and the Moderating Influence of Stressful Life Events." *Psychological Bulletin* 129:614–36.

Soares, R. R. 2010. *Welfare Costs of Crime and Common Violence: A Critical Review*. Working Paper 581, Department of Economics, PUC-Rio.

Solnick, S., and D. Hemenway. 2005. "Are Positional Concerns Stronger in Some Domains Than in Others?" *American Economic Review* 95 (2):147–51.

Steinberg, L., S. D. Lamborn, S. M. Dornbusch, and N. Darling. 1992. "Impact of Parenting Practices on Adolescent Achievement: Authoritative Parenting, School Involvement, and Encouragement to Succeed." *Child Development* 63 (5):1266–81.

Steptoe, A., E. Breeze, J. Banks, and J. Nazroo. 2013. "Cohort Profile: The English Longitudinal Study of Ageing." *International Journal of Epidemiology* 42 (6):1640–48.

Steptoe, A., A. Deaton, and A. Stone. 2015. "Subjective Wellbeing, Health, and Ageing." *Lancet* 385 (9968):640–48.

Steptoe, A., and J. Wardle. 2012. "Enjoying Life and Living Longer." *Archives of Internal Medicine* 172 (3):273–75.

Stern, N. 2007. *The Economics of Climate Change: The Stern Review.* Cambridge: Cambridge University Press.

Stevenson, B., and J. Wolfers. 2008. "Economic Growth and Subjective Well-Being: Reassessing the Easterlin Paradox." *Brookings Papers on Economic Activity* 1:1–87.

———. 2010. "Inequality and Subjective Well-Being." Retrieved from https://editorialexpress.com/cgi-bin/conference/download.cgi?db_name=ALEA2010&paper_id=266.

Stone, A., J. Schwartz, J. Broderick, and A. Deaton. 2010. "A Snapshot of the Age Distribution of Psychological Well-Being in the United States." *Proceedings of the National Academy of Science* 107 (22):9985–90.

Sylva, K., E. Melhuish, P. Sammons, I. Siraj-Blatchford, and B. Taggart. 2004. *The Effective Provision of Pre-school Education (EPPE) Project: Final Report; A Longitudinal Study Funded by the DfES 1997–2004.* DfES Publications.

Talge, N. M., C. Neal, and V. Glover. 2007. "Antenatal Maternal Stress and Long-Term Effects on Child Neurodevelopment: How and Why?" *Journal of Child Psychology and Psychiatry* 48 (3–4):245–61.

Tellegen, A., D. T. Lykken, T. J. Bouchard, K. J. Wilcox, N. L. Segal, and S. Rich. 1988. "Personality Similarity in Twins Reared Apart and Together." *Journal of Personality and Social Psychology* 54 (6):1031–39.

Thoits, P., and L. Hewitt. 2001. "Volunteer Work and Well-Being." *Journal of Health and Social Behavior* 42 (2):115–31.

Tienari, P., L. C. Wynne, J. Moring, I. Lahti, M. Naarala, A. Sorri, et al. 1994. "The Finnish Adoptive Family Study of Schizophrenia:

Implications for Family Research." *British Journal of Psychiatry* 164 (23):20–26.

van den Berg, B., D. Fiebig, and J. Hall. 2014. "Well-Being Losses Due to Care-Giving." *Journal of Health Economics* 35:123–31.

Waldfogel, J., W.-J. Han, and J. Brooks-Gunn. 2002. "The Effects of Early Maternal Employment on Child Cognitive Development." *Demography* 39 (2):369–92.

Walker, I., and Y. Zhu. 2008. "The College Wage Premium and the Expansion of Higher Education in the UK." *Scandinavian Journal of Economics* 110:695–709.

Ward, G. 2015. *Is Happiness a Predictor of Election Results?* CEP Discussion Paper No. 1343. LSE Centre for Economic Performance.

Washbrook, E., P. Gregg, and C. Propper. 2014. "A Decomposition Analysis of the Relationship between Parental Income and Multiple Child Outcomes." *Journal of the Royal Statistical Society: Series A (Statistics in Society)* 177 (4):757–82.

Weitzman, L. J. 1985. *The Divorce Revolution*. New York: Free Press.

Westerlund, H., M. Kivimäki, A. Singh-Manoux, M. Melchior, J. Ferrie, J. Pentti, . . . J. Vahtera. 2009. "Self-Rated Health before and after Retirement in France (GAZEL): A Cohort Study." *Lancet* 374 (9705): 1889–96.

White, L., and J. N. Edwards. 1990. "Emptying the Nest and Parental Well-Being: An Analysis of National Panel Data." *American Sociological Review* 55 (2):235–42. doi: 10.2307/2095629.

Wilkinson, R., and K. Pickett. 2009. *The Spirit Level: Why More Equal Societies Almost Always Do Better*. London: Allen Lane.

Winkelmann, L., and R. Winkelmann. 1998. "Why Are the Unemployed So Unhappy? Evidence from Panel Data." *Economica* 65:1–15.

World Health Organisation (WHO). 2008. The Global Burden of Disease: 2004 Update. Geneva: World Health Organisation.

Yeung, W.-J. J., and D. Conley. 2008. "Black-White Achievement Gap and Family Wealth." *Child Development* 79 (2):303–24.

Yeung, W.-J. J., M. R. Linver, and J. Brooks-Gunn. 2002. "How Money Matters for Young Children's Development: Parental Investment and Family Processes." *Child Development* 73 (6):1861–79.

Zaki, J., and J. P. Mitchell. 2011. "Equitable Decision Making Is Associated with Neural Markers of Intrinsic Value." *Proceedings of the National Academy of Sciences* 108 (49):19761–66.

INDEX

Italics refers to figures and tables

259n13; origins of happiness and, 214, 216, *219, 220,* 221–23, *225,* 226, 233; progress and, *59;* schooling and, 52, 262n6 (*see also* schooling); social comparisons and, 55; United States and, 51, 241
Edwards, J. N., 279n9
Ellison, C. G., 270n37
Elseth Rieck, K. M., 275n5
emotional health, 4; bereavement and, 77–80, 82, 89, 126; British Cohort Study (BCS) and, 90, *92,* 101, *102, 108;* British Household Panel Survey (BHPS) and, *93,* 99; children and, 6–7, 11, 21–30, 161–63, 166, 171–74, 247, 249–51, 259n12, 263n12; conflict and, 24, 27, 153, 155, 166, 171, 179–85, 214, *225,* 226, 249–53, 275n6; cost-effectiveness and, 277n13; crime and, 106, *109;* education and, 57, 58, 263n12; family status and, 86; fathers and, 249–52; genetics and, 7; income and, 25, *40, 48,* 49, 153–56, 159, 249, 271n8; life-satisfaction and, 207, 239–44, 246; loneliness and, 132–35, *136, 138, 140, 143, 145, 146,* 147–49, 215; marital status and, 246, 249–52; mothers and, 21, *154,* 161–63, 214, 250–51; mother survey and, 106; origins of happiness and, 211, 214–15, *216,* 223–27, 279n11; pain and, 61–66, 82, 89, 96–97, 122, 214; parents and, 171–74, 247, 250–51, 273n12, 274n13, 274n21; partnering and, 29, 44, 77–80, 85–87, 215, 222; scarring and, 63–66; schooling and, 188–93, 275n3, 276n8; separation and, 26, 77–82, 89, 155, 180–82, *183,* 213, 222, 244, 249–51, 253, 265n4, 275n6; stress and, 71, 122, 126, 129, 233, 271n11, 274n14, 279n9;

unemployment and, 63–66, *69,* 251; work and, *69,* 161–63; working parents and, 161–63, 166, 171–74, 250
English Longitudinal Study of Aging (ELSA), 102, 130–31, *133, 136, 138, 140, 143, 145, 146,* 237, 248–49, 258n16, 270n7
enjoyment: adaptation and, 43; education and, 51–52, 262n3; family and, 82; health and, 103; income and, 43; measurement of, 1–3; older ages and, 132; origins of happiness and, 212, 218, 233; predictors for, 30; sex and, 70, 121; social capital and, 121; social comparisons and, 43; work and, 61, 68, 71, 75
Enlightenment, 1
epigenetics, 170
equality: Bentham on, 204; income and, 17, 36, 46, 204, 262n27; life-satisfaction and, 269n30; social norms and, 124–25, 127
equity, 204
Ermisch, J., 272n9, 275n5
ethics, 1; ALSPAC and, 236; origins of happiness and, 232; social norms and, 115, 121, 126–27
ethnicity, 11; conflict and, 252; crime and, 106, 247; education and, 58; family status and, 86; health and, 172; income and, 48, 155, 249–50, 271n9; life-satisfaction and, 121, 239–42, 244, 248–49; older ages and, 132, *136,* 137, *138, 140, 146;* parents and, 172, 251; schooling and, 253, 255; social norms and, 121; unemployment and, 58

family, 76; adaptation and, 80–85, 265n2, 265n3, 265n4; ALSPAC and, 179 (*see also* Avon Longitudinal Study of Parents and Children

family (*continued*)
(ALSPAC)); Annexes for, 265n5,
266n12; Australia and, *79–81*,
82–83, 84, *85*; Bath study and,
153; bereavement and, 77–80,
82, 89, 126; birth cohort studies
and, *9, 39*, 179; Bristol study and,
153, 236; British Cohort Study
(BCS) and, 78, *79*, 83, *85*, 265n11;
British Household Panel Survey
(BHPS) and, *78*, 265n2, 265n4;
building, 77–87; child care and,
2, *160*; conflict and, 24, 27, 153,
155, 166, 171, 179–85, 214, *225*,
226, 249–53, 275n6; divorce and,
77–78, 132, *133, 136, 138, 140, 145,
146*, 147, 265n4, 275n2; education
and, *57–59*; emotional health and,
86; enjoyment and, 82; ethnicity
and, *86*; genetics and, 28 (*see also*
genetics); Germany and, *79–81*,
82, 84, *85*; having children and,
83–85, 240–45, 255, 265n2, 265n4;
Household, Income and Labour
Dynamics in Australia (HILDA)
and, 265n2, 265n4; income of,
153–59; intellectual development
and, *86*; life-satisfaction and, 8,
79–85, 180; living as married and,
77–78; marital status and, *136, 138,
140, 146* (*see also* marital status);
mental health and, 87 (*see also*
mental health); origins of happiness and, 212–13, *215, 216, 225*,
226–27; partnering and, 29, 44,
77–80, 85–87, 215, 222; separation
and, *26*, 77–82, 89, 155, 180–82,
183, 213, 222, 244, 249–51, 253,
265n4, 275n6; single people and,
77–79, 213, *220*, 244, 275n2; status
of, *77, 78, 79, 86*, 244–45; well-being
and, 237; widows/widowers and,
77–79, *81*, 132, *133, 136, 138, 140,
145, 146*, 147–48, *220*, 222, 244

Fasani, F., 268n10, 268n9
fathers: adaptation to parenthood
and, 84, *85*, 245; behavioral development and, 274n18; conflict
and, 252; crime and, 106, 247;
divorce and, 77–78, 132, *133, 136,
138, 140, 145, 146*, 147, 265n4,
275n2; education and, 259n13;
emotional health and, 249–52;
life-satisfaction and, *225*, 239–42,
244; marital status and, 243; mental health of, *26*, 27, 155, 172–75,
176, 225, 249–50, 274n13, 275n6;
unemployment and, 21, *22, 26, 48*,
49, 53–54, 57, *58*, 68, 69, 86, 101,
102, 155, 165–66, *225*, 239–42,
244, 249–55, 272n2
Ferrer-i-Carbonell, A., 261n23
Fiebig, D., 267n20
Fischler, C., 265n19
Flèche, S., 254, 258n3, 264n8, 276n6,
276n10
Fließbach, K., 261n23
Ford, T., 271n5
France, *123*, 206, 241, 258n18, 272n9
Francesconi, M., 272n9, 275n5
Fredriksson, P., 275n4
freedom: levels of, 117; mutual
respect and, 125; origins of
happiness and, 228; personal,
115–16, 122–23; social norms
and, 115–17, 122–24, 215, 228–29,
268n4, 269n23, 269n24; of speech,
269n24
Friedman, J., 276n5, 276n9
Friesen, W., 267n24
Frijters, P., 45, 235, 260n4, 264n7,
265n2, 265n7
Fronstin, P., 275n5

Gallup World Poll, 115, 126, 229, 247,
255, 258n2, 258n16, 278n2
gender: conflict and, 252; education
and, *55*; income and, 38, 155, 249;

life-satisfaction and, 239–44, 248,
255; men and, 11 (*see also* men);
mental health and, 251; older ages
and, 130–32, 139–42, 148; origins
of happiness and, 220; schooling
and, 255; unemployment and, 62,
67; well-being and, 19–20; women
and, 11 (*see also* women); work
and, 250

General Certificate of Secondary
Education (GCSE): education
and, 24, *154*, 157–58, 176, 188–89,
225, 226, 250–53, 259n10, 273n12;
income and, *154*, 157–58; intellectual development and, 24, *154*,
157–58, 176, 188–89, 225, 226,
250–53, 259n10, 273n12; mothers
and, 176; schooling and, 188–89,
225, 226

Generalized Linear Model (GLM),
131

generosity, 115–20, 228, *229*, 268n4

genetics: behavioral development
and, 7; children and, 7, 28, 101,
169–71, 173, 215, 273n9; DNA
and, 170, 197; epigenetics and,
170; health and, 7, 101, 169–71,
173, 273n9; intellectual development and, 7; origins of happiness
and, 215; parents and, 7, 28, 101,
169–71, 173, 215, 273n9

Geoergellis, Y., 264n7, 264n12, 265n2,
265n6

German Socio-Economic Panel
(SOEP), 237, 257n15; family and,
265n2, 265n4; income and, 39, *43*;
life-satisfaction and, 246; origins
of happiness and, *230*; unemployment and, 254n7

Germany: adaptation to disability
and, 246–47, 267n21; education
and, *55*, *56*; family and, *79–81*, 82,
84, 85; health and, *99*, 100, 246–47,
267n21; income and, 33, 39, *41*,

43, 45–47; life-satisfaction and, 2,
9; Merkel and, 12, 13, 211, 233;
origins of happiness and, 216, 218,
221, 229, *230*; social norms and,
120, *123*; unemployment and,
62–66, *67*, 72

GHQ-12 measurement, 90–91,
268n10

Gillman, S., 274n15

Glover, V., 274n15

Godechot, O., 261n23

Goldsmith, A. H., 273n11

Goodman, R., 271n5

government: American Time Use
Survey and, 70; corruption and,
115, 119, 124–25; cost-effectiveness
and, 199, 201; distrust and, 127;
misery and, 209; object of, 2;
personal freedom and, 122; policy
makers and, 197 (*see also* policy
makers); quality of, 115, 119,
124–25; reelection and, 4, 208;
schooling and, 187; taxes and, 51,
56, 201, 263n10; votes and, 4, *5*,
51, *56*, 124, 214, 239; well-being
of people and, 12, 127, 207, 209

Green, D., 262n2

Greenberg, D. H., 275n5

Green Book, 204

Gregg, N., 271n9

Gregg, P., 158, 271n5, 271n10, 272n9

Grover, S., 269n26, 269n27, 269n28

Gruber, J., 273n11

Grundy, E., 235

Gunatilaka, R., 269n20

Guo, G., 271n10

Hall, J., 153, 267n20

Halpern, D., 269n19

Hamermesh, D. S., 279n9

Han, W.-J., 272n14, 273n10

Hanson, T. L., 275n6

Hanushek, E. A., 187–88, 275n1,
275n4, 276n5, 276n8

McLoyd, V. C., 273n11
McMunn, A., 272n4
Maimonides' Rule, 275n4
Manning, A., 235
marginal utility, 36, 49, 125, 200,
  203–4
Margolis, R., 266n12
Marie, O., 268n7
marital status: adaptation to parenthood and, 245; conflict and,
  252; emotional health and, 246,
  249–52; fathers and, 243; income
  and, 249; life-satisfaction and,
  241–46; living as married and,
  77–78; misery and, 245; mothers
  and, 240, 250; older ages and, *136,
  138, 140, 146*; schooling and, 253,
  255; unemployment and, 243
Masclet, D., 264n5
Maurin, E., 271n10
Mayr, U., 269n16
Mayraz, G., 257n3, 260n6, 260n12,
  261n23, 269n29
measurement: α-coefficients and,
  18, *92, 93*, 259n7; β-coefficients
  and, 17–18, *48, 58,* 68, *69, 93,
  94–95, 102, 133, 145, 155–59, 172,
  175, 176, 188–92,* 217, *219, 229,*
  245–54, 259n7; Cantril ladder
  and, 115, 228, 268n5; of conflict,
  179–80; cost-effectiveness and,
  197–209; dependent variables
  and, 19, 68, 94, 116, 253–54,
  258n6, 259n8, 267n3, 275n2;
  determinants and, 7, 19–20, 25, 29,
  34, 38, 49, 68, 101–3, 129, 141, 149,
  169, 171, 180, 215, 226, 271n11;
  discount rates and, 204–5, 207; of
  enjoyment, 1–3; equity and, 204;
  Generalized Linear Model (GLM)
  and, 131; GHQ-12 and, 90–91,
  268n10; income and, 33–49,
  153–59; independent variables
  and, 258n6; interpreting results

and, 16–18; life-satisfaction and,
  211 (*see also* life-satisfaction); marginal utility and, 36, 49, 125, 200,
  203–4; origins of happiness and,
  211–33; ratio vs. cardinal scale
  and, 205; standard deviation (SD)
  and, 17–18, 33–36, 52–53, 57, 74,
  108–10, 156–58, 164, 188–90, 207,
  215, 222, 227, 249, 257n10, 258n4,
  259n7, 259n15, 260n9, 262n6,
  267n5, 268n8; by units of money,
  202–3; World Happiness Report
  and, 228, 268n1, 268n5
Meier, S., 269n14
Meltzer, H., 271n5
men, 11; building a family and, *80,
  81, 82, 85,* 265n4; mental illness
  and, 19; older ages and, 130–32,
  139–42, 148; unemployment and,
  243; well-being and, 19; work
  and, 64, *65,* 166, 243, 264n7
mental health, *168,* 267n14; age
  and, 98; anxiety and, 90, *92,* 213,
  219–20, 233, 254–55, 271n11;
  bereavement and, 77–80, 82, 89,
  126; bosses and, 61, 71, 212; children and, 7, *102,* 247, 249, 253,
  271n5; conflict and, 171, 180–81;
  cost-effectiveness and, 207; crime
  and, 112; Crown-Crisp Experiential Index and, 172, 274n13;
  depression and, 90–91, *92,* 149,
  171–73, 213, *219–20,* 222, 233,
  248, 254–55, 274n13; diagnos-
  ing, 19; education and, *55, 58,*
  59; external factors and, 98–99;
  fathers and, *26,* 27, 155, 172–75,
  176, 225, 249–50, 274n13, 275n6;
  gender and, 19, 251; health-care
  spending on, 95; importance
  of, 29; Improving Access to Psychological Therapies and, 207;
  income and, 38, 153, 155–56,
  249; life-satisfaction and, 20, 23,

Moving to Opportunity, 207
Mukuria, C., 268n10
Myers, D. G., 270n33, 270n34
Myrskyla, M., 266n12

National Child Development Study
(NCDS), 158, 271n9
National Dialogue on Wellbeing,
258n19
National Health Service, 199, 231–32
National Institute for Health and
Care Excellence (NICE), 277n5,
277n6
National Institute on Aging, 236
National Longitudinal Survey of
Youth's Child and Young Adult
cohort (CNLSY), 107–10
Neal, C., 274n15
Nehru, Jawaharlal, 167
New Zealand, *123*, 241
Nguyen, A.-M., 269n20
Nickell, S. J., 257n3, 260n6, 260n12,
261n23, 263n4, 264n16, 269n29
Nikolaev, B., 263n9
non-government organizations
(NGOs), 197, 203, 208, 231
Norton, M., 261n23, 269n15
Norway, 118, *123*, 229, 241, 279n14
Nurmi, J. E., 274n16

Ockert, B., 275n4
O'Connor, T. G., 274n15
Odermatt, R., 278n21
O'Donnell, G., 235, 257n4
OECD countries, 12, 235, 257n7,
257n12, 258n18, 260n7, 265n22
Ogborn, H., 235
Okbay, A., 273n8
older ages, *128*; adaptation to disabil-
ity and, 100–101, 246–47, 267n21;
age differences and, 135–39;
Annexes for, 132; autonomy and,
129; divorce and, 132, *133, 136,*
138, 140, 145, 146, 147; English

Longitudinal Study of Aging
(ELSA) and, 102, 130–31, *133,*
136, 138, 140, 143, 145, 146, 237,
248–49, 258n16, 270n7; enjoyment and, 132; ethnicity and, 132,
136, 137, *138, 140, 146;* financial
resources and, 129, 148–49; gender and, 139–41, 148; health and,
131–49; independence and, 129,
149; life-satisfaction and, 129–49,
215, 248; loneliness and, 132–35,
136, 138, 140, 143, 145, 146, 147–49,
215; marital status and, *136, 138,*
140, 146; men and, 130–32, 139–42,
148; mental health and, 98, 131,
139, 148–49; progress and, 129;
regression analysis and, 131–32,
134; retirement and, 98, 129, *136,*
138, 139, *140,* 142, 148; social
relationships and, 129–32, 135,
137, 147; social support and, 132,
135, 149; well-being and, 270n4;
women and, 130–32, 139–42
Olesen, K., 270n9
Olsen, J. A., 270n10
Oosterbeek, H., 275n4
Oreopoulos, P., 262n2, 262n7
origins of happiness, *210;* absolute
effects of experience and, 219–23;
adaptation and, 222; adult outcomes and, 215–16; Australia
and, 216, 218, 221, 229, *230;* Avon
Longitudinal Study of Parents
and Children (ALSPAC) and,
217, *225;* behavioral development
and, 214–15, *216;* Britain and,
216, 221, 229–32; British Cohort
Study (BCS) and, 216, 223, 278n7;
British Household Panel Survey
(BHPS) and, 216, 218, *219, 220,*
230; child outcomes and, 215–16,
223, 225–27; children and, 211,
214–16, 222–27; conflict and,
214, *225,* 226; education and, 214,

also mothers); older ages and, 130–32, 139–42; pregnancy and, 83–85, 240–45, 255, 259n13; well-being and, 19; work and, 68, 71, 161, 166, 264n6
Wooden, M., 279n9
work, *60*; 100 Best Places to Work, 72; American Time Use Survey and, 70; Annexes for, 263n3, 264n7, 264n15; behavioral development and, 163–64, *166*, 273n12; bosses and, 61, 71, 212; Britain and, 62–66, *67*, 72; customers and, *71*, 72; emotional health and, *69*, 161–63; enjoyment and, 61, 68, 71, 75; full-time, 61–63, 242, 259n14; gender and, 250; Germany and, 62–66, *67*, 72; good environment for, 71–74; intellectual development and, 23, 164–65, 251, 272n9; labor force and, 62–64, 242, 264n15, 272n2; men and, 64, *65*, 166, 243, 264n7; mental health and, 94; mothers and, 25, *26*, *48*, *69*, 86, *102*, 155, 161–65, 167, 214, *225*, 239–44, 249–55, 272n2,

272n9; parents and, 161–67; part-time, *63*, 259n14; quality of, 61, 68–74, *220*, 222, 244, 255; quality of workplace and, *74*, 244; regression analysis and, 64, 73, 264n8, 264n11; retirement and, 98, 129, *136*, *138*, 139, *140*, 142, 148; self-employed and, 62, *63*, 264n5; unemployment and, 61–75 (*see also* unemployment); United States and, 62, 163; women and, 68, 71, 161, 166, 264n6; work/life balance and, 73–74
World Happiness Report, 228, 268n1, 268n5
World Health Organization (WHO), 98, 270n1

Xuereb, C., 257n12

Yap, S., 264n7, 265n2, 265n4
Yeung, W.-J. J., 159, 271n5, 271n10, 271n11, 272n13

Zaki, J., 269n16
Zhu, Y., 262n2

CARTOON CREDITS